EDGARDO FERNANDEZ CLIMENT

Mastering CMMC 2.0

A Comprehensive Guide to Implementing
Cybersecurity Maturity in Defense Contracting

First edition

This book was professionally typeset on Reedsy.
Find out more at reedsy.com

To my wife with eternal love.
Thank you for making me happy.
Edgardo

Contents

Preface   vi

*Introduction to the importance of cybersecurity in
the defense industry*   vi

*Overview of CMMC 2.0 and its impact on contractors
and subcontractors in the defense supply chain*   vii

Chapter 1: Understanding CMMC 2.0   1

Background on the development of CMMC and
the transition to CMMC 2.0   1

Overview of the CMMC 2.0 framework   4

Explanation of CMMC 2.0 Levels 1, 2, and 3 and
their Significance   8

Overview of Controlled Unclassified Information
(CUI) and Federal Contract Information (FCI)   13

Best Practices: To streamline CMMC 2.0 adoption, leverage existing compliance efforts (NIST
800-171) and understand regulatory contexts.   17

Chapter 2: CMMC 2.0 Compliance Requirements   23

Detailed breakdown of the requirements for each
CMMC 2.0 level   23

Specific practices and processes at each level (17
practices for Level 1, 110 practices for Level 2, 110+
practices for Level 3)   32

Compliance versus certification   40

Best Practices: Develop a checklist for each
CMMC 2.0 level requirement to ensure no
compliance detail is overlooked.   44

Chapter 3: Preparing for CMMC 2.0   49

Steps to establish a CMMC 2.0 implementation team   49

Initial assessment: Understanding your current
cybersecurity posture   54

Tools and resources for assessment (e.g., NIST
800-171 Self-Assessment)   60

Best Practices: Engage stakeholders from every
department early to ensure alignment and distribute the cybersecurity responsibility across
the organization.   66

Chapter 4: Conducting a Gap Analysis   72

Methodology for performing a gap analysis for
CMMC 2.0   72

Identifying and documenting compliance gaps   78

Prioritizing remediation efforts based on risk assessment   83

Best Practices: Use automated tools to assist in
identifying gaps and ensure documentation is
thorough and regularly updated.   89

Chapter 5: Developing an Implementation Plan   96

Structuring an effective Plan of Action and Milestones (POA&M)   96

Allocating resources and defining timelines   102

Strategies for stakeholder engagement and communication   109

Best Practices: Maintain flexible and scalable
implementation plans to adapt to unforeseen
challenges or changes in requirements.   116

Chapter 6: Cybersecurity Controls and Practices   123

Detailed guidance on specific security controls
required for CMMC 2.0 (based on NIST 800-171)   123
Best practices for implementing technical and
administrative controls   132
Case studies and practical examples   139
Best Practices: Regularly review and test security
controls to ensure they are effective and efficient
in the changing threat landscape.   147
Chapter 7: Training and Awareness   154
Importance of training and security awareness
in achieving CMMC 2.0   154
Developing a continuous training program   160
Measuring training effectiveness   167
Best Practices: Tailor training programs to differ-
ent organizational roles and use engaging, varied
training methods to enhance learning.   173
Chapter 8: Internal Auditing and Continuous Monitoring 180
Strategies for setting up internal audits   180
Tools for continuous monitoring and maintain-
ing compliance   187
Handling non-compliance and corrective actions   194
Best Practices: Establish a routine schedule for
internal audits and continuous monitoring, us-
ing automated tools to assist in regular checks.   202
Chapter 9: Navigating the CMMC 2.0 Assessment Process   210
Understanding the CMMC 2.0 assessment pro-
cess for each level   210
Preparing for self-assessments (Level 1) and
third-party assessments (Levels 2 and 3)   219
What to expect during and after the assessment   227

Best Practices: Start early, be proactive, and maintain open communication throughout the assessment process. 236

Chapter 10: Achieving and Maintaining Certification 243

The certification process explained for each CMMC 2.0 level. 243

Tips for a successful CMMC 2.0 assessment 251

Maintaining compliance and preparing for recertification 258

Best Practices: Develop a culture of continuous improvement and regular compliance review to simplify the recertification process. 265

Chapter 11: Advanced Topics and Future Trends 273

Integrating CMMC 2.0 with other compliance frameworks (e.g., NIST, ISO) 273

Future developments in CMMC 281

The role of CMMC in enhancing national security 287

Best Practices: Stay informed on cybersecurity trends and CMMC updates to adjust your security strategy proactively. 295

Appendix A: Glossary of Terms 302

Appendix B: List of CMMC 2.0 Resources and Tools 307

Appendix C: List of CMMC Controls Ordered by Domain and... 313

Access Control (AC) 313

Asset Management (AM) 317

Audit and Accountability (AU) 318

Awareness and Training (AT) 320

Configuration Management (CM) 320

Identification and Authentication (IA) 322

Incident Response (IR) 326

Maintenance (MA) 328

Media Protection (MP)   329

Personnel Security (PS)   332

Physical Protection (PE)   333

Recovery (RE)   334

Risk Management (RM)   335

Security Assessment (CA)   337

Situational Awareness (SA)   339

System and Communications Protection (SC)   339

System and Information Integrity (SI)   344

Appendix D: Mapping of CMMC 2.0 Practices to

NIST 800-171...   349

Access Control (AC)   349

Audit and Accountability (AU)   355

Configuration Management (CM)   357

Identification and Authentication (IA)   360

Incident Response (IR)   363

Maintenance (MA)   364

Media Protection (MP)   365

Personnel Security (PS)   368

Physical Protection (PE)   368

Risk Assessment (RA)   370

Security Assessment (CA)   371

System and Communications Protection (SC)   372

System and Information Integrity (SI)   377

Appendix E: Templates for Gap Analysis and POA&M   381

Gap Analysis Template: 381

POA&M Template: 386

About the Author   392

Also by Edgardo Fernandez Climent   395

Preface

Introduction to the importance of cybersecurity in the defense industry

In today's rapidly evolving digital landscape, cybersecurity has become a critical concern for organizations across all industries. However, the defense industry faces unique challenges due to the sensitive nature of the information it handles and the potential consequences of a breach. Protecting Controlled Unclassified Information (CUI) and Federal Contract Information (FCI) is paramount to maintaining national security, safeguarding intellectual property, and ensuring the integrity of the defense supply chain.

Cybersecurity threats are becoming increasingly sophisticated, with state-sponsored actors, cybercriminals, and hacktivists targeting defense contractors and subcontractors to gain access to valuable information. A successful cyberattack can result in the theft of sensitive data, disruption of operations, financial losses, and reputational damage. In the context of the defense industry, the impact of a breach can extend beyond individual organizations, compromising military capabilities, exposing vulnerabilities, and endangering lives.

Recognizing the importance of cybersecurity in the defense industry, the U.S. Department of Defense (DoD) has taken proactive steps to strengthen the resilience of its supply chain. The Cybersecurity Maturity Model Certification (CMMC) framework was developed to ensure that defense contractors and subcontractors implement appropriate cybersecurity measures to protect CUI and FCI. By mandating compliance with CMMC, the DoD aims to reduce the risk of cyber incidents and create a more secure and resilient defense industrial base.

Overview of CMMC 2.0 and its impact on contractors and subcontractors in the defense supply chain

CMMC 2.0 is the latest iteration of the Cybersecurity Maturity Model Certification framework, introduced in November 2021 to streamline and simplify the original CMMC framework while maintaining its effectiveness in enhancing cybersecurity within the defense supply chain. The updated framework is designed to be more flexible, affordable, and accessible for defense contractors and subcontractors of all sizes.

CMMC 2.0 consists of three levels of cybersecurity maturity, each with its own set of requirements and assessment processes:

1. Level 1 (Foundational): Focuses on protecting FCI and requires the implementation of 17 basic cybersecurity practices. Contractors can demonstrate compliance through self-assessment.

2. Level 2 (Advanced): This level concentrates on protecting CUI and requires the implementation of 110 cybersecurity practices aligned with NIST SP 800-171. To achieve certification, contractors must undergo a third-party assessment.

3. Level 3 (Expert): This level builds upon Level 2 and includes additional practices based on NIST SP 800-172 to address advanced persistent threats (APTs). To achieve certification, contractors must undergo government-led assessments.

The impact of CMMC 2.0 on contractors and subcontractors in the defense supply chain is significant. Organizations that handle CUI or FCI must now prioritize cybersecurity and invest in the necessary resources, tools, and expertise to achieve and maintain compliance with the appropriate CMMC level. Failure to comply with CMMC requirements may result in the loss of DoD contracts, legal consequences, and reputational damage.

CMMC 2.0 compliance is not a one-time event but an ongoing process that requires continuous monitoring, improvement, and adaptation to the evolving cyber threat landscape. To create a cybersecurity awareness and resilience culture, contractors and subcontractors must develop a robust cybersecurity program encompassing technical controls, policies, procedures, and employee training.

By embracing CMMC 2.0 and prioritizing cybersecurity, defense contractors and subcontractors can protect their organizations and contribute to the defense supply chain's security and resilience. As the framework continues to evolve and mature, organizations must stay informed, collaborate with industry partners, and remain proactive in their approach to cybersecurity.

In the following chapters, we will delve deeper into the intricacies of CMMC 2.0, providing practical guidance, best practices, and case studies to help defense contractors and subcontractors navigate the complexities of cybersecurity maturity and achieve success in their CMMC journey.

Chapter 1: Understanding CMMC 2.0

Background on the development of CMMC and the transition to CMMC 2.0

The Cybersecurity Maturity Model Certification (CMMC) framework was originally developed by the U.S. Department of Defense (DoD) in collaboration with industry partners, academic institutions, and cybersecurity experts. The primary goal of CMMC was to enhance the cybersecurity posture of the defense industrial base (DIB) and protect sensitive information, particularly Controlled Unclassified Information (CUI) and Federal Contract Information (FCI).

The initial version of CMMC, released in January 2020, consisted of five maturity levels, each with its cybersecurity practices and processes. These levels ranged from Basic Cyber Hygiene (Level 1) to Advanced/Progressive (Level 5). The framework aimed to provide a unified standard for cybersecurity assessment and certification across the DIB, ensuring that contractors and subcontractors implemented appropriate security measures commensurate with the sensitivity of the information they handled.

However, the original CMMC framework faced several challenges and concerns from stakeholders. Many small and medium-sized businesses (SMBs) expressed apprehension about the cost and complexity of achieving higher CMMC levels, fearing that it could hinder their ability to compete for DoD contracts. There were also concerns about the capacity and readiness of the CMMC ecosystem, including the availability of qualified assessors and the timeline for widespread adoption.

In response to these concerns and feedback from industry partners, the DoD announced the transition to CMMC 2.0 in November 2021. The updated framework aimed to simplify the model, reduce costs, and increase flexibility for contractors while maintaining the core objective of enhancing cybersecurity within the DIB.

Key changes in CMMC 2.0 include:

1. **Reduction of maturity levels:** CMMC 2.0 streamlines the framework into three levels instead of five, making it more manageable for organizations to understand and implement the required cybersecurity practices.

2. **Alignment with NIST standards:** CMMC 2.0 more closely aligns with the National Institute of Standards and Technology (NIST) Special Publication (SP) 800-171 and 800-172, widely accepted cybersecurity standards. This alignment helps organizations leverage existing compliance efforts and reduces the burden of adopting new requirements.

3. **Flexibility in assessments:** Under CMMC 2.0, Level 1 (Foundational) allows for self-assessment, while Levels 2 (Advanced) and 3 (Expert)

require third-party or government-led assessments, respectively. This approach provides more flexibility for contractors and subcontractors based on the sensitivity of the information they handle.

4. Emphasis on continuous improvement: CMMC 2.0 encourages organizations to view cybersecurity as an ongoing process rather than a one-time event. The framework promotes continuous monitoring, risk management, and the adoption of best practices to maintain a robust cybersecurity posture.

5. Improved rulemaking process: The DoD has committed to engaging in a more collaborative and transparent rulemaking process for CMMC 2.0, allowing for public comment and input from industry stakeholders. This approach ensures the framework remains flexible, effective, and responsive to the evolving cybersecurity landscape.

The transition to CMMC 2.0 demonstrates the DoD's commitment to working with industry partners to create a more secure and resilient defense supply chain. By simplifying the framework, aligning with established standards, and promoting flexibility, CMMC 2.0 seeks to encourage wider adoption and help organizations of all sizes prioritize cybersecurity.

As CMMC 2.0 evolves and matures, defense contractors and subcontractors must stay informed about the latest developments, guidance, and best practices. By understanding the background and rationale behind CMMC 2.0, organizations can better position themselves to achieve compliance, safeguard sensitive information, and contribute to the overall security of the DIB.

Overview of the CMMC 2.0 framework

The Cybersecurity Maturity Model Certification (CMMC) 2.0 framework is a comprehensive approach to assessing and enhancing organizations' cybersecurity posture within the defense industrial base (DIB). The framework consists of three maturity levels, each with its cybersecurity practices and processes that organizations must implement to achieve certification.

The three levels of CMMC 2.0 are:

1. Level 1 (Foundational):

- Focuses on the protection of Federal Contract Information (FCI)
- Requires the implementation of 17 basic cybersecurity practices
- Aligned with the Federal Acquisition Regulation (FAR) clause 52.204-21
- Organizations can demonstrate compliance through self-assessment

Level 1 establishes a foundation of basic cyber hygiene practices that all organizations handling FCI must implement. These practices include:

- Access control
- Identification and authentication
- Media protection
- Physical protection
- System and communications protection

- System and information integrity
- Awareness and training

By achieving Level 1 compliance, organizations demonstrate that they have implemented essential security measures to protect FCI from unauthorized access, modification, or disclosure.

2. Level 2 (Advanced):

- Focuses on the protection of Controlled Unclassified Information (CUI)
- Requires the implementation of 110 cybersecurity practices aligned with NIST SP 800-171
- Organizations must undergo a third-party assessment to achieve certification

Level 2 builds upon the foundational practices of Level 1 and introduces more advanced security requirements to safeguard CUI. The 110 practices at this level are derived from the security controls outlined in NIST SP 800-171, a widely recognized standard for protecting CUI in non-federal systems.

The practices at Level 2 cover a wide range of cybersecurity domains, including:

- Access control
- Audit and accountability
- Configuration management
- Identification and authentication

- Incident response
- Maintenance
- Media protection
- Personnel security
- Physical protection
- Risk assessment
- Security assessment
- System and communications protection
- System and information integrity

To achieve Level 2 certification, organizations must undergo a third-party assessment conducted by a CMMC Third-Party Assessment Organization (C3PAO). The assessment verifies that the organization has implemented the required practices effectively and consistently.

3. Level 3 (Expert):

- Builds upon Level 2 and includes additional practices based on NIST SP 800-172
- Addresses the protection of CUI from advanced persistent threats (APTs)
- Organizations must undergo government-led assessments to achieve certification

Level 3 represents the highest maturity level in CMMC 2.0 and is designed for organizations that handle the most sensitive CUI or operate in high-threat environments. In addition to the 110 practices from Level 2, Level 3 incorporates a subset of the enhanced security requirements from NIST SP 800-172.

The additional practices at Level 3 focus on countering APTs and include:

- Enhanced access control measures
- Advanced threat detection and response capabilities
- Improved incident reporting and information sharing
- Stronger supply chain risk management

Organizations seeking Level 3 certification must undergo a government-led assessment by the Defense Contract Management Agency (DCMA) or other authorized entities. The rigorous assessment process ensures the organization has implemented advanced security measures to defend against sophisticated cyber threats.

Across all three levels, CMMC 2.0 emphasizes the importance of continuous monitoring, incident response, and risk management. Organizations must regularly assess their cybersecurity posture, address identified vulnerabilities, and adapt to the evolving threat landscape.

The framework guides implementation, assessment, and certification processes to support organizations in their CMMC 2.0 journey. The DoD has also established the CMMC Accreditation Body (CMMC-AB) to oversee the training, certification, and quality assurance of CMMC assessors and C3PAOs.

By understanding the structure and requirements of the CMMC 2.0 framework, organizations can effectively plan and execute their cybersecurity initiatives to achieve the appropriate level of certification. The framework's tiered approach allows organizations to prioritize their investments based on the sensitivity of the information they handle and the level of risk they face.

As CMMC 2.0 evolves, organizations must stay informed about updates, guidance, and best practices. Engaging with the CMMC community, participating in training and awareness programs, and collaborating with industry partners can help organizations navigate the framework's complexities and maintain a robust cybersecurity posture.

Ultimately, CMMC 2.0 is critical in safeguarding the nation's sensitive information and strengthening the DIB's resilience. By adopting the framework and prioritizing cybersecurity, organizations not only protect their assets but also contribute to the collective security of the defense supply chain.

Explanation of CMMC 2.0 Levels 1, 2, and 3 and their Significance

CMMC 2.0 consists of three distinct maturity levels, each representing a different level of cybersecurity readiness and the type of information an organization is equipped to handle. Let's delve deeper into each level and understand their significance:

Level 1 (Foundational):

Level 1 is the entry point for organizations in the defense industrial base (DIB) and focuses on protecting Federal Contract Information (FCI). FCI is information provided by or generated for the government under a contract to develop or deliver a product or service to the government. While FCI is not considered sensitive, it still requires a basic level of protection.

At Level 1, organizations must implement 17 basic cybersecurity practices derived from the Federal Acquisition Regulation (FAR) clause 52.204-21. These practices cover essential security hygiene, such as:

- Limiting access to authorized users
- Verifying the identity of users
- Sanitizing or destroying media containing FCI
- Limiting physical access to systems
- Monitoring and controlling communications at system boundaries
- Identifying and correcting information and system flaws
- Providing security awareness training

The significance of Level 1 lies in establishing a foundation of basic cyber hygiene practices that all organizations handling FCI must implement. By achieving Level 1 compliance, organizations demonstrate their commitment to protecting government information and reducing the risk of unauthorized access or disclosure.

Organizations can conduct self-assessments using the CMMC Assessment Guide to demonstrate compliance with Level 1 requirements. Self-assessment allows organizations to evaluate their cybersecurity posture and identify areas for improvement without needing external validation.

Level 2 (Advanced):

Level 2 builds upon the foundational practices of Level 1 and focuses on protecting Controlled Unclassified Information (CUI). CUI is information that requires safeguarding or dissemination controls pursuant to and consistent with laws, regulations, and government-wide policies. Examples of CUI include personally identifiable information (PII), sensitive financial data, and technical specifications.

At Level 2, organizations must implement 110 cybersecurity practices aligned with the security requirements specified in NIST SP 800-171. These practices span across 14 cybersecurity domains and cover a wide range of security controls, such as:

- Limiting system access to authorized users, processes, and devices
- Enforcing a minimum password complexity
- Protecting CUI during transmission and at rest
- Implementing subnetworks for publicly accessible system components
- Employing the principle of least privilege
- Establishing an incident response plan
- Performing periodic scans and real-time monitoring
- Conducting security awareness training

The significance of Level 2 lies in its alignment with NIST SP 800-171, a widely recognized standard for protecting CUI in non-federal systems. By achieving Level 2 certification, organizations demonstrate that they have implemented a comprehensive set of security controls to safeguard CUI from unauthorized access, modification, or disclosure.

To achieve Level 2 certification, organizations must undergo a third-party assessment conducted by a CMMC Third-Party Assessment Organization (C3PAO). The assessment validates that the organization has effectively implemented the required practices and can adequately protect CUI.

Level 3 (Expert):

Level 3 represents the highest maturity level in CMMC 2.0 and is designed for organizations that handle the most sensitive CUI or operate in high-threat environments. In addition to the 110 practices from Level 2, Level 3 incorporates a subset of the enhanced security requirements from NIST SP 800-172.

At Level 3, organizations must implement advanced cybersecurity practices to counter sophisticated threats, such as advanced persistent threats (APTs). These practices may include:

- Employing hardware-based multi-factor authentication
- Implementing network segmentation and micro-segmentation
- Deploying advanced threat detection and response capabilities
- Conducting regular penetration testing and red team exercises
- Participating in threat information-sharing programs

The significance of Level 3 lies in its focus on protecting against APTs and safeguarding the most critical CUI. Organizations that achieve Level 3 certification have demonstrated the highest level of cybersecurity maturity and are well-equipped to operate in high-risk environments.

To achieve Level 3 certification, organizations must undergo a government-led assessment conducted by the Defense Contract Management Agency (DCMA) or other authorized entities. The rigorous assessment process ensures the organization has implemented advanced security measures to defend against sophisticated cyber threats.

In summary, the three levels of CMMC 2.0 provide a structured approach for organizations to enhance their cybersecurity posture based on the sensitivity of the information they handle and the level of risk they face. Each level builds upon the previous one, with Level 1 establishing basic cyber hygiene, Level 2 protecting CUI, and Level 3 safeguarding against APTs.

Organizations must understand the significance of each level and assess their specific cybersecurity needs based on the type of information they handle and the contracts they pursue. By achieving the appropriate level of certification, organizations can demonstrate their commitment to cybersecurity, meet the requirements of their DoD contracts, and contribute to the overall security of the defense supply chain.

It is important to note that CMMC 2.0 is not a one-time achievement but an ongoing continuous improvement process. Organizations must regularly reassess their cybersecurity posture, update their practices, and adapt to the evolving threat landscape to maintain their certification and protect sensitive information.

Overview of Controlled Unclassified Information (CUI) and Federal Contract Information (FCI)

To effectively implement CMMC 2.0, it is crucial to understand the types of information that the framework aims to protect. Two key categories of information are Controlled Unclassified Information (CUI) and Federal Contract Information (FCI). Let's explore each of these categories in detail:

Controlled Unclassified Information (CUI):

CUI is information that requires safeguarding or dissemination controls pursuant to and consistent with applicable laws, regulations, and government-wide policies. While CUI is not classified information, it is still sensitive and requires protection to ensure its confidentiality, integrity, and availability.

The U.S. National Archives and Records Administration (NARA) oversees the CUI program and maintains the CUI Registry, which identifies the categories and subcategories of information that fall under CUI. Some common examples of CUI include:

- Personally Identifiable Information (PII)
- Protected Health Information (PHI)
- Sensitive financial data
- Export-controlled information
- Legal information
- Technical specifications and drawings
- Proprietary business information

Organizations that handle CUI must implement appropriate security controls to safeguard the information from unauthorized access, modification, or disclosure. The protection of CUI is a primary focus of CMMC Level 2, which aligns with the security requirements specified in NIST SP 800-171.

To identify CUI within their systems and processes, organizations should:

1. Review the CUI Registry to understand the categories and sub-categories of CUI that are relevant to their operations.
2. Assess their contracts, agreements, and legal obligations to identify specific CUI requirements.
3. Collaborate with stakeholders, including government agencies and prime contractors, to clarify CUI expectations and flow-down requirements.
4. Conduct data discovery and classification exercises to locate and label CUI within their systems and networks.

Once CUI is identified, organizations must implement technical, administrative, and physical controls to protect the information throughout its lifecycle. These controls include access controls, encryption, incident response, and employee training.

Federal Contract Information (FCI):

FCI is information provided by or generated for the government under a contract to develop or deliver a product or service to the government. While FCI is not considered sensitive information like CUI, it still requires a basic level of protection to prevent unauthorized disclosure.

Examples of FCI include:

- Contract terms and conditions
- Performance data and metrics
- Financial and budget information related to the contract
- Product specifications and deliverables
- Communication between the contractor and the government regarding the contract

The protection of FCI is the primary focus of CMMC Level 1, which establishes a foundation of basic cyber hygiene practices. Organizations at Level 1 must implement 17 cybersecurity practices derived from the Federal Acquisition Regulation (FAR) clause 52.204-21.

To safeguard FCI, organizations should:

1. Identify FCI within their systems and processes by reviewing contracts and communication with the government.
2. Implement access controls to limit FCI access to authorized personnel only.
3. Protect FCI during storage and transmission using appropriate security measures like encryption.
4. Sanitize or destroy media containing FCI when no longer needed.
5. Provide security awareness training to employees handling FCI.

It is important to note that some contracts may involve CUI and FCI. In such cases, organizations must implement the appropriate security controls for each category of information based on the applicable CMMC-level requirements.

Understanding the distinction between CUI and FCI is crucial for organizations to determine the appropriate CMMC level to achieve and implement security controls. Mishandling or inadequate protection of CUI or FCI can lead to compliance violations, contractual penalties, and reputational damage.

To ensure the proper identification and protection of CUI and FCI, organizations should:

1. Establish clear policies and procedures for handling sensitive information.
2. Regular training and awareness programs should be conducted to educate employees on CUI and FCI requirements.
3. Implement robust access controls and monitoring mechanisms to prevent unauthorized access.
4. Regularly assess and update their security controls to address evolving threats and regulatory changes.
5. Collaborate with government agencies, prime contractors, and industry partners to share best practices and stay informed about CUI and FCI protection requirements.

By understanding the nature and importance of CUI and FCI, organizations can develop a comprehensive approach to cybersecurity that aligns with the CMMC 2.0 framework. Protecting sensitive information is not only a regulatory requirement but also a critical factor in maintaining the trust of government agencies, safeguarding national security interests, and ensuring the resilience of the defense industrial base.

Best Practices: To streamline CMMC 2.0 adoption, leverage existing compliance efforts (NIST 800-171) and understand regulatory contexts.

When embarking on the journey to achieve CMMC 2.0 compliance, organizations can benefit greatly by leveraging their existing compliance efforts and understanding the broader regulatory landscape. By doing so, they can streamline their CMMC 2.0 adoption process, avoid duplication of efforts, and ensure a more efficient and cost-effective implementation. Let's explore some best practices in this regard:

1. Leverage NIST SP 800-171 compliance:

NIST SP 800-171 is a set of security requirements for protecting Controlled Unclassified Information (CUI) in non-federal systems. It forms the foundation for CMMC Level 2, focusing on CUI protection.

If your organization has already implemented NIST SP 800-171 controls, you have a significant head start in achieving CMMC Level 2 compliance. Here's how you can leverage your existing efforts:

- **Conduct a gap analysis:** Compare your current NIST SP 800-171 implementation against the CMMC Level 2 requirements. Identify any additional practices or enhancements needed to meet the CMMC requirements.
- **Document your compliance:** Ensure you have comprehensive documentation of your NIST SP 800-171 implementation, including policies, procedures, and evidence of control effectiveness. This documentation will be valuable during your CMMC assess-

ment.

· **Update and refine your controls:** Based on the gap analysis, update and refine your existing controls to align with the CMMC Level 2 requirements. Focus on areas where CMMC introduces additional or more stringent practices.
· **Train your personnel:** Ensure that your personnel are familiar with the CMMC requirements and any updates to your existing controls. Provide training and awareness programs to reinforce the importance of protecting CUI.

By leveraging your NIST SP 800-171 compliance efforts, you can significantly reduce the time and resources needed to achieve CMMC Level 2 certification.

2. Understand the regulatory context:

CMMC 2.0 is not an isolated framework but part of a broader regulatory landscape. Understanding the relationship between CMMC and other relevant regulations can help you streamline compliance efforts and avoid duplication. Some key regulations to consider include:

· **DFARS 252.204-7012:** This Defense Federal Acquisition Regulation Supplement (DFARS) clause requires contractors to implement NIST SP 800-171 controls to protect CUI. If you already comply with DFARS 252.204-7012, you have a solid foundation for CMMC Level 2.
· **FAR 52.204-21:** This Federal Acquisition Regulation (FAR) clause establishes basic safeguarding requirements for Federal Contract Information (FCI). Compliance with FAR 52.204-21 aligns closely with CMMC Level 1 requirements.

- **ITAR and EAR:** The International Traffic in Arms Regulations (ITAR) and Export Administration Regulations (EAR) govern the export of sensitive technologies and information. If your organization handles export-controlled data, you may have already implemented controls that align with CMMC requirements.

By understanding the regulatory context and identifying overlaps between CMMC and other regulations, you can:

- Map your existing compliance efforts to CMMC requirements.
- Identify opportunities for consolidated compliance programs.
- Leverage existing documentation and evidence to support your CMMC assessment.
- Communicate the value of CMMC compliance to stakeholders by highlighting its alignment with other regulatory requirements.

3. Collaborate with industry partners:

Adopting CMMC 2.0 is a collective effort that involves collaboration among contractors, subcontractors, and the wider defense industrial base. Engaging with industry partners can provide valuable insights, best practices, and lessons learned to streamline your CMMC adoption process.

- Participate in industry forums and working groups focused on CMMC implementation.
- Share knowledge and experiences with peer organizations to identify common challenges and solutions.
- Collaborate with your prime contractors or subcontractors to align

CMMC efforts and ensure a consistent approach across the supply chain.
- Engage with CMMC-AB Registered Provider Organizations (RPOs) and Registered Practitioners (RPs) to seek guidance and support in your CMMC journey.

Fostering a collaborative approach can help you benefit from the industry's collective knowledge, avoid common pitfalls, and accelerate your CMMC adoption process.

4. Adopt a risk-based approach:

While CMMC 2.0 prescribes mandatory practices, adopting a risk-based approach to prioritize your implementation efforts is essential. Assess your organization's specific risks, considering factors such as:

- The sensitivity of the information you handle (CUI vs. FCI)
- The criticality of your systems and processes
- The potential impact of a cyber incident on your operations and reputation
- The likelihood and sophistication of the threats you face

By conducting a thorough risk assessment, you can:

- Prioritize the implementation of CMMC practices based on their risk mitigation value.
- Allocate resources effectively to address the most significant risks first.
- Develop a roadmap for CMMC adoption that aligns with your

organization's risk profile and business objectives.
- Communicate the risk-based rationale behind your CMMC implementation decisions to stakeholders.

5. Foster a culture of cybersecurity:

Achieving CMMC compliance is not just about implementing technical controls; it also requires a strong cybersecurity culture within your organization. Engage your leadership, employees, and stakeholders to foster a shared commitment to protecting sensitive information.

- Ensure top management buy-in and support for CMMC adoption.
- Communicate the importance of cybersecurity and the benefits of CMMC compliance to all employees.
- Provide regular training and awareness programs to reinforce cybersecurity best practices.
- Encourage employees to report potential security incidents or vulnerabilities.
- Recognize and reward employees who demonstrate a strong commitment to cybersecurity.

By cultivating a culture of cybersecurity, you can ensure that CMMC practices are not just a checkbox exercise but an integral part of your organization's day-to-day operations.

In summary, leveraging existing compliance efforts, understanding the regulatory context, collaborating with industry partners, adopting a risk-based approach, and fostering a cybersecurity culture are key best practices to streamline your CMMC 2.0 adoption process.

By following these practices, you can efficiently and effectively implement CMMC requirements, safeguard sensitive information, and demonstrate your commitment to cybersecurity excellence in the defense industrial base.

Remember, CMMC 2.0 is an ongoing journey rather than a one-time event. Continuously monitor your cybersecurity posture, update your practices as needed, and stay informed about the latest developments in the CMMC ecosystem. By remaining proactive and adaptive, you can ensure the long-term success of your CMMC compliance efforts and contribute to the overall security and resilience of the defense supply chain.

Chapter 2: CMMC 2.0 Compliance Requirements

Detailed breakdown of the requirements for each CMMC 2.0 level

To effectively implement CMMC 2.0 in your organization, it is crucial to understand the specific requirements for each maturity level thoroughly. Let's dive into the details of the practices and processes required at CMMC Levels 1, 2, and 3.

CMMC Level 1 (Foundational):

Level 1 focuses on protecting Federal Contract Information (FCI) and comprises 17 basic cybersecurity practices. These practices are derived from the Federal Acquisition Regulation (FAR) clause 52.204-21 and cover the following areas:

1. Access Control:

- Limit system access to authorized users, processes, and devices.
- Limit system access to the types of transactions and functions authorized users can execute.

2. Identification and Authentication:

- Verify users' identities, processes, or devices before allowing access to systems.

3. Media Protection:

- Sanitize or destroy system media containing FCI before disposal, release, or reuse.

4. Physical Protection:

- Limit authorized individuals' physical access to systems, equipment, and operating environments.
- Escort visitors and monitor visitor activity.

5. System and Communications Protection:

- Monitor, control, and protect communications at system boundaries.
- Implement subnetworks for publicly accessible system components that are separate from internal networks.

6. System and Information Integrity:

- Identify, report, and correct information and system flaws on time.
- Protect malicious code at appropriate locations.
- Perform periodic scans of systems and real-time scans of files from external sources as files are downloaded, opened, or executed.

7. Awareness and Training:

- Provide security awareness training to system users and managers.

To achieve Level 1 compliance, organizations must implement these 17 practices across their systems and processes that handle FCI. Compliance can be demonstrated through self-assessment using the CMMC Assessment Guide.

CMMC Level 2 (Advanced):

Level 2 builds upon the practices of Level 1 and focuses on protecting Controlled Unclassified Information (CUI). It requires the implementation of 110 cybersecurity practices aligned with NIST SP 800-171. These practices span 14 domains:

1. Access Control (22 practices):

- Limit system access to authorized users, processes, and devices.
- Employ the principle of least privilege.
- Use session lock with pattern-hiding displays to prevent access and viewing of data after a period of inactivity.
- Terminate (automatically) user sessions after a defined condition.

2. Audit and Accountability (9 practices):

- Create and retain system audit logs and records to enable monitoring, analysis, investigation, and reporting of unlawful or unauthorized activity.
- Ensure that the actions of individual system users can be uniquely traced to those users.

3. Awareness and Training (3 practices):

- Provide security awareness training to all system users and managers.
- Ensure that personnel are trained to carry out their assigned information security-related duties.

4. Configuration Management (11 practices):

- Establish and maintain baseline configurations and inventories of systems.
- Establish and enforce security configuration settings for systems.

5. Identification and Authentication (11 practices):

- Identify system users, processes, and devices.
- Authenticate (or verify) the identities of users, processes, or devices.
- Enforce a minimum password complexity and change of characters when new passwords are created.

6. Incident Response (7 practices):

- Establish an operational incident-handling capability for systems.
- Track, document, and report incidents to designated officials and authorities, both internal and external to the organization.

7. Maintenance (6 practices):

- Perform maintenance on systems and provide effective controls on the tools, techniques, mechanisms, and personnel used to conduct system maintenance.

8. Media Protection (8 practices):

- Protect system media containing CUI, both paper and digital.
- Sanitize or destroy system media containing CUI before disposal or release for reuse.

9. Personnel Security (2 practices):

- Screen individuals before authorizing access to systems containing CUI.
- Ensure that CUI and systems containing CUI are protected during and after personnel actions such as terminations and transfers.

10. Physical Protection (6 practices):

- Limit authorized individuals' physical access to systems, equipment, and the respective operating environments.
- Protect and monitor the physical facility and support infrastructure for systems.

11. Risk Assessment (4 practices):

- Periodically assess the risk to operations, assets, and individuals.
- Scan for vulnerabilities in systems and applications periodically and when new vulnerabilities affecting those systems and applications are identified.

12. Security Assessment (4 practices):

- Periodically assess the security controls in systems to determine if the controls are effective.
- Develop and implement action plans designed to correct deficiencies and reduce or eliminate system vulnerabilities.

13. System and Communications Protection (16 practices):

- Monitor, control, and protect communications at system and key internal boundaries.
- Implement subnetworks for publicly accessible system components physically or logically separated from internal networks.
- Deny network communications traffic by default and allow network communications traffic by exception (i.e., deny all, permit by exception).

14. System and Information Integrity (7 practices):

- Identify, report, and correct system flaws promptly.
- Protect malicious code at designated locations.
- Monitor system security alerts and advisories and take action in response.

To achieve Level 2 compliance, organizations must implement these 110 practices and undergo a third-party assessment by a CMMC Third-Party Assessment Organization (C3PAO).

CMMC Level 3 (Expert):

Level 3 builds upon Level 2 and includes additional practices to protect CUI from advanced persistent threats (APTs). It incorporates a subset of the enhanced security requirements from NIST SP 800-172. Some of the additional practices at Level 3 include:

1. Access Control:

- Employ dual authorization to execute critical or sensitive system and organizational operations.

2. Audit and Accountability:

- Protect audit information and tools from unauthorized access, modification, and deletion.
- Analyze and correlate audit records across different repositories to gain organization-wide situational awareness.

3. Configuration Management:

- Employ automated mechanisms to detect unauthorized changes to system configurations.

4. Identification and Authentication:

- Employ automated mechanisms for generating, protecting, rotating, and managing passwords for systems and system components.

5. Incident Response:

- Establish and maintain a security operations center capability that operates continuously.

- Use a combination of manual and automated, real-time responses to anomalous activities that match incident patterns.

6. Risk Assessment:

- Employ threat intelligence to inform the development of system and security architectures, selection of security solutions, monitoring, threat hunting, and response and recovery activities.

7. System and Communications Protection:

- Employ diverse system components to reduce the extent of malicious code propagation.
- Implement internal encryption methods to protect the confidentiality of CUI at rest.

To achieve Level 3 compliance, organizations must implement the additional practices and undergo a government-led assessment conducted by the Defense Contract Management Agency (DCMA) or other authorized entities.

It's important to note that the requirements for each CMMC level are cumulative. To achieve a higher level of compliance, organizations must implement all the practices of the lower levels and those specific to the targeted level.

To streamline compliance efforts, organizations should:

1. Conduct a gap analysis to identify the practices already in place and the ones that must be implemented.
2. Develop a plan of action and milestones (POA&M) to prioritize and track the implementation of missing practices.
3. Assign roles and responsibilities for implementing and maintaining each practice.
4. Provide training and awareness to employees to ensure they understand their roles in maintaining compliance.
5. Regularly assess and monitor the effectiveness of implemented practices through internal audits and continuous monitoring.

By breaking down the requirements for each CMMC level and following a structured approach, organizations can effectively navigate the compliance landscape and safeguard sensitive information by the appropriate maturity level.

Specific practices and processes at each level (17 practices for Level 1, 110 practices for Level 2, 110+ practices for Level 3)

Let's dive deeper into the specific practices and processes required at each CMMC level. Understanding these practices is crucial for implementing effective cybersecurity measures and achieving compliance.

CMMC Level 1 (17 practices):

1. Access Control:

- Limit system access to authorized users, processes, and devices.
- Limit system access to the types of transactions and functions authorized users can execute.

2. Identification and Authentication:

- Verify users' identities, processes, or devices before allowing access to systems.

3. Media Protection:

- Sanitize or destroy system media containing FCI before disposal, release, or reuse.

4. Physical Protection:

- Limit authorized individuals' physical access to systems, equipment, and operating environments.
- Escort visitors and monitor visitor activity.

5. System and Communications Protection:

- Monitor, control, and protect communications at system bound-

aries.
- Implement subnetworks for publicly accessible system components that are separate from internal networks.

6. System and Information Integrity:

- Identify, report, and correct information and system flaws
promptly.
- Protect malicious code at appropriate locations.
- Perform periodic scans of systems and real-time scans of files
from external sources as files are downloaded, opened, or executed.

7. Awareness and Training:

- Provide security awareness training to system users and managers.

CMMC Level 2 (110 practices):

Level 2 includes all 17 practices from Level 1 and 93 practices aligned
with NIST SP 800-171. Some key practices include:

1. Access Control:

- Employ the principle of least privilege.
- Use session lock with pattern-hiding displays to prevent access

and viewing of data after a period of inactivity.
- Terminate (automatically) user sessions after a defined condition.

2. Audit and Accountability:

- Create and retain system audit logs and records to enable monitoring, analysis, investigation, and reporting of unlawful or unauthorized activity.
- Ensure that the actions of individual system users can be uniquely traced to those users.

3. Configuration Management:

- Establish and maintain baseline configurations and inventories of systems.
- Establish and enforce security configuration settings for systems.

4. Identification and Authentication:

- Enforce a minimum password complexity and change of characters when new passwords are created.
- Prohibit password reuse for a specified number of generations.

5. Incident Response:

- Establish an operational incident-handling capability for systems.

- Track, document, and report incidents to designated officials and authorities, both internal and external to the organization.

6. Media Protection:

- Protect system media containing CUI, both paper and digital.
- Sanitize or destroy system media containing CUI before disposal or release for reuse.

7. Risk Assessment:

- Periodically assess the risk to operations, assets, and individuals.
- Scan for vulnerabilities in systems and applications periodically and when new vulnerabilities affecting those systems and applications are identified.

8. System and Communications Protection:

- Implement subnetworks for publicly accessible system components physically or logically separated from internal networks.
- Deny network communications traffic by default and allow network communications traffic by exception (i.e., deny all, permit by exception).

CMMC Level 3 (110+ practices):

Level 3 includes all 110 practices from Level 2, plus additional practices from NIST SP 800-172 to protect against advanced persistent threats (APTs). Some notable practices include:

1. Access Control:

- Employ dual authorization to execute critical or sensitive system and organizational operations.

2. Audit and Accountability:

- Protect audit information and tools from unauthorized access, modification, and deletion.
- Analyze and correlate audit records across different repositories to gain organization-wide situational awareness.

3. Configuration Management:

- Employ automated mechanisms to detect unauthorized changes to system configurations.

4. Identification and Authentication:

- Employ automated mechanisms for generating, protecting, ro-tating, and managing passwords for systems and system components.

5. Incident Response:

- Establish and maintain a security operations center capability that operates continuously.
- Use a combination of manual and automated, real-time responses to anomalous activities that match incident patterns.

6. Risk Assessment:

- Employ threat intelligence to inform the development of system and security architectures, selection of security solutions, monitoring, threat hunting, and response and recovery activities.

7. System and Communications Protection:

- Employ diverse system components to reduce the extent of malicious code propagation.
- Implement internal encryption methods to protect the confidentiality of CUI at rest.

To implement these practices effectively, organizations should:

1. Assign ownership and responsibility for each practice to specific individuals or teams.

2. Develop detailed procedures and guidelines for executing each practice consistently across the organization.
3. Train personnel on the proper implementation of each practice and their roles in maintaining compliance.
4. Establish metrics and key performance indicators (KPIs) to measure each practice's effectiveness and identify areas for improvement.
5. Conduct regular internal assessments and audits to ensure practices are followed and remain effective.
6. Continuously monitor systems and networks for anomalies and potential security incidents and have a well-defined incident response plan.
7. Regularly review and update practices based on changes in the threat landscape, regulatory requirements, and organizational needs.

It's important to note that while the practices are organized into specific levels, organizations should strive to implement as many practices as feasible based on their risk profile and the sensitivity of the information they handle. The more practices implemented, the stronger the organization's cybersecurity posture will be.

Implementing these practices and processes requires a concerted effort from the entire organization, including leadership, IT, security, and business units. It's not just a technical endeavor but also a cultural shift towards prioritizing cybersecurity and making it an integral part of the organization's operations.

By understanding and implementing the specific practices and processes at each CMMC level, organizations can effectively safeguard sensitive information, reduce the risk of cyber incidents, and demonstrate their commitment to cybersecurity excellence in the defense industrial base.

Compliance versus certification

When discussing CMMC 2.0, it's essential to understand the distinction between compliance and certification. Although often used interchangeably, these terms have different implications for organizations seeking to meet CMMC requirements.

Compliance:

Compliance refers to the state of adhering to the cybersecurity practices and processes outlined in the CMMC framework. This means that an organization has implemented the required practices for a specific CMMC level and operates by those practices.

For CMMC Level 1, compliance is achieved through self-assessment. Organizations must implement the 17 basic cybersecurity practices and attest to their compliance. They are not required to undergo a formal assessment by a third party.

Compliance is a prerequisite for certification for CMMC Levels 2 and 3. Organizations must implement the required practices (110 for Level 2 and additional practices for Level 3) and demonstrate their adherence to them through documentation, policies, procedures, and evidence.

Compliance is an ongoing process that requires continuous monitoring, maintenance, and improvement. Organizations must regularly assess their cybersecurity posture, address gaps or deficiencies, and adapt to evolving threats and regulatory requirements.

Certification:

Conversely, certification formally validates an organization's compliance with CMMC requirements. It involves a comprehensive assessment by an authorized third party or government entity to verify that the organization has implemented the required practices effectively and consistently.

Certification is not required for CMMC Level 1. Organizations can self-attest to their compliance with the 17 basic practices.

For CMMC Level 2, certification is achieved through a third-party assessment conducted by a CMMC Third-Party Assessment Organization (C3PAO). The C3PAO evaluates the organization's implementation of the 110 cybersecurity practices, reviews documentation and evidence, and interviews personnel to determine if the organization meets the Level 2 requirements.

For CMMC Level 3, certification is achieved through a government-led assessment conducted by the Defense Contract Management Agency (DCMA) or other authorized entities. The rigorous assessment includes additional practices beyond Level 2 to protect against advanced persistent threats (APTs).

Certification is a point-in-time validation of an organization's compliance. It demonstrates to the Department of Defense (DoD) and other stakeholders that the organization has met cybersecurity requirements and can protect sensitive information.

Certification is valid for a specific duration (usually three years) and must be renewed through reassessment. Organizations must maintain compliance throughout the certification period and be prepared for periodic reviews or audits.

The relationship between compliance and certification:

Compliance and certification are interdependent in the CMMC framework. Compliance is the foundation upon which certification is built. With effective compliance, an organization can achieve certification.

However, compliance alone does not guarantee certification. An organization may have implemented the required practices, but if it fails to demonstrate the effectiveness of those practices during the assessment, it may not achieve certification.

Certification, in turn, formally recognizes an organization's compliance. It assures the DoD and other stakeholders that the organization has met cybersecurity standards and can be trusted with sensitive information.

To navigate the compliance and certification process effectively, organizations should:

1. Understand the specific requirements for their target CMMC

level.

2. Conduct a gap analysis to identify areas where they need to improve their cybersecurity practices.
3. Develop a plan of action and milestones (POA&M) to address gaps and implement the required practices.
4. Document their policies, procedures, and evidence of practice implementation.
5. Provide training and awareness to personnel on their roles and responsibilities in maintaining compliance.
6. Conduct regular internal assessments and audits to ensure ongoing compliance.
7. Engage with a C3PAO (for Level 2) or prepare for a government-led evaluation (for Level 3) to achieve certification.
8. Continuously monitor and improve their cybersecurity posture to maintain compliance and prepare for recertification.

Organizations should view compliance and certification as a journey rather than a destination. The CMMC framework fosters a culture of continuous improvement and proactive cybersecurity practices.

By understanding the distinction between compliance and certification and working towards both, organizations can strengthen their cybersecurity posture, protect sensitive information, and position themselves as trusted partners in the defense industrial base.

It's important to note that the compliance and certification landscape is evolving, and organizations should stay informed about any updates or changes to the CMMC framework. Engaging with industry associations, participating in training and awareness programs, and seeking guidance from qualified professionals can help organizations navigate the compliance and certification process effectively.

Best Practices: Develop a checklist for each CMMC 2.0 level requirement to ensure no compliance detail is overlooked.

Developing a comprehensive checklist for each CMMC 2.0 level requirement is a crucial best practice for ensuring compliance and avoiding oversights. A well-structured checklist serves as a roadmap for implementing the necessary cybersecurity practices and helps organizations track their progress towards compliance.

Here's a step-by-step guide to creating and utilizing a CMMC 2.0 compliance checklist:

1. Understand the requirements:

- Review the CMMC 2.0 documentation thoroughly, including the model, assessment guides, and supplementary materials.
- Identify the specific practices and processes required for each CMMC level (17 for Level 1, 110 for Level 2, and additional practices for Level 3).
- Familiarize yourself with the objectives and intent behind each practice to understand its purpose in enhancing cybersecurity.

2. Create a master checklist:

- Develop a comprehensive master checklist that includes all the practices and processes for each CMMC level.

- Organize the checklist by domain (e.g., Access Control, Audit and Accountability, Configuration Management) to provide a logical structure.
- Break down each practice into specific, actionable items or sub-tasks to provide a granular level of detail.
- Include columns for status (e.g., not started, in progress, completed), responsible party, target completion date, and any relevant notes or comments.

3. Customize the checklist:

- Tailor the master checklist to your organization's specific needs and environment.
- Consider the scope of your CMMC assessment, including the systems, networks, and data involved.
- Identify any additional practices or requirements that may be applicable based on your organization's unique circumstances (e.g., specific contractual obligations, industry standards).
- Add or modify checklist items to ensure comprehensive coverage of all relevant requirements.

4. Assign responsibilities:

- Assign ownership and responsibility for each checklist item to specific individuals or teams within your organization.
- Ensure the assigned parties have the knowledge, skills, and resources to implement and maintain the required practices.
- Communicate the expectations and deadlines to all stakeholders

involved in the compliance effort.

5. Implement and track progress:

- Use the checklist to implement the required practices and processes systematically.
- Update the checklist regularly to reflect the progress made on each item.
- Conduct periodic reviews and status meetings to assess progress, identify roadblocks or challenges, and make necessary adjustments.
- Maintaining detailed documentation and evidence of practice implementation will be crucial during the assessment process.

6. Validate and assess:

- Perform internal assessments and audits to validate the effectiveness of the implemented practices and identify any gaps or deficiencies.
- Engage with a CMMC Third-Party Assessment Organization (C3PAO) for Level 2 or prepare for a government-led assessment for Level 3.
- Use the checklist as a reference during the assessment process to demonstrate compliance and provide evidence of practice implementation.

7. Continuously improve:

- Treat the checklist as a living document that evolves with your organization's cybersecurity posture.
- Regularly review and update the checklist based on changes in the CMMC framework, regulatory requirements, or your organization's environment.
- Incorporate lessons learned and best practices from your compliance journey to refine and optimize your checklist over time.
- To enhance the checklist's effectiveness, foster a culture of continuous improvement, and encourage ongoing feedback and suggestions from stakeholders.

By developing and utilizing a comprehensive checklist for each CMMC level, organizations can:

1. Ensure that no compliance requirement is overlooked or forgotten.
2. Provide a structured approach to implementing and managing the required cybersecurity practices.
3. Assign clear ownership and accountability for each practice, promoting a shared responsibility for compliance.
4. Track progress and identify areas where additional effort or resources may be needed.
5. Facilitate effective communication and collaboration among stakeholders involved in the compliance effort.
6. Streamline the assessment process by providing a centralized reference for demonstrating compliance.
7. Enable continuous improvement and adaptation to evolving cybersecurity challenges.

It's important to note that while a checklist is a valuable tool, it should not be treated as a mere "checkbox" exercise. Organizations should strive to understand the intent behind each practice and implement it meaningfully and effectively.

Compliance checklists should complement robust policies, procedures, and training programs to ensure cybersecurity becomes integral to the organization's culture and operations.

Organizations should also consider leveraging automated tools and platforms to facilitate creating, managing, and tracking compliance checklists. These tools can provide real-time visibility into compliance status, generate reports and dashboards, and enable collaboration among team members.

In summary, developing a comprehensive checklist for each CMMC 2.0 level requirement is a critical best practice for ensuring compliance and strengthening an organization's cybersecurity posture. By following a structured approach to checklist creation, implementation, and continuous improvement, organizations can navigate the CMMC compliance journey with greater confidence and effectiveness.

Chapter 3: Preparing for CMMC 2.0

Steps to establish a CMMC 2.0 implementation team

Establishing a dedicated and competent CMMC 2.0 implementation team is crucial for successfully adopting and maintaining the required cybersecurity practices. A well-structured team ensures that all aspects of CMMC compliance are addressed effectively and efficiently. Here are the key steps to establish a CMMC 2.0 implementation team:

1. Secure executive sponsorship:

- Identify and engage an executive sponsor to champion the CMMC implementation effort and provide strategic guidance.
- Ensure the executive sponsor understands the importance of CMMC compliance and its impact on the organization's ability to secure and maintain DoD contracts.
- Obtain the executive sponsor's commitment to allocate the necessary resources, budget, and support for the implementation team.

2. Define team structure and roles:

- Determine the size and composition of the implementation team based on your organization's size, complexity, and CMMC-level requirements.
- Identify the key roles and responsibilities needed within the team, such as:
- Project Manager: Oversees the overall implementation effort, co-ordinates activities and communicates progress to stakeholders.
- Technical Lead: Provides expertise in cybersecurity technologies, tools, and best practices and guides the technical implementation of CMMC practices.
- Compliance Specialist: Ensures alignment with CMMC require-ments, conducts assessments, and maintains documentation and evidence.
- Domain Experts: Provide subject matter expertise in specific CMMC domains (e.g., Access Control, Incident Response, Risk Management).
- Training and Awareness Coordinator: Develops and delivers training programs to educate employees on CMMC practices and their roles in maintaining compliance.
- Consider including representatives from various departments (e.g., IT, security, legal, HR) to foster cross-functional collabora-tion and ensure a holistic approach to compliance.

3. Select team members:

- Identify individuals within your organization with the necessary skills, knowledge, and experience to fulfill the defined roles.
- Consider factors such as cybersecurity expertise, project manage-

ment experience, familiarity with CMMC or similar frameworks, and communication skills.

- Ensure that selected team members have the capacity and availability to dedicate sufficient time to the CMMC implementation effort.
- If necessary, consider hiring external consultants or subject matter experts to fill any skill gaps or provide additional support.

4. Establish clear objectives and timelines:

- Define the objectives and goals for the CMMC implementation team that align with your organization's overall cybersecurity strategy and compliance requirements.
- Develop a high-level project plan that outlines the key milestones, deliverables, and timelines for achieving CMMC compliance.
- Break down the project plan into smaller, manageable tasks and assign responsibilities to team members.
- Establish regular progress review meetings to track the team's performance against the project plan and make necessary adjustments.

5. Foster a collaborative and inclusive environment:

- Encourage open communication, knowledge sharing, and collaboration among team members.
- Create a safe space for team members to raise concerns, ask questions, and provide feedback on the implementation process.
- Promote a continuous learning and improvement culture, encouraging team members to stay up-to-date with the latest CMMC

developments and cybersecurity best practices.
- Recognize and celebrate the team's achievements and milestones to maintain motivation and engagement.

6. Provide necessary resources and support:

- Ensure the implementation team has access to the tools, technologies, and resources to implement and manage CMMC practices effectively.
- Allocate sufficient budget for training, certifications, and external support, if required.
- Provide the team with the authority and decision-making power to implement changes and drive the compliance effort forward.
- Ensure that the team has the full support and backing of the executive sponsor and senior management.

7. Establish communication and reporting channels:

- Define clear communication channels and protocols for the implementation team to share progress, updates, and challenges with stakeholders.
- Develop a reporting framework that regularly updates the executive sponsor, senior management, and other relevant stakeholders.
- Ensure that the team communicates the importance and impact of CMMC compliance to all employees, fostering a culture of cybersecurity awareness and shared responsibility.

8. Continuously assess and improve:

- Regularly assess the implementation team's performance and effectiveness, identifying improvement areas.
- Encourage team members to provide feedback and suggestions for enhancing the team's processes, communication, and collaboration.
- Continuously refine the team's structure, roles, and responsibilities based on lessons learned and evolving CMMC requirements.
- Foster a culture of innovation and continuous improvement within the team, encouraging the adoption of new technologies, methodologies, and best practices.

Establishing a dedicated CMMC 2.0 implementation team is critical in ensuring a successful and sustainable compliance effort. By carefully selecting team members, defining clear roles and objectives, and providing the necessary resources and support, organizations can create a high-performing team that effectively navigates the complexities of CMMC compliance.

It's important to note that the CMMC implementation team should not operate in isolation but actively engage and collaborate with stakeholders across the organization. The team should catalyze change, driving the adoption of cybersecurity best practices and fostering a culture of compliance.

As the organization progresses through the CMMC compliance journey, the implementation team should continuously assess its performance, adapt to new challenges, and seek opportunities for improvement. By embracing continuous learning and growth, the team can stay ahead of evolving cybersecurity threats and ensure the organization's ongoing compliance with CMMC requirements.

In summary, establishing a CMMC 2.0 implementation team is a critical success factor for organizations seeking to achieve and maintain compliance. By following the steps outlined above and fostering a collaborative, inclusive, and improvement-oriented environment, organizations can build a high-performing team that effectively leads the CMMC compliance effort and strengthens the organization's overall cybersecurity posture.

Initial assessment: Understanding your current cybersecurity posture

Before embarking on the CMMC 2.0 implementation journey, conducting a thorough initial assessment of your organization's cybersecurity posture is crucial. This assessment is a foundation for understanding your strengths, weaknesses, and gaps in the CMMC requirements. It helps you prioritize your efforts, allocate resources effectively, and develop a roadmap for achieving compliance. Let's explore the key steps involved in conducting an initial assessment:

1. Determine the scope of the assessment:

- Identify the systems, networks, and data relevant to your CMMC compliance efforts.
- Consider your organization's boundaries, including any external partners, suppliers, or service providers that handle Controlled Unclassified Information (CUI) or Federal Contract Information

(FCI) on your behalf.

- Clearly define the scope of the assessment to ensure a comprehensive evaluation of your cybersecurity posture.

2. Review existing documentation and policies:

- Gather and review all relevant documentation related to your cybersecurity practices organization, such as policies, procedures, standards, and guidelines.
- Assess these documents' completeness, accuracy, and effectiveness in addressing the CMMC requirements.
- Identify any gaps or inconsistencies in your documentation that need to be addressed.

3. Conduct interviews and workshops:

- Engage with key stakeholders, including executives, managers, and subject matter experts, to gain insights into your organization's cybersecurity practices and challenges.
- Conduct interviews or workshops to gather information about current security controls, incident response procedures, risk management processes, and employee awareness and training programs.
- Encourage open and honest communication to understand your organization's cybersecurity posture comprehensively.

4. Perform technical assessments:

- Conduct vulnerability scans and penetration tests to identify technical weaknesses and potential entry points for attackers.
- Assess the configuration and security settings of your systems, networks, and applications against industry best practices and CMMC requirements.
- Evaluate the effectiveness of your security controls, such as firewalls, intrusion detection/prevention systems, and access controls.
- Analyze log files and audit trails to detect any suspicious activities or anomalies.

5. Evaluate incident response and business continuity:

- Assess your organization's incident response plan and procedures to ensure they are comprehensive, up-to-date, and regularly tested.
- Evaluate your ability to detect, respond to, and recover from cybersecurity incidents promptly and effectively.
- Review your business continuity and disaster recovery plans to ensure they address potential disruptions caused by cybersecurity events.

6. Assess third-party risks:

- Identify and assess the cybersecurity risks associated with your external partners, suppliers, and service providers.
- Evaluate the security controls and practices your third parties implement to ensure they align with your organization's security requirements and CMMC standards.

- Review contracts and service level agreements (SLAs) to ensure appropriate security clauses and obligations are in place.

7. Conduct a gap analysis:

- Compare your current cybersecurity posture against the CMMC requirements for your targeted level (Level 1, 2, or 3).
- Identify the gaps between your existing practices and the CMMC practices and processes.
- Prioritize the identified gaps based on their criticality and potential impact on your organization's ability to protect CUI or FCI.

8. Develop a findings and recommendations report:

- Document the results of your initial assessment in a comprehensive report.
- Include an executive summary highlighting the key findings, risks, and recommendations for improvement.
- Provide detailed observations and evidence to support your findings and recommendations.
- Present the report to senior management and relevant stakeholders to obtain their buy-in and support for the CMMC implementation effort.

9. Establish a baseline and set targets:

- Use the initial assessment results to establish a baseline for your organization's cybersecurity posture.

- Set realistic and measurable targets to improve cybersecurity practices and achieve CMMC compliance.
- Develop key performance indicators (KPIs) and metrics to track progress and measure the effectiveness of your improvement efforts.

10. Develop a roadmap and action plan:

- Based on the gap analysis and prioritized findings, develop a detailed roadmap and action plan to address the identified gaps and achieve CMMC compliance.
- Break down the roadmap into manageable phases and milestones, considering the resources, time, and budget required for each activity.
- Assign responsibilities and timelines to specific individuals or teams to ensure accountability and progress.
- Communicate the roadmap and action plan to all relevant stakeholders and obtain their commitment and support.

A thorough initial assessment is a critical step in preparing for CMMC 2.0. It provides a clear understanding of your organization's cybersecurity posture, identifies areas for improvement, and lays the foundation for a successful compliance journey.

It's important to approach the initial assessment with an open and honest mindset, acknowledging that no organization has a perfect cybersecurity posture. The assessment should be seen as an opportunity to identify strengths, weaknesses, and opportunities for improvement rather than a punitive exercise.

Throughout the assessment process, engage with organizational stakeholders, including IT, security, legal, HR, and business units. Encourage collaboration and knowledge sharing to comprehensively and accurately understand your cybersecurity posture.

Consider leveraging external expertise, such as cybersecurity consultants or CMMC Registered Provider Organizations (RPOs), to assist with the initial assessment. These experts can bring valuable insights, best practices, and tools to enhance the quality and efficiency of the assessment process.

Once the initial assessment is complete, use the findings and recommendations to drive meaningful change and improve your organization's cybersecurity practices. Regularly communicate progress and successes to maintain momentum and engagement throughout the CMMC implementation journey.

Remember, the initial assessment is not a one-time event but a continuous evaluation and improvement process. As your organization evolves and new threats emerge, regularly reassess your cybersecurity posture to ensure ongoing alignment with CMMC requirements and industry best practices.

In summary, conducting a comprehensive initial assessment is vital in preparing for CMMC 2.0. It provides a clear understanding of your cybersecurity posture, identifies gaps and priorities, and sets the stage for a successful compliance journey. By approaching the assessment with an open and collaborative mindset, leveraging external expertise when needed, and using the findings to drive continuous improvement, your organization can effectively navigate the path to CMMC compliance and strengthen its overall cybersecurity resilience.

Tools and resources for assessment (e.g., NIST 800-171 Self-Assessment)

Several tools and resources are available to effectively assess your organization's readiness for CMMC 2.0 and identify areas for improvement. These tools can help streamline the assessment process, guide best practices, and comprehensively evaluate your cybersecurity posture. Let's explore some key tools and resources:

1. NIST SP 800-171 Self-Assessment:

- The NIST SP 800-171 Self-Assessment is a valuable tool for organizations seeking to comply with CMMC Level 2, which aligns closely with the NIST SP 800-171 requirements.
- The self-assessment helps organizations evaluate their current implementation of the 110 security controls outlined in NIST SP 800-171.
- It provides a structured approach to assess the effectiveness of each control and identify areas where improvements are needed.
- The self-assessment includes a scoring system that allows organizations to measure their progress and benchmark their performance against industry standards.
- By conducting the NIST SP 800-171 Self-Assessment, organizations can clearly understand their gaps and prioritize their remediation efforts.

2. CMMC Assessment Guides:

- The CMMC Accreditation Body (CMMC-AB) provides assessment guides for each CMMC level, which offer detailed guidance on the assessment process and requirements.
- The assessment guides include information on the practices and processes organizations must implement to achieve compliance at each level.
- They guide the evidence and artifacts organizations should maintain to demonstrate compliance during the assessment.
- The assessment guides also include assessment procedures and objectives, which help organizations understand how assessors will evaluate their compliance.
- By leveraging the CMMC Assessment Guides, organizations can better prepare for the assessment process and ensure they have the necessary evidence and documentation.

3. CMMC Maturity Level Scoping Guides:

- The CMMC-AB provides scoping guides for each CMMC maturity level, which help organizations determine the scope of their assessment based on the specific contracts and information they handle.
- The scoping guides identify the systems, networks, and data relevant to CMMC compliance.
- They help organizations understand the boundaries of their assessments and ensure they focus on the most critical assets and processes.
- By using the CMMC Maturity Level Scoping Guides, organizations can streamline their assessment process and allocate resources

effectively.

4. Cybersecurity Maturity Model Certification (CMMC) Version 2.0 Model:

- The CMMC Version 2.0 Model is the foundational document that outlines the requirements and practices for each CMMC level.
- It provides a comprehensive overview of the CMMC framework, including the domains, capabilities, and practices organizations must implement to achieve compliance.
- The model serves as a reference guide for organizations, helping them understand the specific requirements and expectations for each CMMC level.
- By thoroughly reviewing and understanding the CMMC Version 2.0 Model, organizations can align their cybersecurity practices with the framework and ensure they meet the requirements.

5. CMMC Marketplace:

- The CMMC Marketplace is an online platform provided by the CMMC-AB that connects organizations with CMMC ecosystem partners, including Registered Provider Organizations (RPOs), Registered Practitioners (RPs), and Licensed Training Providers (LTPs).
- RPOs and RPs can provide expert guidance, consulting services, and support to organizations preparing for CMMC assessments.
- LTPs offer training and education programs to help organizations understand the CMMC requirements and develop the necessary skills and knowledge within their workforce.

- By leveraging the CMMC Marketplace, organizations can access a network of qualified professionals and resources to support their CMMC assessment and compliance efforts.

6. Cybersecurity Assessment Tools:

- Various cybersecurity assessment tools help organizations evaluate their security controls and identify vulnerabilities.
- Tools such as vulnerability scanners, penetration testing platforms, and security information and event management (SIEM) systems can provide valuable insights into an organization's cybersecurity posture.
- These tools can automate the assessment process, identify potential weaknesses, and provide recommendations for remediation.
- By incorporating cybersecurity assessment tools into their assessment process, organizations can gain a more comprehensive and accurate understanding of their security gaps and prioritize their improvement efforts.

7. Industry-specific Resources:

- Industry associations, such as the National Defense Industrial Association (NDIA) and the Aerospace Industries Association (AIA), provide resources and guidance specific to the defense industrial base.
- These resources may include industry best practices, templates, and tools tailored to the defense sector's unique requirements and challenges.
- By leveraging industry-specific resources, organizations can

benefit from their peers' collective knowledge and experience and stay informed about the latest developments and trends in CMMC compliance.

When selecting tools and resources for CMMC assessment, consider the following factors:

- Applicability to your organization's specific CMMC level and scope
- Ease of use and integration with existing processes and systems
- Cost and resource requirements
- Reputation and credibility of the tool or resource provider
- Availability of support and training materials

It's important to note that while tools and resources can greatly facilitate the assessment process, they should not be relied upon exclusively. Organizations should also engage in manual review, analysis, and validation to ensure a comprehensive and accurate assessment of their cybersecurity posture.

Additionally, organizations should strive to build internal competencies and expertise in CMMC compliance. Investing in employee training and education can help foster a culture of cybersecurity awareness and enable the organization to maintain ongoing compliance beyond the initial assessment.

Ultimately, the selection and use of tools and resources should be guided by the organization's specific needs, goals, and resources. By leveraging a combination of self-assessments, CMMC-specific guides, cybersecurity assessment tools, and industry resources, organizations can conduct a thorough and effective assessment of their readiness for CMMC 2.0 and identify areas for improvement.

Regular assessment and continuous monitoring should be ongoing, allowing organizations to track their progress, identify emerging risks, and adapt their cybersecurity practices to the evolving threat landscape. By embracing a proactive and iterative approach to assessment, organizations can strengthen their cybersecurity posture and maintain compliance with CMMC requirements over time.

Best Practices: Engage stakeholders from every department early to ensure alignment and distribute the cybersecurity responsibility across the organization.

Engaging stakeholders from every department is a critical best practice when preparing for CMMC 2.0. Cybersecurity is not solely an IT responsibility; it requires the active participation and commitment of the entire organization. By involving stakeholders early in the process, you can foster a shared sense of ownership, ensure alignment with business objectives, and distribute the responsibility for cybersecurity across the organization. Let's explore the key steps and considerations for effective stakeholder engagement:

1. Identify relevant stakeholders:

- Map out your organization's various departments and functions, including IT, security, operations, finance, legal, and human resources.
- Identify the key individuals within each department involved in the CMMC compliance effort, such as department heads, managers, and subject matter experts.
- Consider external stakeholders, such as customers, suppliers, and partners, whom your CMMC compliance journey may impact.

2. Communicate the importance of CMMC:

- Develop a clear and compelling message articulating CMMC

compliance's significance for your organization.

- Highlight the potential benefits, such as securing DoD contracts, enhancing cybersecurity posture, and protecting sensitive information.
- Explain the consequences of non-compliance, including the risk of losing business opportunities and potential legal and reputational repercussions.
- Tailor your communication to the specific interests and concerns of each stakeholder group.

3. Conduct awareness sessions and workshops:

- Organize awareness sessions and workshops to educate stakeholders about CMMC and its requirements.
- Provide an overview of the CMMC framework, the different maturity levels, and the specific practices and processes required for compliance.
- Explain the roles and responsibilities of each department in achieving and maintaining CMMC compliance.
- Use real-world examples and case studies to demonstrate the impact of cybersecurity incidents and the importance of a collaborative approach to cybersecurity.

4. Establish a cross-functional CMMC team:

- Form a dedicated CMMC implementation team that includes representatives from various departments.
- Ensure the team has the skills, knowledge, and authority to drive the CMMC compliance effort forward.

- Foster a collaborative and inclusive environment within the team, encouraging open communication and knowledge sharing.
- Assign clear roles and responsibilities to each team member, aligning with their expertise and departmental focus.

5. Engage stakeholders in risk assessment and planning:

- Involve stakeholders in the initial assessment of your organization's cybersecurity posture and the identification of gaps and risks.
- Seek input from stakeholders on the potential impact of CMMC practices on their specific operations and processes.
- Collaborate with stakeholders to develop a comprehensive CMMC implementation plan that addresses the identified risks and aligns with business objectives.
- Ensure the plan includes clear milestones, timelines, and resource requirements, and communicate it to all relevant stakeholders.

6. Establish regular communication and reporting channels:

- Set up regular communication channels to keep stakeholders informed about the progress of the CMMC compliance effort.
- Provide periodic updates on the status of key initiatives, milestones achieved, and any challenges or roadblocks encountered.
- Encourage stakeholders to provide feedback, raise concerns, and share ideas for improvement.
- Establish a reporting structure that ensures transparency and accountability at all levels of the organization.

7. Provide training and support:

- Develop and deliver targeted training programs to equip stakeholders with the necessary knowledge and skills to fulfill their CMMC-related responsibilities.
- Tailor the training content to each stakeholder group's needs and roles, making it relevant and actionable.
- Provide ongoing support and resources to help stakeholders navigate the challenges of CMMC implementation and maintain compliance over time.

8. Celebrate successes and recognize contributions:

- Acknowledge and celebrate the achievements and milestones reached throughout the CMMC compliance journey.
- Recognize the contributions of individual stakeholders and teams who have gone above and beyond in supporting the CMMC effort.
- Share success stories and best practices across the organization to inspire and motivate others.
- Foster a continuous improvement and learning culture, encouraging stakeholders to share their experiences and insights.

9. Continuously engage and adapt:

- Regularly assess the effectiveness of your stakeholder engagement approach and make necessary adjustments.
- Seek stakeholders' feedback on improving communication, collaboration, and support.
- Stay attuned to changes in the CMMC landscape and evolving

stakeholder needs, and adapt your engagement strategies accordingly.

· Maintain open lines of communication and continue to involve stakeholders throughout the CMMC compliance journey, not just during the initial preparation phase.

By engaging stakeholders from every department early and continuously, you can cultivate a shared sense of responsibility for cybersecurity and ensure that CMMC compliance becomes an integral part of your organization's culture and operations.

Remember, effective stakeholder engagement is not a one-time event but an ongoing process that requires sustained effort, communication, and collaboration. It involves building trust, fostering a shared vision, and empowering stakeholders to take ownership of their roles in the CMMC compliance journey.

Key success factors for stakeholder engagement include:

· Clear and compelling communication
· Tailored messaging for different stakeholder groups
· Regular updates and progress reports
· Opportunities for feedback and input
· Collaborative decision-making and problem-solving
· Recognition and celebration of successes
· Continuous improvement and adaptation

By investing in stakeholder engagement, you can overcome silos, align efforts, and create a strong foundation for CMMC success.

When everyone in the organization understands the importance of cybersecurity and their role in maintaining compliance, you can build a culture of shared responsibility and resilience.

Effective stakeholder engagement is not just about achieving CMMC compliance; it's about transforming your organization's approach to cybersecurity and embedding it into the fabric of your operations. By engaging stakeholders early and often, you can position your organization for long-term success in the evolving landscape of cybersecurity and defense contracting.

Chapter 4: Conducting a Gap Analysis

Methodology for performing a gap analysis for CMMC 2.0

Conducting a thorough gap analysis is crucial in preparing for CMMC 2.0 compliance. A gap analysis involves comparing your organization's current cybersecurity practices against the requirements of the CMMC framework, identifying areas where improvements are needed, and prioritizing remediation efforts. By following a structured methodology, you can ensure a comprehensive and effective gap analysis process. Let's explore the key steps involved:

1. Define the scope:

- Clearly define the scope of your gap analysis, including the systems, networks, and data relevant to your CMMC compliance efforts.
- Determine the CMMC level (1, 2, or 3) that applies to your organization based on the types of information you handle and the contracts you seek to pursue.
- Identify the practices and processes within each CMMC domain

that apply to your organization's scope.

2. Assemble the gap analysis team:

- Form a dedicated team to conduct the gap analysis, including representatives from key IT, security, operations, and compliance departments.
- Ensure team members have the knowledge, skills, and expertise to assess your organization's cybersecurity practices against the CMMC requirements.
- Assign roles and responsibilities to each team member, clearly defining their focus areas and expected contributions.

3. Gather and review relevant documentation:

- Collect and review all relevant documentation related to your organization's cybersecurity practices, such as policies, procedures, standards, and guidelines.
- Identify existing compliance efforts, such as NIST SP 800-171 or ISO 27001, and map them to the corresponding CMMC practices.
- Review past assessment reports, audit findings, and remediation plans to gain insights into your organization's cybersecurity posture.

4. Conduct interviews and workshops:

- Schedule interviews and workshops with key stakeholders and subject matter experts to gather information about your organization's current cybersecurity practices.

- Use structured questionnaires or interview guides to ensure consistent and comprehensive data collection.
- Encourage open and honest communication, creating a safe space for participants to share their knowledge, experiences, and concerns.

5. Perform technical assessments:

- Conduct technical assessments of your organization's systems, networks, and applications to evaluate the effectiveness of existing security controls.
- Automated tools, such as vulnerability scanners and configuration analyzers, can be used to identify potential weaknesses and misconfigurations.
- Perform manual testing and validation to complement automated assessments and gain a deeper understanding of your cybersecurity posture.

6. Map current practices to CMMC requirements:

- Create a matrix or spreadsheet that maps your organization's cybersecurity practices to the corresponding CMMC practices and processes.
- Assess whether your organization fully meets, partially meets, or does not meet the requirements for each CMMC practice.
- Document the evidence and rationale for each assessment, providing clear and concise explanations.

7. Identify gaps and prioritize remediation efforts:

- Analyze the results of your gap analysis to identify the areas where your organization falls short of the CMMC requirements.
- Prioritize the identified gaps based on their criticality, potential impact, and alignment with your organization's risk management strategy.
- Consider factors such as the sensitivity of the information involved, the likelihood and potential consequences of a breach, and the required resources and timeline for remediation.

8. Develop a remediation plan:

- Create a detailed remediation plan that outlines the specific actions, resources, and timelines required to address the identified gaps.
- Break down the remediation efforts into manageable tasks and assign ownership and accountability to specific individuals or teams.
- Establish milestones and key performance indicators (KPIs) to track progress and measure the effectiveness of remediation activities.

9. Validate and document results:

- Validate the results of your gap analysis through independent review and quality assurance processes.
- Ensure that the gap analysis findings, including the identified gaps, prioritization criteria, and remediation plans, are accurately

documented.

- Maintain a centralized repository of gap analysis documentation, making it easily accessible to relevant stakeholders and auditors.

10. Communicate and report findings:

- Communicate the gap analysis results to key stakeholders, including senior management, the CMMC implementation team, and affected departments.
- Develop executive summaries and visual representations of the findings, such as heat maps or dashboards, to facilitate understanding and decision-making.
- Present the remediation plan and obtain buy-in and support from leadership to ensure the necessary resources and commitment for addressing the identified gaps.

11. Monitor and update the gap analysis:

- Establish a process for regularly monitoring and updating the gap analysis as remediation efforts progress and new cybersecurity practices are implemented.
- Conduct periodic reassessments to validate the effectiveness of remediation activities and identify any new gaps that may emerge.
- Update the gap analysis documentation and remediation plans based on the results of ongoing monitoring and reassessments.

When conducting a gap analysis for CMMC 2.0, it's important to keep the following considerations in mind:

- **Objectivity and impartiality:** Ensure the gap analysis is conducted objectively and without bias, using consistent criteria and evidence-based assessments.
- **Collaboration and communication:** Foster a collaborative and transparent environment that encourages open communication and input from stakeholders across the organization.
- **Scalability and adaptability:** Design the gap analysis methodology to be scalable and adaptable to your organization's size, complexity, and unique cybersecurity needs.
- **Continuous improvement:** View the gap analysis as an ongoing process rather than a one-time event, continuously refining and updating your assessment as your organization's cybersecurity posture evolves.

By following a structured methodology for performing a gap analysis, you can clearly understand your organization's current cybersecurity state, identify areas for improvement, and develop a prioritized plan for achieving CMMC 2.0 compliance.

Remember, the gap analysis is not an end but a means to drive meaningful change and enhance your organization's cybersecurity resilience. You can use the insights from the gap analysis to inform your remediation efforts and continuously monitor progress to ensure a successful and sustainable CMMC implementation journey.

Identifying and documenting compliance gaps

Once you have conducted a thorough gap analysis by comparing your organization's current cybersecurity practices against the CMMC 2.0 requirements, the next crucial step is identifying and documenting the compliance gaps. This process involves analyzing the gap analysis results, categorizing the identified gaps, and creating clear and comprehensive documentation to support remediation efforts and compliance tracking. Let's delve into the key activities involved in identifying and documenting compliance gaps:

1. Analyze gap analysis results:

- Review the gap analysis results, including mapping your current practices to the CMMC 2.0 practices and processes.
- Examine each CMMC practice and assess whether your organization fully meets, partially meets, or does not meet the requirements.
- Pay close attention to the areas where your organization's practices fall short of the CMMC expectations.

2. Categorize compliance gaps:

- Group the identified compliance gaps into meaningful categories based on factors such as the CMMC domains, the severity of the gaps, or the level of effort required to address them.
- Common categories for compliance gaps may include:
- Technical gaps: Gaps related to specific technical controls, such as access control, encryption, or incident response capabilities.

- Policy and procedure gaps: Gaps in cybersecurity-related policies and procedures' existence, adequacy, or implementation.
- Documentation gaps: Gaps in the documentation of cybersecurity practices, such as missing or incomplete policies, procedures, or evidence.
- Awareness and training gaps: There are gaps in the cybersecurity awareness and training of personnel, including employees, contractors, and third-party partners.
- Categorizing gaps helps understand the nature and scope of the compliance challenges and facilitates targeted remediation efforts.

3. Determine the impact and priority of gaps:

- Assess the potential impact of each identified compliance gap on your organization's cybersecurity posture and CMMC compliance.
- Consider factors such as the sensitivity of the information involved, the potential consequences of a breach, and the level of risk exposure.
- Assign a priority level to each gap based on its impact and criticality. Common priority levels may include high, medium, and low.
- Prioritizing gaps helps allocate resources and focus remediation efforts on the most significant and time-sensitive issues.

4. Document compliance gaps:

- Create a comprehensive and structured document that captures the identified compliance gaps and their relevant details.

- For each gap, include the following information:
- CMMC domain and practice: Specify the CMMC domain and the specific practice or process where the gap exists.
- Gap description: Provide a clear and concise description of the gap, highlighting the specific shortcomings or deviations from the CMMC requirements.
- Evidence and observations: Include any evidence, observations, or findings that support the identification of the gap, such as assessment results, interviews, or technical analysis.
- Impact and priority: Document the gap's assessed impact and priority level and the rationale behind the assigned priority.
- Recommended remediation actions: Outline the suggested remediation actions or steps needed to address the gap and achieve compliance with the CMMC practice.
- Use a consistent and standardized format for documenting gaps to ensure clarity, comparability, and ease of tracking.

5. Validate and review gap documentation:

- Engage relevant stakeholders, such as subject matter experts, process owners, and the CMMC implementation team, to review and validate the documented compliance gaps.
- Seek input and feedback to ensure the gap descriptions' accuracy, completeness, and relevance and recommended remediation actions.
- Incorporate any necessary revisions or clarifications based on the stakeholder review process.

6. Establish a centralized gap tracking system:

- Implement a centralized system or tool to track and manage the identified compliance gaps.
- Consider using a spreadsheet, database, or specialized compliance management software to maintain a single source of truth for gap information.
- Ensure the tracking system captures key details such as gap descriptions, priority levels, assigned owners, target remediation dates, and status updates.
- Establish access controls and version control mechanisms to maintain the integrity and confidentiality of the gap-tracking system.

7. Communicate and report compliance gaps:

- Share the documented compliance gaps with relevant stakeholders, including senior management, the CMMC implementation team, and affected departments.
- Develop clear and concise reports or dashboards highlighting the most critical gaps, their potential impact, and the progress of remediation efforts.
- Regularly update stakeholders on the status of gap remediation activities and any gap landscape changes.
- Foster a culture of transparency and accountability in addressing compliance gaps, encouraging open communication and collaboration.

8. Integrate gap documentation into remediation planning:

- Use the documented compliance gaps to develop a comprehensive remediation plan.

- Map the identified gaps to specific remediation tasks, assign ownership and timelines, and allocate the necessary resources.
- Ensure the remediation plan aligns with your organization's cybersecurity strategy and risk management objectives.
- Review and update the remediation plan regularly based on the progress of gap closure activities and any newly identified gaps.

When identifying and documenting compliance gaps, keep the following best practices in mind:

- **Be thorough and systematic:** Ensure the gap analysis and documentation cover all relevant CMMC domains and practices.
- **Use clear and consistent language:** Describe gaps and remediation actions clearly, concisely, and consistently to avoid ambiguity and ensure a common understanding among stakeholders.
- **Prioritize based on risk:** Focus on the gaps that pose the highest risk to your organization's cybersecurity posture and CMMC compliance, allocating resources and attention accordingly.
- **Collaborate and communicate:** Engage stakeholders throughout the gap identification and documentation process, fostering a collaborative and transparent environment.
- **Maintain evidence and audit trails:** Document and retain evidence supporting the identification and remedy of compliance gaps, facilitating future audits and assessments.

Identifying and documenting compliance gaps can create a solid foundation for your CMMC remediation efforts. The gap documentation serves as a roadmap, guiding your organization in addressing the identified weaknesses and progressively enhancing your cybersecurity posture to achieve CMMC compliance.

Remember, identifying and documenting compliance gaps is not a one-time exercise but an ongoing process. As your organization's cybersecurity practices evolve and new threats emerge, it is essential to regularly reassess and update the gap documentation to ensure its relevance and effectiveness.

By maintaining a proactive and diligent approach to identifying and documenting compliance gaps, you can demonstrate your organization's commitment to cybersecurity excellence and position yourself for success in the CMMC assessment and certification process.

Prioritizing remediation efforts based on risk assessment

After identifying and documenting the compliance gaps through a thorough gap analysis, the next critical step is prioritizing the remediation efforts based on a risk assessment. Prioritization ensures that your organization focuses its resources and attention on addressing the gaps that pose the highest risk to your cybersecurity posture and CMMC compliance. By conducting a risk assessment and aligning remediation efforts accordingly, you can maximize the effectiveness and efficiency of your CMMC implementation journey. Let's explore the key considerations and steps involved in prioritizing remediation efforts based on risk assessment:

1. Establish a risk assessment framework:

- Define a risk assessment framework that aligns with your organization's risk management practices and industry standards, such as NIST SP 800-30 or ISO 27005.
- The framework should provide a structured approach to identifying, analyzing, and evaluating risks associated with the identified compliance gaps.
- Ensure the framework considers your organization's specific context, including its mission, objectives, and risk appetite.

2. Identify potential threats and vulnerabilities:

- For each identified compliance gap, assess the potential threats and vulnerabilities that could exploit or exacerbate the gap.
- Consider internal and external threats, such as malicious insiders, cybercriminals, nation-state actors, or accidental breaches.
- Identify the vulnerabilities in your systems, networks, processes, or human factors that the identified threats could leverage.

3. Determine the likelihood of occurrence:

- Assess the likelihood or probability of each identified threat exploiting the associated vulnerability, resulting in a cybersecurity incident or breach.
- Consider factors such as the ease of exploitation, the target's attractiveness, the threat actor's capability and motivation, and the effectiveness of existing controls.
- Use a consistent scale or rating system to assign likelihood levels, such as low, medium, or high, based on predefined criteria.

4. Assess the potential impact:

- Evaluate each identified risk's potential impact or consequences on your organization's operations, assets, and individuals.
- Consider the confidentiality, integrity, and availability aspects of the affected systems and data and the potential financial, reputational, and legal implications of a breach.
- Determine the criticality of the affected assets and processes to your organization's mission and objectives.
- Use a consistent scale or rating system to assign impact levels, such as low, medium, or high, based on predefined criteria.

5. Calculate risk levels:

- Combine the likelihood and impact assessments to determine the overall risk level for each identified gap.
- Use a risk matrix or heat map to visually represent the risk levels, typically using a low, moderate, or high-risk scale.
- Consider using a quantitative or semi-quantitative approach to assign numerical values to likelihood and impact, which would allow for more granular risk calculations.

6. Prioritize remediation efforts:

- Based on the calculated risk levels, prioritize the remediation efforts for the identified compliance gaps.
- Focus on addressing the gaps that pose the highest risk first, as they have the greatest potential impact on your organization's cybersecurity posture and CMMC compliance.

- Consider the feasibility, cost, and time required for remediation when determining the prioritization order.
- Align the prioritization with your organization's risk appetite and tolerance levels, ensuring that the remediation efforts are commensurate with the acceptable level of risk.

7. Develop a risk-based remediation plan:

- Create a detailed remediation plan incorporating the prioritized compliance gaps and associated risk levels.
- Define specific remediation tasks, assign ownership and responsibilities, and establish timelines for completion.
- Allocate the necessary resources to support the remediation efforts, including budget, personnel, and tools.
- Ensure the remediation plan aligns with your organization's cybersecurity strategy and CMMC implementation roadmap.

8. Implement and monitor remediation efforts:

- Execute the remediation plan, starting with the highest priority gaps and progressing through the prioritized list.
- Regularly monitor the progress of remediation efforts, tracking the completion of tasks and the effectiveness of implemented controls.
- Conduct periodic reassessments to validate the successful remediation of gaps and ensure the risk levels have been effectively mitigated.
- Update the risk assessment and prioritization as new gaps are identified or as the threat landscape evolves.

9. Communicate and report progress:

- Keep stakeholders, including senior management, the CMMC implementation team, and affected departments, informed about the progress of remediation efforts.
- Provide regular updates on the status of high-priority gaps, the risk levels associated with each gap, and the effectiveness of implemented controls.
- Communicate the overall risk posture and the impact of remediation efforts using visualizations, such as risk dashboards or heat maps.
- Celebrate successes and milestones in mitigating high-risk gaps and improving the organization's cybersecurity posture.

When prioritizing remediation efforts based on risk assessment, consider the following best practices:

- **Adopt a risk-based mindset:** Embed risk management principles into all aspects of your CMMC implementation, ensuring that decisions are guided by a thorough understanding of risks and their potential impact.
- **Use industry standards and frameworks:** Align your risk assessment approach with widely accepted standards and frameworks to ensure a comprehensive and consistent evaluation of risks.
- **Engage stakeholders:** Involve relevant stakeholders, including business owners, IT professionals, and cybersecurity experts, in the risk assessment and prioritization to gain diverse perspectives and ensure buy-in.
- **Document and maintain risk assessment records:** Maintain clear and comprehensive documentation of the risk assessment

process, including the identified risks, likelihood and impact assessments, and prioritization decisions.

· **Continuously reassess and adapt:** Review and update the risk assessment and prioritization regularly as the threat landscape evolves, new vulnerabilities are discovered, or organizational changes occur.

By prioritizing remediation efforts based on a thorough risk assessment, you can ensure that your organization allocates resources effectively and efficiently to address the most critical compliance gaps. This risk-based approach helps minimize the overall cybersecurity risk exposure and accelerates the journey toward CMMC compliance.

Remember, risk assessment and prioritization are ongoing processes that require continuous monitoring, review, and adaptation. As your organization progresses in its CMMC implementation, it is essential to regularly reassess the risk landscape and adjust the remediation priorities accordingly.

By integrating risk assessment into the core of your CMMC implementation strategy, you can demonstrate a proactive and mature approach to cybersecurity risk management. This strengthens your organization's resilience against cyber threats and enhances your credibility and competitiveness in the eyes of DoD customers and partners.

Ultimately, prioritizing remediation efforts based on risk assessment is critical in ensuring a risk-informed and effective CMMC implementation journey. By focusing on the highest-risk gaps first, you can systematically enhance your cybersecurity posture, protect sensitive information, and achieve CMMC compliance in a prioritized and strategic manner.

Best Practices: Use automated tools to assist in identifying gaps and ensure documentation is thorough and regularly updated.

When conducting a gap analysis for CMMC 2.0, leveraging automated tools can significantly streamline the process, improve accuracy, and ensure that documentation is comprehensive and current. Automated tools offer a range of capabilities that can assist in identifying gaps, managing documentation, and tracking progress throughout the CMMC implementation journey. Let's explore some best practices for using automated tools effectively:

1. Identify relevant automated tools:

- Research and evaluate various automated tools available in the market to support your CMMC gap analysis and documentation efforts.
- Consider tools specializing in cybersecurity assessments, compliance management, vulnerability scanning, and documentation management.
- Look for tools that align with the specific requirements and practices of CMMC 2.0, ensuring that they cover the relevant domains and levels.

2. Assess tool capabilities and features:

- Evaluate the capabilities and features of each automated tool to determine its suitability for your organization's needs.
- Consider factors such as:
- Compatibility with your existing IT infrastructure and systems
- Ease of use and user-friendly interface
- Customization options to tailor the tool to your specific CMMC requirements
- Integration capabilities with other tools and systems, such as security information and event management (SIEM) or governance, risk, and compliance (GRC) platforms
- Reporting and analytics functionalities to generate meaningful insights and visualizations
- Scalability to accommodate your organization's size and growth
- Vendor support, training, and documentation resources

3. Use automated tools for gap identification:

- Leverage automated tools to scan your systems, networks, and applications to identify potential gaps against CMMC requirements.
- Configure the tools to align with the specific CMMC practices and processes relevant to your organization's target level.
- Conduct regular scans and assessments using automated tools to identify new or evolving gaps as your cybersecurity posture changes.
- Use the tools to assess the effectiveness of existing security controls and identify areas where improvements are needed.

4. Integrate automated tools into your documentation processes:

- Utilize computerized tools to centralize and manage your CMMC-related documentation, including policies, procedures, evidence, and assessment results.
- Establish a structured and consistent documentation framework within the tool, aligning with the CMMC domains and practices.
- Automate the collection and organization of evidence, such as system configurations, logs, and audit trails, to support your compliance efforts.
- Leverage the tool's version control and collaboration features to ensure that documentation is regularly updated and easily accessible to relevant stakeholders.

5. Automate gap tracking and remediation:

- Automated tools track and manage the identified gaps throughout the remediation process.
- Assign ownership, prioritize gaps based on risk, and set target remediation dates within the tool.
- Utilize the tool's workflow and task management capabilities to assign remediation tasks, track progress, and monitor the status of gap closure activities.
- Integrate the tool with your ticketing or project management systems to ensure seamless coordination and accountability.

6. Generate reports and dashboards:

- Leverage automated tools' reporting and analytics features to generate comprehensive reports and dashboards on your CMMC compliance status.

- Customize reports to highlight key metrics, such as the number of gaps identified, the progress of remediation efforts, and the overall risk posture.
- Use visualizations, such as heat maps or trend charts, to communicate the impact of your gap analysis and remediation efforts to stakeholders.
- Regularly share reports with senior management, the CMMC implementation team, and relevant departments to keep them informed and engaged.

7. Ensure data accuracy and quality:

- Implement processes to validate the accuracy and quality of the data captured by automated tools.
- Conduct periodic manual reviews and spot checks to verify the tool's findings and ensure that gaps are accurately identified and documented.
- Establish data governance practices to maintain the integrity, consistency, and confidentiality of the information stored within the tool.

8. Provide training and support:

- Offer users comprehensive training on effectively utilizing automated gap analysis and documentation tools.
- Develop user guides, video tutorials, and FAQ resources to help users navigate the tool's features and functionalities.

- Encourage users to share best practices and lessons learned when using automated tools to foster a culture of collaboration and knowledge sharing.

9. Continuously monitor and update:

- Regularly monitor the performance and effectiveness of the automated tools in supporting your CMMC gap analysis and documentation efforts.
- Stay informed about updates, patches, and new features released by the tool vendors, and ensure timely implementation of relevant enhancements.
- Continuously assess the tool's alignment with evolving CMMC requirements and industry best practices, making necessary adjustments as needed.

10. Integrate with other cybersecurity tools and processes:

- Explore opportunities to integrate your automated gap analysis and documentation tools with other cybersecurity tools and processes within your organization.
- Consider integration with vulnerability management systems, security information and event management (SIEM) platforms, or governance, risk, and compliance (GRC) solutions to create a holistic and unified approach to cybersecurity management.

When using automated tools for CMMC gap analysis and documentation, keep the following considerations in mind:

- **Automated tools are not a silver bullet:** While computerized tools can significantly streamline and enhance your efforts, they should not be relied upon exclusively. Manual reviews, expert judgment, and human oversight are critical for a comprehensive and effective gap analysis.
- **Customize and configure tools appropriately:** Ensure the automated tools are properly configured and customized to align with your organization's specific CMMC requirements, environment, and processes. Regularly review and update the tool configurations to maintain their relevance and effectiveness.
- **Maintain data security and confidentiality:** Implement strong access controls, encryption, and data protection measures to safeguard the sensitive information stored within the automated tools. Ensure compliance with relevant data privacy regulations and industry standards.
- **Foster a continuous improvement culture:** Encourage constant improvement using automated tools for gap analysis and documentation. Regularly seek user feedback, assess the tool's performance, and make iterative enhancements to optimize its value and impact.

By leveraging automated tools effectively and following these best practices, you can significantly enhance the efficiency, accuracy, and comprehensiveness of your CMMC gap analysis and documentation efforts. Automated tools can help you quickly identify gaps, manage documentation more effectively, and track progress more easily throughout your CMMC implementation journey.

However, it is important to remember that automated tools are just one piece of the puzzle. They should be complemented by human expertise, manual reviews, and a strong governance framework to ensure a thorough and reliable gap analysis process.

Ultimately, by combining the power of automated tools with human oversight and a commitment to continuous improvement, you can streamline your CMMC gap analysis efforts, ensure comprehensive and up-to-date documentation, and accelerate your progress towards achieving CMMC compliance and strengthening your organization's cybersecurity posture.

Chapter 5: Developing an Implementation Plan

Structuring an effective Plan of Action and Milestones (POA&M)

Once you have conducted a thorough gap analysis and prioritized the identified gaps based on risk assessment, the next crucial step is to develop a comprehensive implementation plan. A key component of this plan is the Plan of Action and Milestones (POA&M), which serves as a roadmap for addressing the identified gaps and achieving CMMC compliance. A well-structured POA&M is essential for effectively managing and tracking the progress of your CMMC implementation efforts. Let's explore the best practices for structuring an effective POA&M:

1. Define the POA&M purpose and scope:

- Clearly articulate the purpose of the POA&M, which is to outline the specific actions, resources, and timelines required to address the identified gaps and achieve CMMC compliance.
- Define the scope of the POA&M, including the CMMC level tar-

geted, the systems and assets in scope, and the timeline for implementation.

- Ensure the POA&M aligns with your organization's cybersecurity strategy and business objectives.

2. Identify and prioritize gaps:

- Use the results of your gap analysis to identify the specific gaps that need to be addressed in the POA&M.
- Based on the risk assessment conducted, prioritize the gaps, focusing on those that pose the highest risk to your organization's cybersecurity posture and CMMC compliance.
- Group related gaps together to facilitate a logical and efficient implementation approach.

3. Define clear and measurable milestones:

- Break down the overall implementation plan into clear and measurable milestones that represent significant achievements or progress points.
- Milestones should be specific, achievable, and time-bound as checkpoints to assess progress and make necessary adjustments.
- Examples of milestones could include:
- Completion of specific CMMC practices or processes
- Implementation of critical security controls
- Development and approval of policies and procedures
- Completion of employee training and awareness programs
- Ensure that milestones are sequenced logically and aligned with the prioritization of gaps.

4. Develop detailed action items:

- Identify the specific action items or tasks that must be completed to achieve each milestone.
- Action items should be granular, actionable, and assignable to specific individuals or teams.
- Include a description of each action item, the expected deliverables, and the estimated effort required.
- Consider dependencies between action items and ensure that they are properly sequenced.

5. Assign ownership and responsibilities:

- Assign clear ownership and responsibilities for each action item in the POA&M.
- Identify the individuals or teams responsible for executing the tasks and ensuring their completion.
- Ensure the assigned owners have the skills, knowledge, and resources to carry out their responsibilities effectively.
- Communicate the assignments clearly and obtain a commitment from the designated owners.

6. Establish realistic timelines:

- Set realistic timelines for each action item and milestone, considering the complexity of the tasks, the resources available, and any dependencies.
- Be specific with start and end dates for each action item, allowing for sufficient time to complete the work while maintaining a sense

of urgency.
- Consider potential risks or obstacles impacting the timelines and build contingency plans or buffers where necessary.
- Ensure the timeline aligns with your organization's CMMC compliance deadlines and contractual obligations.

7. Allocate necessary resources:

- Identify the resources required to execute each action item and milestone successfully in the POA&M.
- Resources may include personnel, budget, tools, technologies, and external expertise or support.
- Ensure that the necessary resources are allocated and available when needed to avoid delays or bottlenecks in the implementation process.
- Consider the impact of resource allocation on other organizational initiatives and priorities and make necessary trade-offs or adjustments.

8. Establish progress tracking and reporting mechanisms:

- Implement a systematic approach to track and report progress against the POA&M.
- Define key performance indicators (KPIs) and metrics to measure progress, such as the percentage of action items completed, the number of milestones achieved, or the reduction in risk levels.
- Establish regular reporting cadences, such as weekly or monthly status updates, to inform stakeholders of progress, challenges, and successes.

- Use a centralized tool or platform to manage and update the POA&M, ensuring transparency and accessibility for all relevant stakeholders.

9. Monitor and update the POA&M:

- Regularly monitor the execution of the POA&M, tracking progress against the defined action items and milestones.
- Conduct periodic reviews to assess the effectiveness of the implementation efforts and identify any deviations or challenges.
- Update the POA&M as necessary based on progress, priority changes, or newly identified gaps or risks.
- Ensure that the POA&M remains a living document that reflects the most up-to-date status and plans for CMMC implementation.

10. Communicate and collaborate:

- Foster open communication and collaboration among the teams and individuals executing the POA&M.
- Establish regular status meetings or check-ins to discuss progress, challenges, and dependencies.
- Encourage a culture of transparency, accountability, and continuous improvement, where team members feel empowered to raise issues, share lessons learned, and propose improvements to the POA&M.
- Regularly engage senior management and key stakeholders to ensure ongoing support and alignment with the POA&M.

When structuring an effective POA&M, consider the following best practices:

- **Align with CMMC requirements:** Ensure the POA&M is explicitly mapped to the specific CMMC practices, processes, and domains relevant to your organization's target level.
- **Prioritize based on risk:** First, focus on addressing the gaps that pose the highest risk to your organization's cybersecurity posture and CMMC compliance, ensuring that critical vulnerabilities are remediated promptly.
- **Break down complex tasks:** Divide large or complex action items into smaller, more manageable sub-tasks to facilitate execution and progress tracking.
- **Assign clear ownership:** Ensure that each action item has a designated owner accountable for its completion and has the authority and resources to execute the task effectively.
- **Set realistic timelines:** Establish achievable and realistic timelines for each action item and milestone, considering dependencies, resource constraints, and potential risks or obstacles.
- **Monitor and adapt:** Continuously monitor the execution of the POA&M, assess progress, and make necessary adjustments based on changing circumstances, new information, or lessons learned.
- **Communicate and report:** Maintain regular communication with stakeholders, providing clear and concise updates on the progress of the POA&M and highlighting achievements, challenges, and next steps.

By structuring an effective POA&M, you can establish a clear and actionable roadmap for addressing the identified gaps and achieving CMMC compliance. The POA&M is a central tool for managing and coordinating the various activities, resources, and stakeholders involved in your CMMC implementation efforts.

Remember, the POA&M is a living document that should be regularly reviewed, updated, and adapted as your organization progresses through the CMMC implementation journey. It should be a dynamic tool for driving progress, accountability, and continuous improvement.

A well-structured and effectively executed POA&M ensures a systematic, prioritized, and successful approach to achieving CMMC compliance and strengthening your organization's overall cybersecurity posture.

Allocating resources and defining timelines

When developing an implementation plan for CMMC compliance, allocating resources effectively and defining realistic timelines are critical for success. These elements ensure that your organization has the necessary capabilities, budget, and personnel to execute the plan effectively and achieve compliance within the desired timeframe. Let's explore the key considerations and best practices for allocating resources and defining timelines:

1. Identify resource requirements:

- Based on the identified gaps and the actions outlined in your Plan of Action and Milestones (POA&M), determine the specific resources required for each task or milestone.

- Resources may include:
- Personnel: Identify the roles, skills, and expertise needed to execute the tasks effectively. Consider both internal staff and external consultants or contractors.
- Technology: Determine the software, hardware, and tools necessary to implement and maintain CMMC practices and controls.
- Budget: Estimate the financial resources required for each task, including costs for personnel, technology, training, and any external services or support.
- Facilities: Consider any physical space or infrastructure requirements, such as secure storage areas or network upgrades.
- Be comprehensive in identifying resource needs, considering both one-time investments and ongoing operational costs.

2. Assess available resources:

- Evaluate your organization's current resources and capabilities against the identified requirements.
- Determine which resources are available in-house and which must be acquired or procured externally.
- Consider the capacity and workload of existing personnel and assess their ability to take on additional CMMC-related responsibilities.
- Identify any skill gaps or expertise that may need to be filled through training, hiring, or engaging external support.

3. Prioritize resource allocation:

- Prioritize the allocation of resources based on the criticality and risk level of each task or milestone in the POA&M.

- First, prioritize allocating resources to the most critical and high-risk areas, ensuring the essential CMMC practices and controls are implemented promptly.
- Consider the dependencies between tasks and allocate resources to avoid bottlenecks or delays.
- Allocating resources across different CMMC domains and practices should be balanced to ensure a comprehensive and balanced approach to compliance.

4. Develop a resource allocation plan:

- Create a detailed resource allocation plan that maps the identified resources to specific tasks and milestones in the POA&M.
- Specify the type and quantity of resources required for each task, along with the estimated duration of the resource commitment.
- Assign clear ownership and accountability for each resource, ensuring a designated individual or team is responsible for its management and utilization.
- Identify resource constraints or conflicts and develop contingency plans or alternative approaches to mitigate potential risks.

5. Establish realistic timelines:

- Establish realistic timelines for completing the CMMC implementation activities based on the resource allocation plan and the complexity of each task.
- Break down the implementation timeline into specific phases or milestones, each with its deliverables and target completion dates.

- Consider the dependencies between tasks and ensure the timelines account for any prerequisite activities or approvals.
- Factor in potential risks or uncertainties that may impact the timelines, such as resource availability, technology challenges, or changes in CMMC requirements.
- Build contingency time or buffers to accommodate unexpected delays or issues during implementation.

6. Align timelines with business priorities:

- Ensure the CMMC implementation timelines align with your organization's overall business priorities and objectives.
- Consider the impact of CMMC compliance on other projects, initiatives, or operational activities and adjust timelines accordingly to minimize disruptions.
- Communicate the timelines and their importance to key stakeholders, including senior management, to secure their support and ensure alignment across the organization.

7. Monitor and adjust resources and timelines:

- Regularly monitor the utilization of resources and the progress against defined timelines throughout the CMMC implementation process.
- Track key metrics and indicators, such as resource utilization rates, task completion percentages, and milestone achievements.
- Identify any deviations or challenges in resource allocation or timeline adherence and take proactive measures to address them.
- Adjust resource allocations or timelines based on changing cir-

cumstances, new information, or lessons learned during implementation.

· Communicate any significant changes or updates to resource
allocations or timelines to relevant stakeholders, ensuring transparency and alignment.

8. Foster collaboration and communication:

· Promote a culture of collaboration and open communication
among the teams and individuals involved in CMMC implementation.
· Establish regular status meetings or check-ins to discuss resource
utilization, timeline progress, and any challenges or roadblocks.
· Encourage cross-functional collaboration and knowledge sharing
to optimize resource usage and ensure a coordinated approach to
CMMC compliance.
· Provide clear channels for escalating issues or concerns related to
resource constraints or timeline delays and ensure that they are
addressed promptly.

9. Continuously optimize resource allocation:

· Regularly assess the effectiveness and efficiency of resource
allocation throughout the CMMC implementation process.
· Identify areas where resources may be underutilized or overallo-
cated and make necessary adjustments to optimize usage.
· Explore opportunities for resource sharing, cross-training, or
leveraging external expertise to maximize the value of available
resources.

- Continuously seek ways to streamline processes, automate tasks, or adopt best practices to optimize resource utilization and improve timeline adherence.

10. Celebrate milestones and successes:

- Recognize and celebrate the achievement of key milestones and successes throughout the CMMC implementation process.
- Acknowledge the efforts and contributions of individuals and teams who have effectively managed resources and met timeline targets.
- Share success stories and lessons learned across the organization to motivate and inspire others involved in CMMC compliance efforts.
- Use milestones and successes to reinforce the importance of effective resource allocation and timeline management in achieving CMMC compliance.

When allocating resources and defining timelines for CMMC implementation, consider the following best practices:

- **Be realistic and pragmatic:** Ensure that resource allocations and timelines are grounded in reality, considering the available budget, personnel, and technology constraints.
- **Prioritize based on risk:** Focus resource allocation and timeline priorities on the areas that pose the highest risk to your organization's cybersecurity posture and CMMC compliance.
- **Communicate and collaborate:** Foster open communication and collaboration among stakeholders to ensure a shared under-

standing of resource requirements, timeline expectations, and progress.

· **Monitor and adapt:** Regularly monitor resource utilization and timeline adherence, and be prepared to make necessary adjustments based on changing circumstances or lessons learned.

· **Optimize continuously:** Continuously seek opportunities to optimize resource allocation and streamline processes to maximize the efficiency and effectiveness of your CMMC implementation efforts.

By effectively allocating resources and defining realistic timelines, you can ensure that your organization has the capability and capacity to execute the CMMC implementation plan successfully. This helps align efforts, manage expectations, and achieve compliance within the desired timeframe.

Resource allocation and timeline management require regular review, monitoring, and adaptation. By staying proactive, flexible, and responsive to changing needs and circumstances, you can optimize your CMMC implementation efforts and achieve compliance in a structured and efficient manner.

Ultimately, effective resource allocation and timeline definition are essential for driving progress, ensuring accountability, and achieving the desired outcomes of your CMMC implementation plan. By dedicating the right resources at the right time and adhering to well-defined timelines, you can position your organization for success in achieving CMMC compliance and strengthening your overall cybersecurity posture.

Strategies for stakeholder engagement and communication

Effective stakeholder engagement and communication are critical to a successful CMMC implementation plan. Engaging stakeholders throughout the implementation process helps to ensure buy-in, alignment, and support for the CMMC compliance efforts. It also promotes a shared understanding of cybersecurity's importance and each stakeholder's roles and responsibilities in achieving compliance. Let's explore key strategies for stakeholder engagement and communication:

1. Identify and map stakeholders:

- Identify all relevant stakeholders who have a vested interest in or are impacted by the CMMC implementation process.
- Stakeholders may include senior management, IT and security teams, legal and compliance departments, business unit leaders, employees, contractors, suppliers, and customers.
- Create a stakeholder map that categorizes stakeholders based on their influence, interest, and involvement in the CMMC implementation process.
- Understand each stakeholder group's needs, concerns, and expectations to tailor engagement and communication strategies accordingly.

2. Develop a communication plan:

- Create a comprehensive communication plan that outlines the objectives, key messages, target audiences, communication channels, and timelines for stakeholder engagement.

- Define clear goals and objectives for communication, such as raising awareness, providing updates, seeking input, or addressing concerns.
- Identify each stakeholder group's most effective communication channels, such as email, intranet, meetings, workshops, or newsletters.
- Establish a regular communication cadence, ensuring stakeholders receive timely and relevant information throughout the implementation process.

3. Engage senior management:

- Secure the support and commitment of senior management for the CMMC implementation initiative.
- Clearly articulate the business case for CMMC compliance, highlighting the benefits, risks, and potential consequences of non-compliance.
- Update senior management regularly on the progress of the implementation plan, key milestones achieved, and any significant challenges or roadblocks encountered.
- Seek their guidance and decision-making support when needed, and involve them in key communications to demonstrate leadership commitment.

4. Conduct awareness and training sessions:

- Develop and deliver awareness and training sessions to educate stakeholders about CMMC, its requirements, and the importance of compliance.

- Tailor the content and format of the sessions to the specific needs and roles of each stakeholder group.
- Cover topics such as the CMMC framework, the organization's implementation plan, individual roles and responsibilities, and best practices for cybersecurity.
- Use engaging and interactive formats, such as workshops, webinars, or e-learning modules, to maximize participation and information retention.

5. Establish a CMMC champion network:

- Identify and appoint CMMC champions or advocates within each business unit, department, or team.
- These champions serve as local points of contact, promoting CMMC awareness, answering questions, and facilitating two-way communication between their teams and the CMMC implementation team.
- Provide champions with the necessary training, resources, and support to fulfill their roles effectively.
- Regularly engage with the champion network to gather feedback, address concerns, and share best practices and lessons learned.

6. Foster cross-functional collaboration:

- Establish cross-functional teams or working groups that bring together stakeholders from different departments and disciplines.
- These teams can collaborate on specific aspects of CMMC im-

plementation, such as policy development, risk assessment, or incident response planning.

- Encourage open dialogue, knowledge sharing, and problem-solving among team members to break down silos and foster a collaborative approach to compliance.
- Regularly facilitate meetings or workshops to review progress, discuss challenges, and identify opportunities for improvement.

7. Provide regular updates and progress reports:

- Keep stakeholders informed about the progress of the CMMC implementation plan through regular updates and progress reports.
- Use various communication channels, such as email updates, newsletters, or dashboards, to share key milestones achieved, upcoming activities, and any changes or updates to the plan.
- Highlight success stories, best practices, and lessons learned to maintain momentum and engagement.
- Be transparent about challenges or setbacks, and communicate the steps to address them.

8. Seek feedback and input:

- Actively seek feedback and input from stakeholders throughout the CMMC implementation process.
- Conduct surveys, focus groups, or interviews to gather insights, concerns, and suggestions for improvement.
- Encourage open and honest feedback and create a safe and confidential environment for stakeholders to share their perspectives.
- Use feedback to inform decision-making, refine the implementa-

tion plan, and address any gaps or areas of concern.

9. Celebrate successes and milestones:

- Recognize and celebrate the achievement of key milestones and successes throughout the CMMC implementation journey.
- Acknowledge the contributions and efforts of individuals and teams who have made significant progress or demonstrated exemplary commitment to CMMC compliance.
- Share success stories and best practices widely to inspire and motivate others and reinforce the importance of CMMC compliance.
- Use celebrations as opportunities to build a positive culture around cybersecurity and compliance and to foster a sense of shared accomplishment.

10. Continuously evaluate and improve:

- Assess the effectiveness of stakeholder engagement and communication strategies regularly and make necessary adjustments based on feedback and lessons learned.
- Monitor key metrics, such as stakeholder participation rates, awareness levels, or compliance progress, to measure the impact of engagement efforts.
- Continuously seek opportunities to enhance communication channels, content, and frequency to meet stakeholders' evolving needs and expectations.
- Encourage ongoing dialogue and maintain open lines of communication to ensure that stakeholders remain engaged and informed throughout the CMMC implementation process.

When developing strategies for stakeholder engagement and communication, consider the following best practices:

- **Tailor communication to the audience:** Adapt the content, language, and format of communication to the specific needs, roles, and preferences of each stakeholder group.
- **Be transparent and consistent:** Provide clear, accurate, and consistent information to build stakeholder trust and credibility.
- **Listen actively and respond promptly:** Demonstrate a genuine interest in stakeholder concerns and feedback and provide timely and meaningful responses to their inquiries or suggestions.
- **Encourage two-way communication:** Create opportunities for stakeholders to ask questions, provide input, and engage in dialogue to foster a sense of ownership and collaboration.
- **Leverage visual aids and storytelling:** Use visual aids, such as infographics, videos, or case studies, to simplify complex concepts and make communication more engaging and memorable.
- **Continuously reinforce the importance of CMMC:** Regularly communicate the benefits, risks, and responsibilities associated with CMMC compliance to maintain stakeholder commitment and motivation.

Effective stakeholder engagement and communication are essential for securing buy-in, aligning efforts, and driving successful CMMC implementation. By developing a comprehensive communication plan, engaging stakeholders at all levels, fostering collaboration, and continuously evaluating and improving engagement strategies, organizations can build a strong foundation for CMMC compliance and create a culture of cybersecurity awareness and responsibility.

Remember, stakeholder engagement and communication are ongoing processes that require consistent effort and attention throughout the CMMC implementation journey. By maintaining open, transparent, and responsive communication channels, organizations can effectively navigate the challenges of CMMC compliance, build trust and credibility among stakeholders, and achieve their compliance goals collaboratively and sustainably.

Effective stakeholder engagement and communication are key enablers of CMMC's success. They help organizations align priorities, mobilize resources, and drive continuous improvement in their cybersecurity practices. By investing in robust engagement strategies and fostering a culture of open communication, organizations can position themselves for long-term success in achieving and maintaining CMMC compliance.

Best Practices: Maintain flexible and scalable implementation plans to adapt to unforeseen challenges or changes in requirements.

In the dynamic landscape of cybersecurity and CMMC compliance, it is crucial to develop implementation plans that are flexible and scalable. The ability to adapt to unforeseen challenges, changes in requirements, or evolving threat landscapes is essential for the success of your CMMC implementation efforts. Let's explore the best practices for maintaining flexible and scalable implementation plans:

1. Embrace an agile mindset:

- Adopt an agile mindset and approach to CMMC implementation planning, recognizing that change is inevitable and adaptability is key.
- Break down the implementation plan into smaller, manageable iterations or sprints, allowing for regular review, feedback, and adjustment.
- Prioritize flexibility and responsiveness over rigid adherence to a fixed plan, enabling your team to pivot and adapt as needed.

2. Build modular and scalable architectures:

- Design your technical architectures and solutions to be modular, scalable, and adaptable to changing requirements or emerging technologies.
- Use a layered approach to security controls, allowing for adding,

modifying, or removing controls without significantly disrupting the overall architecture.
- Leverage cloud-based or virtualized environments with scalability, flexibility, and rapid provisioning capabilities.

3. Develop contingency plans:

- Identify potential risks, uncertainties, and challenges that may impact your CMMC implementation plan, such as changes in CMMC requirements, resource constraints, or technology disruptions.
- Develop contingency plans or alternative approaches to mitigate these risks and ensure business continuity.
- Consider scenarios such as accelerating or decelerating implementation timelines, adapting to new CMMC practices or controls, or responding to security incidents.
- Document and communicate contingency plans to relevant stakeholders, ensuring everyone understands their roles and responsibilities in the event of plan deviations.

4. Foster a culture of continuous improvement:

- Embed a culture of continuous improvement throughout your CMMC implementation process, encouraging ongoing learning, experimentation, and adaptation.
- Regularly assess the effectiveness and efficiency of your implementation plan, seeking opportunities for optimization and refinement.
- Encourage team members to identify areas for improvement

proactively, suggest innovative solutions, and share lessons learned.

· Celebrate successes and milestones and embrace failures as opportunities for growth and learning.

5. Leverage automation and tools:

· Utilize automation and tools to enhance the flexibility and scalability of your CMMC implementation efforts.
· Implement automated testing, continuous integration, and continuous deployment (CI/CD) practices to streamline the implementation process and reduce manual effort.
· Leverage configuration management and version control tools to manage policy, procedure, and technical configuration changes.
· Utilize security orchestration, automation, and response (SOAR) tools to automate incident response and adapt to evolving threat landscapes.

6. Establish change management processes:

· Develop robust change management processes to handle modifications to your CMMC implementation plan effectively.
· Define clear roles, responsibilities, and approval workflows for initiating, reviewing, and implementing changes to the plan.
· Establish criteria for assessing the impact and prioritization of proposed changes, considering urgency, risk, and resource requirements.
· Communicate changes to relevant stakeholders, providing clear rationale and guidance on implementing them and their expected

outcomes.

7. Monitor and adapt to external factors:

- Stay informed about external factors that may impact your CMMC implementation plan, such as changes in CMMC requirements, regulatory updates, or industry best practices.
- Regularly monitor CMMC-related news, publications, and guidance from the CMMC Accreditation Body (CMMC-AB) and other authoritative sources.
- Participate in CMMC-focused forums, working groups, or industry associations to stay connected with the CMMC community and learn from others' experiences.
- Adapt your implementation plan proactively to align with evolving CMMC requirements or industry standards, minimizing the need for significant rework or disruption.

8. Foster cross-functional collaboration:

- To enhance flexibility and adaptability, promote cross-functional collaboration and communication throughout the CMMC implementation process.
- Engage stakeholders from various departments, such as IT, security, legal, compliance, and business units, to gather diverse perspectives and insights.
- Establish cross-functional teams or working groups to collaboratively address challenges, brainstorm solutions, and adapt to changing requirements.
- Encourage a shared sense of ownership and accountability for

the success of the CMMC implementation plan across all relevant functions.

9. Conduct regular plan reviews and updates:

- Schedule regular reviews and updates of your CMMC implementation plan to assess its relevance, effectiveness, and alignment with changing circumstances.
- Evaluate progress against milestones, identify any deviations or challenges, and make necessary adjustments to the plan.
- Solicit feedback from team members, stakeholders, and external partners to gather insights and suggestions for improvement.
- Update the plan based on lessons learned, new information, or changes in requirements, ensuring that it remains a living and evolving document.

10. Invest in workforce development:

- Invest in your workforce's continuous development and up-skilling to enhance their ability to adapt to new challenges and requirements.
- Provide ongoing training and education opportunities to keep team members up-to-date with the latest CMMC practices, technologies, and industry trends.
- Foster a learning culture encouraging experimentation, knowledge sharing, and continuous improvement.
- Develop a workforce that is agile, resilient, and equipped with the skills and mindset to navigate the evolving landscape of CMMC compliance.

When maintaining flexible and scalable implementation plans, consider the following best practices:

- **Embrace iterative planning:** Break down the implementation plan into smaller, iterative cycles, allowing for regular review, feedback, and adjustment based on changing circumstances or new information.
- **Build in buffer time:** Include buffer time or contingency allowances in your implementation plan to accommodate unforeseen delays, challenges, or changes in requirements.
- **Prioritize risk-based decision-making:** Use risk assessment to prioritize and adapt your implementation plan, focusing on the highest-risk or highest-impact areas.
- **Communicate transparently:** Maintain open and transparent communication with stakeholders about the flexibility and scalability of the implementation plan, setting realistic expectations, and managing potential concerns.
- **Leverage lessons learned:** Continuously capture and apply lessons learned throughout the implementation process to inform future planning and adaptation efforts.

Organizations can effectively navigate the uncertainties and challenges associated with CMMC compliance by maintaining flexible and scalable implementation plans. The ability to adapt and pivot as needed enables organizations to respond proactively to changes in requirements, mitigate risks, and ensure the ongoing effectiveness of their CMMC implementation efforts.

Remember, flexibility and scalability are not about abandoning structure or planning altogether. Rather, they involve striking a balance between having a clear direction and being open to adjustments and improvements. By embracing an agile mindset, fostering a culture of continuous improvement, and leveraging the right tools and processes, organizations can develop implementation plans that are resilient, adaptable and well-positioned to achieve CMMC success in a dynamic and evolving landscape.

Ultimately, maintaining flexible and scalable implementation plans is a critical best practice for organizations seeking to navigate the complexities of CMMC compliance. By building adaptability into the core of their implementation approach, organizations can proactively manage change, mitigate risks, and drive continuous improvement in their cybersecurity practices, ensuring a successful and sustainable CMMC journey.

Chapter 6: Cybersecurity Controls and Practices

Detailed guidance on specific security controls required for CMMC 2.0 (based on NIST 800-171)

CMMC 2.0 Level 2 requires organizations to implement the security controls outlined in NIST Special Publication 800-171, which provides comprehensive requirements for protecting Controlled Unclassified Information (CUI) in non-federal systems. Let's dive into the specific security controls and practices based on NIST 800-171 that organizations need to implement to achieve CMMC 2.0 Level 2 compliance:

1. Access Control:

- Limit system access to authorized users, processes, and devices.
- Employ the principle of least privilege, granting users only the access rights necessary to perform their job functions.
- Implement access controls based on user roles and responsibilities.
- Enforce separation of duties to prevent individuals from having excessive control over critical functions.

- Use multifactor authentication for local and network access to privileged accounts and remote access to the system.
- Employ session lock mechanisms to prevent unauthorized access to unattended workstations.
- Terminate user sessions automatically after a defined period of inactivity.
- Monitor and control remote access sessions.
- Authorize wireless access before allowing such connections.

2. Audit and Accountability:

- Create and retain system audit logs to enable monitoring, analysis, investigation, and reporting of unauthorized or inappropriate activity.
- Ensure that the actions of individual system users can be uniquely traced to those users.
- Review and update logged events periodically.
- Alert designated personnel in the event of an audit logging process failure.
- Correlate audit record review, analysis, and reporting processes for investigation and response to indications of unlawful, unauthorized, suspicious, or unusual activity.
- Provide audit record reduction and report generation capabilities to support on-demand analysis and reporting.
- Protect audit information and logging tools from unauthorized access, modification, and deletion.

3. Configuration Management:

- Establish and maintain baseline configurations and inventories of systems.
- Establish and enforce security configuration settings for systems and components.
- Track, review, approve, and log changes to systems.
- Analyze the security impact of changes before implementation.
- Define, document, approve, and enforce physical and logical access restrictions associated with system changes.
- Employ the principle of least functionality by configuring systems to provide only essential capabilities.
- Restrict, disable, or prevent the use of nonessential programs, functions, ports, protocols, and services.
- Apply a deny-by-exception (blocklist) policy to prevent the use of unauthorized software or a deny-all, permit-by-exception (allowlist) policy to allow the execution of authorized software.

4. Identification and Authentication:

- Identify system users, processes, and devices.
- Authenticate (or verify) the identities of users, processes, or devices before allowing access to systems.
- Enforce a minimum password complexity and change of characters when new passwords are created.
- Prohibit password reuse for a specified number of generations.
- Allow temporary password use for system logins with an immediate change to a permanent password.
- Store and transmit only cryptographically protected passwords.
- Obscure feedback of authentication information during the authentication process.

5. Incident Response:

- Establish an operational incident-handling capability for systems.
- Track, document, and report incidents to designated officials and authorities, both internal and external to the organization.
- Test the incident response capability periodically.
- Implement security safeguards to protect the confidentiality and integrity of incident information.
- Develop and maintain an incident response plan that addresses purpose, scope, roles, responsibilities, management commitment, coordination among organizational entities, and compliance.
- Distribute copies of the incident response plan to key incident response personnel.
- Review and update the incident response plan periodically.

6. Maintenance:

- Perform maintenance on systems and components.
- Provide controls on the tools, techniques, mechanisms, and personnel used to conduct system maintenance.
- Ensure that only authorized personnel perform maintenance activities.
- Sanitize or remove system components containing CUI before disposal or release for reuse.
- Check media containing diagnostic and test programs for malicious code before the media are used in systems.
- Multifactor authentication is required to establish nonlocal maintenance sessions via external network connections and terminate

such connections when nonlocal maintenance is complete.

- Supervise the maintenance activities of maintenance personnel without required access authorization.

7. Media Protection:

- Protect system media containing CUI, both paper and digital.
- Restrict access to CUI on system media to authorized users.
- Sanitize or destroy system media containing CUI before disposal or release for reuse.
- Mark media with necessary CUI markings and distribution limitations.
- Control access to media containing CUI and maintain accountability for media during transport outside of controlled areas.
- Implement cryptographic mechanisms to protect the confidentiality of CUI stored on digital media during transport unless otherwise protected by alternative physical safeguards.

8. Personnel Security:

- Screen individuals before authorizing access to systems containing CUI.
- Ensure that CUI and systems containing CUI are protected during and after personnel actions such as terminations and transfers.
- Revoke system access within a defined period following the formal transfer action or the termination of an individual.

9. Physical Protection:

- Limit authorized individuals' physical access to systems, equipment, and the respective operating environments.
- Protect and monitor the physical facility and support infrastructure for systems.
- Escort visitors and monitor visitor activity.
- Maintain audit logs of physical access.
- Control and manage physical access devices.
- Enforce safeguarding measures for CUI at alternate work sites.

10. Risk Assessment:

- Periodically assess the risk to operations, assets, and individuals.
- Scan for vulnerabilities in systems and applications periodically and when new vulnerabilities are identified.
- Remediate vulnerabilities by risk assessments.
- Develop and implement action plans designed to correct deficiencies and reduce or eliminate system vulnerabilities.

11. Security Assessment:

- Periodically assess the security controls in systems to determine if they are effective in their application.
- Develop and implement action plans designed to correct deficiencies and reduce or eliminate system vulnerabilities.
- Monitor security controls on an ongoing basis to ensure the continued effectiveness of the controls.
- Employ an independent assessor or assessment team to conduct security control assessments.
- Ensure that the assessors or assessment team have the necessary

access and information to conduct comprehensive assessments.

12. System and Communications Protection:

- Monitor, control, and protect communications at external and key internal boundaries.
- Employ architectural designs, software development techniques, and systems engineering principles that promote effective information security.
- Separate user functionality from system management functionality.
- Prevent unauthorized and unintended information transfer via shared system resources.
- Deny network communications traffic by default and allow network communications traffic by exception (i.e., deny all, permit by exception).
- Implement subnetworks for publicly accessible system components physically or logically separated from internal networks.
- Prevent remote devices from simultaneously establishing non-remote connections with organizational systems and communicating via some other connection to resources in external networks (i.e., split tunneling).
- Implement cryptographic mechanisms to prevent unauthorized disclosure of CUI during transmission unless otherwise protected by alternative physical safeguards.
- Terminate network connections associated with communications sessions at the end of the sessions or after a defined period of inactivity.

13. System and Information Integrity:

- Identify, report, and correct system flaws promptly.
- Protect malicious code at designated locations within organizational systems.
- Monitor system security alerts and advisories and take action in response.
- Update malicious code protection mechanisms when new releases are available.
- Perform periodic scans of systems and real-time scans of files from external sources as files are downloaded, opened, or executed.
- Monitor systems and detect attacks and indicators of potential attacks.
- Identify unauthorized use of systems.

When implementing these security controls and practices, consider the following guidance:

- **Prioritize controls based on risk:** First, focus on implementing the controls that address the highest risks to your organization's systems and data.
- **Tailor controls to your environment:** Adapt the controls to fit your organization's needs, requirements, and operational constraints.
- **Document control implementation:** Maintain comprehensive documentation of how each control is implemented, including policies, procedures, and technical configurations.
- **Regularly assess and monitor controls:** Conduct periodic assessments to ensure that the controls are operating effectively

and monitor them continuously to detect and respond to any deviations or weaknesses.

· **Provide training and awareness:** Educate personnel on their roles and responsibilities in implementing and maintaining the security controls.

· **Continuously improve:** Review and update the controls regularly based on changes in the threat landscape, technological advancements, and organizational requirements.

By implementing the security controls outlined in NIST 800-171 and following the guidance provided, organizations can establish a strong foundation for protecting CUI and meeting the requirements of CMMC 2.0 Level 2. It is important to note that while these controls serve as a baseline, organizations should also consider additional controls and best practices based on their specific industry, regulatory requirements, and risk profile.

Implementing effective cybersecurity controls and practices is an ongoing process that requires continuous monitoring, assessment, and improvement. Organizations should strive to create a security awareness and accountability culture where everyone understands their role in protecting sensitive information and systems.

By dedicating the necessary resources, expertise, and commitment to implementing and maintaining robust cybersecurity controls, organizations can achieve CMMC 2.0 compliance, strengthen their overall security posture, and build trust with their customers, partners, and stakeholders.

Best practices for implementing technical and administrative controls

Implementing effective technical and administrative controls is crucial for achieving CMMC 2.0 compliance and strengthening an organization's cybersecurity posture. Let's explore the best practices for implementing these controls:

1. Conduct a thorough risk assessment:

- Perform a comprehensive risk assessment to identify the critical assets, systems, and data that require protection.
- Evaluate the potential threats, vulnerabilities, and impacts associated with each asset.
- Prioritize the identified risks based on their likelihood and potential consequences.
- Use the risk assessment results to guide selecting and implementing appropriate technical and administrative controls.

2. Develop and maintain policies and procedures:

- Establish clear and comprehensive policies and procedures that define the organization's cybersecurity requirements, roles, and responsibilities.
- Ensure that policies and procedures align with the CMMC 2.0 requirements and industry best practices.
- Review and update policies and procedures regularly to reflect changes in the organization's environment, regulatory requirements, and threat landscape.

- Communicate policies and procedures to all relevant personnel and provide training to ensure understanding and compliance.

3. Implement strong access controls:

- Enforce the principle of least privilege, granting users only the access rights necessary to perform their job functions.
- Implement robust authentication mechanisms, such as multifactor authentication, for all user accounts, especially for privileged accounts and remote access.
- Regularly review and update user access rights based on job responsibilities or employment status changes.
- Monitor and log access activities to detect and respond to unauthorized attempts or suspicious behavior.

4. Secure network infrastructure:

- Segment networks based on security requirements and data sensitivity, separating critical assets from less sensitive systems.
- Implement firewalls, intrusion detection/prevention systems (IDS/IPS), and other network security controls to monitor and protect network traffic.
- To protect data in transit, use secure protocols for network communications, such as HTTPS, SSH, and VPN.
- Regularly update and patch network devices and software to address known vulnerabilities and maintain a secure configuration.

5. Protect endpoints and devices:

- Deploy endpoint protection solutions, such as antivirus software, on all devices connected to the organization's network.
- Implement device management policies to ensure only authorized devices can access the network and critical resources.
- Encrypt sensitive data stored on endpoints, such as laptops and mobile devices, to protect against unauthorized access in case of loss or theft.
- Regularly update and patch operating systems, applications, and firmware on endpoints to address security vulnerabilities.

6. Implement secure configuration management:

- Establish secure baseline configurations for all systems, devices, and applications.
- Implement configuration management tools and processes to control and track changes to system configurations.
- Regularly assess and audit system configurations to ensure compliance with security policies and best practices.
- Employ automated tools to scan for misconfigurations, vulnerabilities, and deviations from the approved baseline configurations.

7. Conduct security awareness and training:

- Develop comprehensive security awareness and training programs for all personnel, including employees, contractors, and third-party users.
- Cover topics such as password security, phishing awareness, data handling, incident reporting, and compliance requirements.

- Tailor training content to specific roles and responsibilities, ensuring personnel understand their obligations to protect sensitive information and systems.
- Conduct regular security awareness campaigns and simulated phishing exercises to reinforce secure behaviors and identify areas for improvement.

8. Implement incident response and recovery:

- Establish a well-defined incident response plan that outlines the procedures for detecting, reporting, investigating, and responding to security incidents.
- Form an incident response team with clearly defined roles and responsibilities, including communication protocols and escalation paths.
- Conduct regular incident response drills and tabletop exercises to test the plan's effectiveness and identify areas for improvement.
- Implement data backup and recovery mechanisms to ensure the availability and integrity of critical data in the event of a security incident or disaster.

9. Monitor and log security events:

- Implement centralized logging and monitoring solutions to collect and analyze security events from various sources, such as servers, network devices, and applications.
- Establish baseline normal behavior and configure alerts to detect and notify of anomalous activities or potential security incidents.
- Regularly review and analyze log data to identify trends, patterns,

and indicators of compromise.
- Retain log data for a sufficient period to support incident investigation and compliance requirements.

10. Perform regular security assessments and audits:

- Conduct periodic security assessments, including vulnerability
scans, penetration testing, and configuration reviews, to identify
weaknesses and areas for improvement.
- Engage third-party security experts to perform independent
assessments and objectively evaluate the organization's security
posture.
- Conduct internal audits to assess compliance with CMMC 2.0
requirements, security policies, and procedures.
- Use assessment and audit findings to prioritize and implement
remediation efforts and continuously improve the organization's
cybersecurity controls.

11. Manage third-party risks:

- Assess the security practices and controls of third-party vendors,
suppliers, and partners with access to the organization's sensitive
information or systems.
- Establish contractual requirements and service level agreements
(SLAs) defining security expectations and responsibilities.
- Conduct regular security assessments and audits of third-party
entities to ensure compliance with the organization's security
standards.
- Implement processes for timely notification and response to

security incidents or breaches involving third-party entities.

12. Continuously monitor and improve:

- Establish metrics and key performance indicators (KPIs) to measure the effectiveness of technical and administrative controls.
- Regularly review and analyze security metrics to identify trends, gaps, and opportunities for improvement.
- Implement continuous monitoring solutions to detect and respond to real-time security events and anomalies.
- Foster a culture of continuous improvement, encouraging personnel to report security concerns, suggest enhancements, and share lessons learned.

When implementing technical and administrative controls, consider the following best practices:

- **Align controls with business objectives:** Ensure the selected controls support and enable the organization's goals and mission.
- **Prioritize based on risk:** Focus on implementing controls that address the highest risks and have the greatest potential impact on the organization's security posture.
- **Document and communicate:** Maintain comprehensive documentation of control implementations, including policies, procedures, and technical configurations. Communicate the controls and their importance to all relevant personnel.
- **Provide adequate resources:** Allocate sufficient resources, including budget, personnel, and tools, to effectively implement and maintain the controls.

- **Regularly test and validate:** Conduct regular testing and validation of controls to ensure their effectiveness and identify gaps or weaknesses.
- **Monitor and adapt:** Continuously monitor the performance of controls and adjust them as needed based on changes in the threat landscape, regulatory requirements, or organizational needs.

Implementing effective technical and administrative controls is an ongoing process that requires commitment, collaboration, and continuous improvement. By following these best practices and aligning controls with the CMMC 2.0 requirements, organizations can strengthen their cybersecurity posture, protect sensitive information, and demonstrate their commitment to cybersecurity excellence.

It is important to note that the specific controls and their implementation may vary based on the organization's size, industry, and risk profile. Organizations should tailor their control implementation to their unique needs and requirements while ensuring compliance with the CMMC 2.0 framework.

By dedicating the necessary resources, expertise, and leadership support to implementing robust technical and administrative controls, organizations can establish a strong foundation for cybersecurity and build trust with their customers, partners, and stakeholders. Effective control implementation helps achieve CMMC 2.0 compliance, enhances the organization's resilience against cyber threats, and supports long-term business success.

Case studies and practical examples

To better understand the implementation of cybersecurity controls and practices in the context of CMMC 2.0, let's explore some case studies and practical examples that demonstrate how organizations have successfully navigated the compliance journey.

Case Study 1: Secure Access Management at Acme Aerospace

Acme Aerospace, a mid-sized defense contractor, recognized the importance of implementing strong access controls to protect sensitive data and meet CMMC 2.0 requirements. They took the following steps:

1. Role-based access control (RBAC):

- Acme Aerospace thoroughly analyzed job roles and responsibilities within the organization.
- They defined granular access permissions based on the principle of least privilege, ensuring that users only had access to the resources required for their specific tasks.
- RBAC policies were implemented across all systems and applications, with regular reviews and updates to maintain the accuracy of access rights.

2. Multifactor authentication (MFA):

- Acme Aerospace implemented MFA for all user accounts, requiring users to provide two or more forms of authentication, such as a password and a hardware token or biometric factor.
- MFA was enforced for remote access to the organization's network and for accessing critical systems and applications.
- The organization provided training and support to users to ensure smooth adoption and understanding of MFA processes.

3. Privileged access management (PAM):

- Acme Aerospace identified privileged accounts, such as system administrators and database administrators, with elevated access rights.
- They implemented a PAM solution to secure and monitor privileged access, including features like password vaulting, session recording, and real-time monitoring.
- Privileged access was granted on a need-to-use basis, with regular reviews and audits to ensure compliance with the organization's access control policies.

By implementing RBAC, MFA, and PAM, Acme Aerospace significantly enhanced its access control posture, reducing the risk of unauthorized access and ensuring compliance with CMMC 2.0 requirements. The organization also experienced improved productivity and streamlined access management processes.

Case Study 2: Incident Response and Recovery at Beta Industries

Beta Industries, a small defense supplier, recognized the importance of having a robust incident response and recovery plan to handle cybersecurity incidents and meet CMMC 2.0 requirements effectively. They took the following steps:

1. Incident response plan development:

- Beta Industries formed a cross-functional incident response team, including IT, security, legal, and executive management representatives.
- They developed a comprehensive incident response plan outlining team members' roles and responsibilities, communication protocols, and step-by-step procedures for handling different incidents.
- The plan was regularly reviewed, updated, and tested through tabletop exercises and simulated incident scenarios.

2. Incident detection and analysis:

- Beta Industries implemented a security information and event management (SIEM) solution to centralize log collection and analysis from various sources.
- They established baseline normal behavior and configured alerts to detect anomalous activities and potential security incidents.
- The incident response team regularly monitored and analyzed the SIEM data, investigating any suspicious events and correlating

information to identify potential threats.

3. Containment and eradication:

- When a security incident was detected, the incident response team quickly isolated the affected systems and networks to prevent the incident from spreading further.
- They followed established procedures to gather evidence, analyze the root cause, and determine the extent of the compromise.
- The team worked diligently to eradicate the threat, remove malicious artifacts, and restore affected systems to a secure state.

4. Recovery and lessons learned:

- Beta Industries had a well-defined recovery plan that included data backup and restoration procedures to minimize downtime and ensure business continuity.
- After the incident was resolved, the team conducted a thorough post-incident review to identify lessons learned and areas for improvement.
- Based on the findings, they updated their incident response plan and security controls and shared the insights with relevant stakeholders to enhance cybersecurity awareness.

Beta Industries implemented a comprehensive incident response and recovery program to demonstrate its ability to detect, respond to, and recover effectively from cybersecurity incidents. This helped them meet CMMC 2.0 requirements, strengthen their resilience against cyber threats, and minimize the potential impact of incidents on their business operations.

Case Study 3: Continuous Monitoring and Improvement at Gamma Solutions

Gamma Solutions, a large defense systems integrator, recognized the importance of continuous monitoring and improvement to maintain a strong cybersecurity posture and meet CMMC 2.0 requirements. They took the following steps:

1. Security metrics and KPIs:

- Gamma Solutions defined a set of meaningful security metrics and key performance indicators (KPIs) to measure the effectiveness of their cybersecurity controls and practices.
- They aligned these metrics with CMMC 2.0 requirements and industry best practices, covering vulnerability management, access control, incident response, and user awareness.
- The security team regularly reviewed and analyzed the metrics and reported to senior management to provide visibility into the organization's security posture.

2. Continuous monitoring:

- Gamma Solutions implemented a comprehensive continuous monitoring program to detect and respond to real-time security events and anomalies.

- They deployed security tools and technologies, such as intrusion detection systems (IDS), security information and event management (SIEM), and endpoint detection and response (EDR), to monitor their networks, systems, and applications.
- The security team continuously monitored the data generated by these tools, investigating and responding promptly to any potential security incidents.

3. Vulnerability management:

- Gamma Solutions established a robust vulnerability management process to identify, assess, and remediate vulnerabilities in their systems and applications.
- They conducted regular vulnerability scans, penetration testing, and security assessments to identify weaknesses and prioritize remediation efforts based on risk severity.
- The organization implemented a patch management program to ensure the timely application of security patches and updates across their technology environment.

4. Security awareness and training:

- Gamma Solutions recognized that employees are critical in maintaining a strong cybersecurity posture.
- They developed and delivered comprehensive security awareness and training programs to educate employees on cybersecurity best practices, policies, and procedures.
- The training content was tailored to different roles and departments, with regular refresher sessions and phishing simulation

exercises to reinforce secure behaviors.

5. Continuous improvement:

- Gamma Solutions fostered a culture of continuous improvement, encouraging employees to report security concerns, suggest enhancements, and share lessons learned.
- They conducted regular security audits and assessments to identify gaps and opportunities for improvement in their cybersecurity controls and practices.
- The organization actively participated in industry forums, threat intelligence sharing communities, and cybersecurity research to stay informed about emerging threats and best practices.

By implementing a comprehensive continuous monitoring and improvement program, Gamma Solutions demonstrated its commitment to maintaining a strong cybersecurity posture and meeting CMMC 2.0 requirements. The organization's proactive approach to security metrics, continuous monitoring, vulnerability management, and employee awareness helped them identify and address potential risks promptly, reducing the likelihood and impact of cybersecurity incidents.

These case studies and practical examples highlight the importance of implementing effective cybersecurity controls and practices in CMMC 2.0. Organizations should tailor their approaches based on their unique needs, risk profiles, and operational environments. By learning from the experiences and best practices of others, organizations can gain valuable insights and guidance on their own CMMC 2.0

compliance journeys.

It is important to note that the case studies presented here are fictitious and serve as illustrative examples only. The specific implementation details and outcomes may vary in real-world scenarios based on the organization's size, industry, and resources.

Regardless of the specific approach taken, the key to successful CMMC 2.0 compliance lies in a holistic and proactive approach to cybersecurity. Organizations should prioritize risk management, employee awareness, and continuous improvement to build a strong foundation for protecting sensitive information and meeting the evolving cybersecurity challenges in the defense industry.

Best Practices: Regularly review and test security controls to ensure they are effective and efficient in the changing threat landscape.

In the dynamic world of cybersecurity, regularly reviewing and testing security controls is a critical best practice for ensuring their ongoing effectiveness and efficiency. As cyber threats evolve and new vulnerabilities emerge, organizations must proactively assess and adapt their security controls to avoid potential risks. Let's explore the key steps and considerations for regularly reviewing and testing security controls in the context of CMMC 2.0.

1. Establish a review and testing schedule:

- Develop a comprehensive schedule for reviewing and testing security controls, considering the criticality of assets, the frequency of changes, and the organization's risk tolerance.
- Determine the appropriate frequency for different types of controls, such as quarterly reviews for high-risk systems and annual reviews for lower-risk areas.
- Ensure the schedule aligns with regulatory requirements, industry standards, and contractual obligations, including CMMC 2.0 guidelines.

2. Identify relevant security controls:

- Create an inventory of all security controls implemented across the organization, including technical, administrative, and physical controls.

- Categorize the controls based on their relevance to CMMC 2.0 requirements and the organization's security objectives.
- Prioritize the controls that have the greatest impact on protecting sensitive information, such as Controlled Unclassified Information (CUI), and ensuring compliance with CMMC 2.0.

3. Develop testing procedures and criteria:

- Establish clear and consistent testing procedures and criteria for each security control, aligned with CMMC 2.0 requirements and industry best practices.
- Define the objectives, scope, and methodology for testing, including the required tools, techniques, and resources.
- Determine each control's expected outcomes and success criteria, considering effectiveness, efficiency, and alignment with security policies and procedures.

4. Conduct regular control reviews:

- Perform regular reviews of security controls to assess their design, implementation, and operating effectiveness.
- Evaluate the controls against the defined testing procedures and criteria, considering factors such as configuration settings, access controls, and monitoring capabilities.
- Review relevant documentation, such as policies, procedures, and system configurations, to ensure they are current and aligned with CMMC 2.0 requirements.
- Identify any gaps, weaknesses, or areas for improvement in the

controls and document the findings and recommendations.

5. Perform comprehensive control testing:

- Conduct in-depth testing of security controls to validate their effectiveness in preventing, detecting, and responding to potential cyber threats.
- To identify potential weaknesses and vulnerabilities, use manual and automated testing techniques, such as vulnerability scanning, penetration testing, and security assessments.
- Simulate real-world attack scenarios and test the controls' ability to withstand and mitigate the impact of different cyber threats.
- Document the testing results, including any identified vulnerabilities, exploits, or areas for improvement, and prioritize remediation efforts based on risk severity.

6. Assess control efficiency and resource optimization:

- Evaluate the efficiency of security controls in terms of their resource utilization, performance impact, and overall cost-effectiveness.
- Identify redundant or overlapping controls that may be streamlined or consolidated to optimize resource allocation and reduce complexity.
- Assess the automation and integration capabilities of controls to minimize manual effort and improve efficiency in security operations.
- Consider the scalability and adaptability of controls to accommodate changes in the organization's environment, such as business

growth or technological advancements.

7. Incorporate threat intelligence and industry best practices:

- Leverage threat intelligence sources and industry best practices to inform the review and testing of security controls.
- Monitor emerging threats, vulnerabilities, and attack techniques relevant to the organization's industry and technology environment.
- Participate in information-sharing communities, such as Information Sharing and Analysis Centers (ISACs), to gain insights into cybersecurity trends and mitigation strategies.
- Adapt the testing procedures and criteria based on the evolving threat landscape and incorporate lessons learned from industry peers and security experts.

8. Engage independent assessors and auditors:

- Engage independent assessors or auditors to evaluate the organization's security controls and CMMC 2.0 compliance posture objectively.
- Leverage the expertise of third-party professionals specializing in cybersecurity assessments and having experience in CMMC 2.0 requirements.
- Collaborate with the assessors to identify potential blind spots, gaps, or areas for improvement in the security controls and overall cybersecurity program.
- Use the assessment findings and recommendations to prioritize remediation efforts and strengthen the organization's cybersecu-

rity posture.

9. Implement continuous monitoring and alerting:

- Establish a continuous monitoring program to detect and respond to real-time security events and anomalies proactively.
- Deploy security monitoring tools and technologies, such as security information and event management (SIEM) systems, intrusion detection/prevention systems (IDS/IPS), and endpoint detection and response (EDR) solutions.
- Configure automated alerts and notifications to promptly notify security teams of potential incidents or deviations from baseline security controls.
- Review and fine-tune the monitoring and alerting thresholds regularly to minimize false positives and ensure timely detection and response to security events.

10. Foster a culture of continuous improvement:

- Promote a culture of continuous improvement in cybersecurity, encouraging employees to actively review and test security controls.
- Provide regular training and awareness programs to educate employees about the importance of security controls, their roles and responsibilities, and the latest cybersecurity best practices.
- Encourage open communication and feedback channels for employees to report security concerns, suggest improvements, or share lessons learned from their experiences.
- Celebrate successes and recognize individuals or teams demon-

strating exceptional commitment to strengthening the organization's cybersecurity posture.

11. Document and report on control effectiveness:

- Maintain comprehensive documentation of the review and testing processes, including the scope, methodology, findings, and recommendations.
- Develop clear and concise reports highlighting the effectiveness of security controls, identify gaps or weaknesses, and propose remediation actions.
- Present the reports to relevant stakeholders, including senior management, the security team, and the CMMC 2.0 implementation team, to ensure transparency and facilitate informed decision-making.
- During assessments or audits, use the documentation and reports as evidence of the organization's ongoing commitment to cyber-security and CMMC 2.0 compliance.

By regularly reviewing and testing security controls, organizations can proactively identify and address potential weaknesses before adversaries can exploit them. This best practice helps ensure that the controls remain effective and efficient in the face of evolving cyber threats and changing business requirements.

It is important to note that the specific approach to reviewing and testing security controls may vary based on the organization's size, industry, and risk profile. Organizations should tailor their review and testing processes to align with their unique needs and CMMC 2.0

compliance objectives.

Additionally, organizations should consider leveraging automated tools and technologies to streamline the review and testing processes, reduce manual effort, and improve the accuracy and consistency of results. However, automated tools should be used with human expertise and judgment to ensure a comprehensive and context-aware evaluation of security controls.

Overall, regularly reviewing and testing security controls is a critical best practice for maintaining a strong and resilient cybersecurity posture in the face of evolving threats. By proactively assessing and adapting their controls, organizations can better protect sensitive information, meet CMMC 2.0 requirements, and build trust with their customers, partners, and stakeholders in the defense industry.

Chapter 7: Training and Awareness

Importance of training and security awareness in achieving CMMC 2.0

Training and security awareness play critical roles in achieving CMMC 2.0 compliance and maintaining a strong cybersecurity posture within an organization. As the human element is often considered the weakest link in cybersecurity, investing in comprehensive training and awareness programs is essential to mitigate risks and foster a culture of security consciousness. Let's explore the significance of training and security awareness in the context of CMMC 2.0.

1. Ensuring compliance with CMMC 2.0 requirements:

- CMMC 2.0 explicitly emphasizes the importance of training and awareness as part of its requirements.
- Level 2 of CMMC 2.0 includes security awareness and training practices, such as providing security awareness training to all system users and managers (AT.2.056) and ensuring that personnel are trained to carry out their assigned information security-related duties and responsibilities (AT.2.057).

- By implementing comprehensive training and awareness programs, organizations demonstrate their commitment to meeting CMMC 2.0 requirements and establishing a foundation for a strong cybersecurity culture.

2. Reducing human-related cybersecurity risks:

- Human error, negligence, and lack of security awareness contribute to cybersecurity incidents and data breaches.
- Employees may unknowingly fall victim to phishing scams, disclose sensitive information, use weak passwords, or bypass security controls, putting the organization's assets and reputation at risk.
- Regular training and awareness initiatives help educate employees about common cybersecurity threats, best practices for secure behavior, and their roles and responsibilities in protecting sensitive information.
- Organizations can significantly reduce the likelihood and impact of human-related cybersecurity incidents by equipping employees with the knowledge and skills to identify and respond to potential security risks.

3. Fostering a culture of security consciousness:

- Effective training and awareness programs go beyond mere compliance and aim to create a culture of security consciousness throughout the organization.
- By regularly reinforcing the importance of cybersecurity and promoting secure practices, organizations can instill a sense of

shared responsibility and accountability among employees.

- A strong security culture encourages employees to report potential security incidents proactively, suggest improvements to security processes, and advocate for cybersecurity best practices.
- When security becomes integral to the organization's values and day-to-day operations, it enhances overall resilience against cyber threats and supports long-term CMMC 2.0 compliance.

4. Enhancing incident response and reporting:

- Comprehensive training and awareness programs equip employees with the knowledge and skills to identify and respond promptly to potential cybersecurity incidents.
- Well-trained employees in incident response procedures, reporting mechanisms, and escalation protocols can be an early warning system for detecting and mitigating security breaches.
- Timely reporting and effective incident response are crucial for minimizing the impact of security incidents, protecting sensitive information, and maintaining compliance with CMMC 2.0 requirements.
- Regular training exercises and simulations can help employees develop muscle memory and confidence in handling real-world cybersecurity incidents, reducing response times and improving overall incident management.

5. Addressing evolving cybersecurity threats and best practices:

- The cybersecurity landscape constantly evolves, with new threats, vulnerabilities, and attack techniques emerging regularly.

- Training and awareness programs provide an opportunity to keep employees updated on the latest cybersecurity trends, emerging risks, and best practices for risk mitigation.
- Organizations can ensure that employees are well-prepared to face the ever-changing cybersecurity challenges by incorporating up-to-date threat intelligence and industry insights into training content.
- Continuous learning and skill development also help employees adapt to new technologies, security tools, and processes, enhancing the organization's overall cybersecurity capabilities.

6. Promoting secure behavior beyond the workplace:

- Effective training and awareness initiatives extend beyond workplace boundaries and encourage employees to adopt secure practices in their personal lives as well.
- As employees increasingly use personal devices for work purposes and access organizational resources remotely, educating them about secure remote working practices, device security, and safe online behavior is crucial.
- By promoting a holistic approach to cybersecurity, organizations can create a more secure ecosystem that encompasses the professional and personal aspects of employees' lives.
- This holistic approach helps mitigate risks associated with bring-your-own-device (BYOD) policies, remote work arrangements, and the blurring lines between work and personal technology use.

7. Demonstrating commitment to stakeholders and partners:

- Investing in robust training and awareness programs demonstrates an organization's commitment to cybersecurity excellence to its stakeholders, including customers, partners, and regulatory bodies.
- By showcasing a well-trained and security-conscious workforce, organizations can build trust and confidence in protecting sensitive information and maintaining compliance with CMMC 2.0 requirements.
- Strong training and awareness initiatives can serve as a competitive advantage, differentiating organizations from their peers and positioning them as reliable and secure partners in the defense industry supply chain.

8. Enabling continuous improvement and feedback:

- Training and awareness programs provide valuable opportunities for gathering employee feedback and insights on the effectiveness of security controls, policies, and processes.
- Encouraging open communication and feedback loops during training sessions can help identify potential gaps, challenges, or areas for improvement in the organization's cybersecurity posture.
- By actively listening to employees' concerns, suggestions, and experiences, organizations can continuously refine their training content, delivery methods, and overall cybersecurity strategies.
- Continuous improvement based on employee feedback helps ensure that training and awareness programs remain relevant, engaging, and impactful over time.

To maximize the benefits of training and security awareness in achieving CMMC 2.0 compliance, organizations should consider the following best practices:

- Develop a comprehensive training and awareness plan that aligns with CMMC 2.0 requirements and the organization's specific needs and risks.
- Tailor training content to different roles, responsibilities, and skill levels within the organization, ensuring relevance and applicability to each audience.
- Employ various training delivery methods, such as in-person sessions, online courses, workshops, simulations, and gamification, to engage employees and cater to different learning styles.
- Conduct regular training sessions, including initial onboarding training, annual refresher courses, and ad-hoc training to reinforce key concepts and address emerging threats.
- To keep security at the forefront, supplement formal training with ongoing awareness initiatives, such as newsletters, posters, phishing simulation exercises, and cybersecurity awareness events.
- Measure the effectiveness of training and awareness programs through assessments, quizzes, and behavioral metrics, and use the results to inform continuous improvement efforts.
- Foster a culture of open communication, encouraging employees to ask questions, report concerns, and share their experiences related to cybersecurity.
- Lead by example, with senior management and executives actively promoting and participating in training and awareness activities to demonstrate the organization's commitment to cybersecurity.

In conclusion, training and security awareness are vital to achieving CMMC 2.0 compliance and building a robust cybersecurity posture. By investing in comprehensive training and awareness programs, organizations can empower employees to become active participants in defending against cyber threats, foster a culture of security consciousness, and demonstrate their commitment to protecting sensitive information. Effective training and awareness initiatives help meet CMMC 2.0 requirements and contribute to organizations' overall resilience and competitiveness in the face of evolving cybersecurity challenges.

Developing a continuous training program

Organizations must develop and implement a continuous training program to effectively support CMMC 2.0 compliance and maintain a strong cybersecurity posture. A well-designed continuous training program ensures employees receive ongoing education and skill development to stay current with evolving cybersecurity threats, best practices, and CMMC 2.0 requirements. Explore the key steps and considerations for developing a comprehensive and effective continuous training program.

1. Assess training needs and goals:

- Begin by thoroughly assessing your organization's training needs and goals in the context of CMMC 2.0 compliance.
- Identify the specific knowledge, skills, and competencies required for different organizational roles and responsibilities.
- Consider the employees' cybersecurity awareness and expertise

level and determine the gaps that need to be addressed through training.

· Align the training goals with the organization's cybersecurity strategy and CMMC 2.0 implementation roadmap.

2. Develop a training curriculum:

· Based on the identified training needs and goals, develop a comprehensive training curriculum that covers the essential topics and concepts related to CMMC 2.0 and cybersecurity.

· Break the curriculum into modules or courses that address specific CMMC 2.0 domains, practices, and procedures.

· Ensure the curriculum is tailored to different roles and skill levels within the organization, providing relevant and applicable content for each audience.

· Incorporate a mix of foundational knowledge, practical skills, and scenario-based learning to engage learners and promote retention.

· Align the curriculum with industry standards, best practices, and the latest cybersecurity trends to ensure relevance and effectiveness.

3. Determine the training delivery methods:

· Based on your organization's resources, preferences, and the nature of the content, select the most appropriate training delivery methods.

· Consider a blended approach that combines various delivery methods, such as:

- Instructor-led training: In-person or virtual classroom sessions led by knowledgeable trainers or subject matter experts.
- Online learning: Self-paced e-learning courses, webinars, or video tutorials allow learners to access training materials conveniently.
- Hands-on labs and simulations: These practical exercises and simulations allow learners to apply their knowledge and skills in a safe environment.
- Workshops and group discussions: Interactive sessions that encourage collaboration, knowledge sharing, and problem-solving among learners.
- Ensure that the chosen delivery methods are accessible, engaging, and effective in achieving the desired learning outcomes.

4. Establish a training schedule and timeline:

- Develop a comprehensive training schedule and timeline that outlines the sequence and frequency of training activities.
- Determine the appropriate frequency for different types of training, such as:
- Initial onboarding training for new employees to cover foundational CMMC 2.0 concepts and security practices.
- Annual refresher training to reinforce key concepts, update employees on new threats and best practices, and maintain CMMC 2.0 compliance.
- Periodic role-specific training to address different job functions' unique needs and responsibilities.
- Ad-hoc training sessions to respond to emerging threats and changes in CMMC 2.0 requirements or identify employee knowledge or skills gaps.

- Ensure the training schedule is feasible, allows for flexibility, and minimizes disruption to regular work activities.

5. Identify and train instructors:

- Identify qualified instructors or subject matter experts who can deliver the training effectively.
- Consider a mix of internal resources, such as experienced cybersecurity professionals or CMMC 2.0 implementation team members, and external experts, such as certified trainers or consultants.
- Provide train-the-trainer programs to equip internal instructors with the necessary skills and knowledge to deliver the training content effectively.
- Ensure that instructors are well-versed in adult learning principles, facilitation techniques, and the specific requirements of CMMC 2.0.

6. Develop training materials and resources:

- Create high-quality training materials and resources that support the delivery of the training curriculum.
- Develop clear and concise presentations, handouts, exercises, and assessments that align with the learning objectives and engage learners.
- To ensure accuracy and relevance, leverage existing CMMC 2.0 documentation, such as the CMMC 2.0 Model, assessment guides, and best practice frameworks.
- Incorporate real-world examples, case studies, and scenarios that illustrate the practical application of CMMC 2.0 concepts and

practices.
- Ensure that training materials are accessible, visually appealing, and easy to navigate, regardless of the delivery method.

7. Implement the training program:

- Roll out the continuous training program according to the established schedule and timeline.
- Communicate the training objectives, expectations, and benefits to employees, emphasizing the importance of their active participation and engagement.
- Provide necessary support and resources to ensure employees can access and complete the training effectively.
- Monitor training progress, attendance, and completion rates, and promptly address any issues or challenges.
- Encourage open communication and participant feedback to identify improvement areas and gather insights for future training iterations.

8. Evaluate and measure training effectiveness:

- Establish metrics and key performance indicators (KPIs) to measure the effectiveness of the continuous training program.
- Conduct assessments, quizzes, and practical exercises to evaluate learners' knowledge retention, skill acquisition, and ability to apply CMMC 2.0 concepts in real-world scenarios.
- Gather participant feedback through surveys, focus groups, or interviews to assess the training's quality, relevance, and impact.
- Monitor behavioral changes and improvements in cybersecurity

practices following the training, such as increased reporting of security incidents or reduced non-compliance incidents.

· Use the evaluation results to identify gaps, refine the training content and delivery methods, and continuously improve the overall effectiveness of the training program.

9. Provide ongoing support and reinforcement:

· Recognize that training is not a one-time event but an ongoing process that requires continuous reinforcement and support.

· Provide job aids, reference materials, and quick guides that employees can refer to after the training to reinforce their learning and apply the concepts in their daily work.

· Encourage managers and supervisors to actively support and reinforce the training by discussing cybersecurity topics in team meetings, providing coaching and feedback, and recognizing employees who demonstrate strong cybersecurity practices.

· Promote informal learning opportunities, such as lunch and learn sessions, cybersecurity awareness events, and online learning communities, to establish a culture of continuous learning.

10. Continuously update and improve the training program:

· Regularly review and update the training curriculum, materials, and delivery methods to ensure alignment with the latest CMMC 2.0 requirements, industry best practices, and emerging cyberse-curity threats.

· Incorporate feedback and lessons learned from training sessions, assessments, and real-world incidents to refine and enhance the

training content and approach.
- Stay informed about advancements in training technologies, techniques, and platforms, and explore opportunities to leverage them to improve the effectiveness and efficiency of the training program.
- Collaborate with industry peers, professional associations, and training providers to exchange ideas, share best practices, and stay updated on cybersecurity training trends and innovations.

Developing a continuous training program is critical to achieving and maintaining CMMC 2.0 compliance. It ensures that employees have the necessary knowledge, skills, and awareness to protect sensitive information, identify and respond to cybersecurity threats, and adhere to security policies and procedures.

Organizations can create a sustainable and effective learning environment that supports their CMMC 2.0 compliance efforts and overall cybersecurity posture by following a structured approach, leveraging various delivery methods, and continuously evaluating and improving the training program.

Remember, a successful continuous training program requires ongoing commitment, resources, and support from leadership and employees at all levels. It should be an integral part of the organization's cybersecurity strategy and culture, fostering a shared sense of responsibility and vigilance in the face of evolving cybersecurity challenges.

Measuring training effectiveness

Measuring training effectiveness is a critical component of a successful continuous training program for CMMC 2.0 compliance. It helps organizations assess the impact of their training efforts, identify areas for improvement, and ensure that employees acquire the necessary knowledge, skills, and behaviors to protect sensitive information and maintain compliance. Let's explore the key strategies and methods for measuring training effectiveness in CMMC 2.0.

1. Establish clear training objectives and metrics:

- Define specific, measurable, achievable, relevant, and time-bound (SMART) objectives for each training module or program.
- Align the objectives with the desired outcomes of CMMC 2.0 compliance, such as increased awareness of security policies, improved incident reporting, or reduced non-compliance incidents.
- Identify key performance indicators (KPIs) and metrics that will measure the achievement of the training objectives.
- Examples of metrics may include:
- Knowledge retention rates: Percentage of learners who demonstrate mastery of the training content through assessments or quizzes.
- Behavioral changes: Observed improvements in cybersecurity practices, such as increased use of strong passwords or timely reporting of security incidents.
- Compliance metrics: Reduction in non-compliance incidents or audit findings related to CMMC 2.0 requirements.

2. Conduct pre and post-training assessments:

- Administer assessments or quizzes before and after each training session to measure learners' knowledge and understanding of the content.
- To evaluate different aspects of learning, use a variety of assessment formats, such as multiple-choice questions, scenario-based exercises, or hands-on simulations.
- Compare the pre and post-training assessment results to determine the knowledge gained and identify areas where learners may need additional support or clarification.
- Use the assessment results to improve effectiveness and refine the training content, delivery methods, and instructional strategies.

3. Gather feedback from learners:

- Use surveys, feedback forms, or interviews to collect learners' perceptions and opinions about the training program.
- Ask questions about the relevance, clarity, and usefulness of the training content, the effectiveness of the delivery methods, and the overall learning experience.
- Encourage learners to provide specific examples of how they plan to apply the knowledge and skills acquired from the training in their job roles.
- Analyze the feedback to identify trends, common challenges, or areas for improvement, and use the insights to enhance future training iterations.

4. Observe and assess behavioral changes:

- Conduct observations or assessments of employees' cybersecurity behaviors and practices following the training.
- Look for evidence of improved security hygiene, such as strong passwords, proper handling of sensitive information, or adherence to security policies and procedures.
- Use scenario-based exercises or simulations to assess employees' ability to apply the knowledge and skills acquired from the training in real-world situations.
- Provide feedback and coaching to reinforce positive behaviors and address any gaps or areas for improvement.

5. Monitor and analyze training-related metrics:

- Track and analyze training-related metrics to assess the training program's impact on overall CMMC 2.0 compliance and cybersecurity posture.
- Monitor metrics such as:
- Training completion rates: Percentage of employees who have completed the required training modules within the specified timeframe.
- Phishing simulation results: Success rates of employees in identifying and reporting simulated phishing emails.
- Security incident metrics: Number and severity of security incidents reported, response times, and resolution rates.
- Compliance audit results: Findings and recommendations from internal or external audits related to CMMC 2.0 requirements.
- Use data analytics and visualization tools to identify trends, correlations, and areas for improvement.

6. Conduct skills assessments and certifications:

- Implement skills assessments or certification programs to validate employees' proficiency in specific CMMC 2.0 domains or practices.
- Use industry-recognized certifications, such as CompTIA Security+, CISSP, or CMMC-specific certifications, to assess employees' knowledge and skills against established standards.
- Encourage employees to pursue relevant certifications and provide support, such as study materials, training, or exam vouchers, to facilitate professional development.
- Track certification rates and use them to measure the effectiveness of the training program in building the necessary competencies for CMMC 2.0 compliance.

7. Seek input from managers and supervisors:

- Engage managers and supervisors in assessing the effectiveness of the training program and its impact on their teams' cybersecurity practices.
- Conduct regular check-ins or surveys to gather feedback on the observed changes in employees' knowledge, skills, and behaviors following the training.
- Ask managers to provide specific examples of how the training has improved cybersecurity practices, reduced incidents, or enhanced team compliance.
- Use the feedback to identify areas where additional training, support, or resources may be needed to reinforce the learning and drive continuous improvement.

8. Conduct post-training follow-ups and reinforcement:

- Implement post-training follow-up activities to reinforce the learning and assess the long-term retention and application of acquired knowledge and skills.
- Use techniques such as spaced repetition, micro-learning, or gamification to provide ongoing reinforcement and practice opportunities.
- Conduct periodic refresher sessions or mini-assessments to review key concepts and ensure employees remain current with the latest CMMC 2.0 requirements and best practices.
- Provide job aids, reference materials, or performance support tools that employees can access on-demand to apply the learning in their daily work.

9. Benchmark against industry standards and best practices:

- Compare your organization's training effectiveness measures against industry benchmarks and best practices for CMMC 2.0 training and cybersecurity education.
- Participate in industry forums, working groups, or benchmarking studies to exchange insights, share experiences, and learn from other organizations' successes and challenges.
- Use the benchmarking data to identify areas where your training program excels or lags behind industry standards and make data-driven decisions for improvement.

10. Continuously review and improve the measurement approach:

- Regularly review and assess the effectiveness of your training measurement approach itself.
- Seek feedback from stakeholders, including learners, managers, and training professionals, on the metrics and measurement methods' relevance, validity, and usefulness.
- Stay updated on the latest research, trends, and innovations in training evaluation and measurement, and adapt your approach accordingly.
- Continuously refine and improve the measurement framework based on the insights gained, making sure that it's aligned with the evolving needs and goals of your CMMC 2.0 training program.

Measuring training effectiveness is an ongoing process that requires a multi-faceted approach, combining quantitative and qualitative data from various sources. By establishing clear objectives and metrics, conducting assessments, gathering feedback, monitoring behavioral changes, and benchmarking against industry standards, organizations can understand the impact and value of their CMMC 2.0 training efforts.

It is important to note that measuring training effectiveness is not a one-size-fits-all endeavor. Organizations should tailor their measurement approach to their specific context, goals, and resources. The key is establishing a consistent and systematic framework that provides actionable insights for continuous improvement.

Effective measurement of training effectiveness enables organizations to justify the investment in training, identify areas for optimization, and demonstrate the tangible benefits of the training program in terms of enhanced CMMC 2.0 compliance, reduced cybersecurity risks, and improved organizational performance.

By making training measurement an integral part of the continuous training program, organizations can ensure that their CMMC 2.0 training efforts remain relevant, impactful, and aligned with the evolving needs of their workforce and the dynamic landscape of cybersecurity threats and compliance requirements.

Best Practices: Tailor training programs to different organizational roles and use engaging, varied training methods to enhance learning.

When developing and delivering training programs for CMMC 2.0 compliance, it is crucial to tailor the content and approach to different organizational roles and use various engaging training methods to maximize learning effectiveness. By customizing training to each role's specific needs and responsibilities and employing interactive and diverse instructional strategies, organizations can ensure that employees acquire the necessary knowledge, skills, and mindset to support CMMC 2.0 compliance efforts. Let's explore the best practices for tailoring training programs using engaging, varied training methods.

1. Conduct a role-based training needs analysis:

- Begin by comprehensively analyzing the training needs for different organizational roles involved in CMMC 2.0 compliance.
- Identify the specific knowledge, skills, and competencies required

for each role, considering their level of interaction with sensitive information, cybersecurity responsibilities, and CMMC 2.0 requirements.

- Engage with managers, supervisors, and subject matter experts to gather insights into each role's unique challenges, gaps, and learning preferences.
- Use the findings from the needs analysis to inform the design and development of role-specific training programs.

2. Develop role-specific learning objectives:

- Based on the identified training needs, define clear and measurable learning objectives for each role.
- Ensure that the objectives are aligned with the specific CMMC 2.0 practices, processes, and responsibilities relevant to each role.
- Consider the desired outcomes, such as identifying and reporting security incidents, adhering to security policies, or implementing specific technical controls.
- Communicate the learning objectives to learners and stakeholders to set clear expectations and provide a roadmap for the training program.

3. Customize training content and examples:

- Tailor the training content, examples, and scenarios to each role's specific context and responsibilities.
- Use real-world examples and case studies that resonate with the learners' day-to-day experiences and challenges.
- Highlight the practical applications and implications of CMMC

2.0 requirements within each role's work environment.
- Adapt the language, terminology, and level of technical depth to match the learners' background and expertise.

4. Employ a blended learning approach:

- Utilize a combination of training methods and modalities to cater to different learning styles and preferences.
- Incorporate a mix of instructor-led sessions, online self-paced modules, hands-on labs, simulations, and group discussions to provide a well-rounded learning experience.
- Leverage the strengths of each training method to reinforce key concepts, provide practical application opportunities, and foster collaboration and knowledge sharing among learners.
- Ensure that the blended learning approach is flexible, accessible, and accommodates the schedules and workload of different roles.

5. Incorporate interactive and experiential learning:

- Engage learners through interactive and experiential learning activities that promote active participation and hands-on practice.
- Use simulations, role-playing exercises, and scenario-based learning to immerse learners in realistic cybersecurity situations and decision-making processes.
- Incorporate gamification elements, such as quizzes, challenges, and rewards, to motivate learners and reinforce key concepts.
- Encourage learners to work in teams or pairs to solve problems, share insights, and learn from each other's experiences.

6. Leverage storytelling and real-world examples:

- Use storytelling techniques to make the training content more relatable, memorable, and impactful.
- Share real-world examples of cybersecurity incidents, breaches, or compliance challenges that highlight the importance of CMMC 2.0 practices and the consequences of non-compliance.
- Invite guest speakers or subject matter experts to share their experiences and lessons learned, which will provide learners with practical insights and inspiration.
- Use case studies and scenarios that showcase the application of CMMC 2.0 principles in different organizational contexts and roles.

7. Incorporate micro-learning and just-in-time training:

- Break down complex CMMC 2.0 topics into bite-sized, easily digestible micro-learning modules that can be accessed on-demand.
- Provide just-in-time training resources, such as quick reference guides, checklists, or video tutorials, that learners can refer to when needed in their daily work.
- Use mobile learning platforms or apps to deliver micro-learning content and support learning in the workflow.
- Update and curate the micro-learning library regularly to ensure that the content remains relevant, accurate, and aligned with the latest CMMC 2.0 requirements and best practices.

8. Foster a culture of continuous learning:

- Encourage a culture of continuous learning and knowledge sharing among employees, regardless of their roles.
- Provide opportunities for learners to participate in communities of practice, discussion forums, or peer-to-peer learning sessions to exchange ideas, best practices, and lessons learned.
- Recognize and reward individuals actively engaging in training activities, demonstrating strong cybersecurity practices, or contributing to the knowledge base.
- Encourage managers and supervisors to support and reinforce the importance of continuous learning and applying CMMC 2.0 principles in daily work.

9. Provide performance support and reinforcement:

- Develop performance support tools and resources to help learners apply the knowledge and skills acquired from training in their roles.
- Create job aids, quick reference guides, or decision-making frameworks to help learners navigate CMMC 2.0 requirements and best practices in their work environment.
- Implement a system of regular reinforcement, such as periodic emails, newsletters, or micro-learning modules, to keep the training content fresh and top of mind.
- Encourage managers and supervisors to provide ongoing coaching, feedback, and support to help learners transfer the learning to their job roles.

10. Continuously evaluate and improve training programs:

- Regularly assess the effectiveness and impact of role-specific training programs using various evaluation methods, such as surveys, assessments, performance metrics, and feedback from learners and managers.
- Analyze the evaluation data to identify areas of strength, gaps, or opportunities for improvement in the training content, delivery, and learner engagement.
- Continuously refine and update the training programs based on the evaluation findings, evolving CMMC 2.0 requirements, and changes in the cybersecurity landscape.
- Seek input and feedback from learners, managers, and subject matter experts to ensure that the training programs remain relevant, engaging, and aligned with the needs and expectations of different roles.

By tailoring training programs to different organizational roles and using engaging, varied training methods, organizations can create a dynamic and effective learning environment that supports CMMC 2.0 compliance efforts. The key is to understand the unique needs, challenges, and learning preferences of each role and design training experiences that are relevant, interactive, and memorable.

It is essential to recognize that training is not a one-time event but an ongoing process that requires continuous reinforcement, support, and improvement. By fostering a culture of continuous learning, providing performance support tools, and regularly evaluating and refining training programs, organizations can ensure that employees remain engaged, knowledgeable, and well-equipped to meet the evolving demands of CMMC 2.0 compliance.

Ultimately, investing in role-specific, engaging, and varied training programs helps organizations meet CMMC 2.0 requirements and enhances overall cybersecurity awareness, skills, and culture. By empowering employees with the knowledge and tools they need to protect sensitive information and maintain compliance in their specific roles, organizations can build a strong foundation for long-term cybersecurity success and resilience.

Chapter 8: Internal Auditing and Continuous Monitoring

Strategies for setting up internal audits

Internal audits are a crucial component of an effective CMMC 2.0 compliance program. They provide organizations with a systematic and independent assessment of their cybersecurity practices, controls, and processes, helping to identify gaps, vulnerabilities, and areas for improvement. Organizations can proactively monitor their compliance posture, mitigate risks, and prepare for external assessments by setting up a robust internal audit function. Let's explore the key strategies for implementing effective internal audits in CMMC 2.0.

1. Establish an internal audit charter and framework:

- Develop a formal internal audit charter that defines the purpose, scope, authority, and responsibilities of the internal audit function within the organization.
- Align the internal audit framework with the CMMC 2.0 model, ensuring it covers all the relevant domains, capabilities, and practices.

- Obtain approval and support from senior management and the board of directors to establish the internal audit function as an independent and objective assurance mechanism.
- Communicate the internal audit charter and framework to all relevant stakeholders, including employees, contractors, and third-party partners.

2. Identify and prioritize audit areas:

- Conduct a risk assessment to identify the critical assets, systems, and processes in scope for CMMC 2.0 compliance.
- Prioritize the audit areas based on factors such as the sensitivity of the information handled, the criticality of the systems, and the inherent risks associated with each area.
- Consider the CMMC 2.0 assessment objectives and the organization's cybersecurity strategy when determining the audit priorities.
- Develop an annual audit plan that outlines the specific audits to be conducted, their timing, and the resources required.

3. Assign roles and responsibilities:

- Establish a dedicated internal audit team with the necessary skills, knowledge, and experience to conduct CMMC 2.0 audits effectively.
- Assign clear roles and responsibilities to each team member, including the lead auditor, subject matter experts, and support staff.
- Ensure the internal audit team has sufficient independence and

objectivity to perform their duties without undue influence or bias.

· Provide the internal audit team with the necessary resources, tools, and authority to access relevant information, systems, and personnel.

4. Develop audit procedures and checklists:

· Create detailed audit procedures and checklists that align with the CMMC 2.0 requirements and assessment objectives.
· When developing the audit procedures, use the CMMC 2.0 assessment guides, practice descriptions, and other authoritative sources as references.
· To ensure consistency and thoroughness, the audit procedures should be broken down into specific steps, test objectives, and expected outcomes.
· Incorporate industry best practices, regulatory requirements, and organizational policies into the audit procedures as applicable.

5. Conduct audit planning and scoping:

· Conduct a planning and scoping exercise prior to each audit to define the specific objectives, scope, and criteria for the audit.
· Identify the key stakeholders, systems, and processes involved in the audit and communicate the audit scope and expectations to them.
· Develop an audit timeline and resource plan, considering the availability of personnel, systems, and documentation.
· Obtain necessary approvals and coordinate with relevant depart-

ments to ensure minimal disruption to business operations during the audit.

6. Perform audit fieldwork and testing:

- Execute the audit procedures and checklists, collecting evidence and documenting observations, findings, and recommendations.
- Use a combination of techniques, such as interviews, documentation reviews, system inspections, and technical testing, to gather audit evidence.
- Validate the effectiveness of controls through a combination of manual and automated testing methods, such as vulnerability scans, penetration testing, and configuration reviews.
- Maintain detailed audit work papers and documentation to support the audit findings and ensure the auditability of the process.

7. Communicate and report audit results:

- Prepare clear and concise audit reports summarizing the objectives, scope, methodology, findings, and recommendations.
- Use a risk-based approach to prioritize the audit findings based on their potential impact and likelihood of occurrence.
- Provide actionable recommendations for remediation, including specific steps, timelines, and responsible parties.
- Present the audit results to senior management, the board of directors, and other relevant stakeholders, highlighting the key risks, gaps, and improvement opportunities.

8. Establish a remediation and follow-up process:

- Work with the audited departments and process owners to develop corrective action plans for each audit finding.
- Assign clear ownership and accountability for remediation actions, along with realistic timelines for completion.
- Establish a tracking mechanism to monitor the progress of remediation efforts and ensure timely closure of audit findings.
- Conduct follow-up audits or reviews to validate the effectiveness of remediation actions and ensure sustained compliance.

9. Foster a culture of continuous improvement:

- Use the internal audit process as a catalyst for continuously improving the organization's cybersecurity practices and compliance posture.
- Encourage open communication and collaboration between the internal audit team and the audited departments to identify root causes and implement systemic improvements.
- Share the lessons learned and best practices identified during organizational audits to promote awareness and drive positive change.
- Recognize and reward individuals and teams demonstrating a strong commitment to cybersecurity and compliance through the audit process.

10. Continuously enhance the internal audit function:

- Regularly assess the effectiveness and efficiency of the internal audit function against established performance metrics and stake-holder feedback.

- Invest in the internal audit team's ongoing training and professional development to keep them updated with the latest CMMC 2.0 requirements, cybersecurity trends, and auditing techniques.
- Leverage technology and automation tools to streamline audit processes, enhance data analysis capabilities, and improve quality and consistency.
- Benchmark the internal audit function against industry best practices and seek continuous improvement and innovation opportunities.

When setting up internal audits for CMMC 2.0, consider the following best practices:

- **Align with organizational objectives:** Ensure the internal audit function aligns with the organization's overall cybersecurity strategy, risk management framework, and business objectives.
- **Maintain independence and objectivity:** Establish reporting lines and oversight mechanisms that ensure the internal audit function remains independent and objective, free from undue influence or conflicts of interest.
- **Collaborate with stakeholders:** Foster a collaborative and transparent relationship with stakeholders, including business units, IT, and compliance teams, to ensure a shared understanding of audit objectives and expectations.
- **Use a risk-based approach:** Prioritize audit efforts based on the inherent risks, criticality, and sensitivity of the systems and processes being audited, focusing on areas with the highest potential impact on CMMC 2.0 compliance.

- **Leverage technology and automation:** Implement audit management tools, data analytics solutions, and automated testing frameworks to enhance the efficiency, consistency, and coverage of internal audits.
- **Communicate effectively:** Develop clear and concise audit reports that provide actionable insights and recommendations tailored to the needs and understanding of different stakeholder groups.
- **Foster a culture of learning:** Encourage a mindset of continuous learning and improvement, using the internal audit process to identify gaps, share best practices, and drive positive change in the organization's cybersecurity posture.

Setting up effective internal audits is a critical step in achieving and maintaining CMMC 2.0 compliance. By establishing a robust internal audit function, organizations can proactively identify and address risks, improve their cybersecurity practices, and demonstrate their commitment to protecting sensitive information.

However, it is important to recognize that internal audits are not a one-time exercise but an ongoing process that requires continuous monitoring, evaluation, and improvement. Organizations should regularly assess the effectiveness of their internal audit function, adapt to changes in the CMMC 2.0 requirements and the evolving cybersecurity landscape, and strive for excellence in their auditing practices.

Ultimately, a well-designed and executed internal audit program helps organizations meet CMMC 2.0 requirements, strengthen their overall cybersecurity posture, build trust with stakeholders, and operate with greater confidence and resilience in the face of ever-evolving cyber threats.

Tools for continuous monitoring and maintaining compliance

Continuous monitoring is a critical component of an effective CMMC 2.0 compliance program. It involves the ongoing assessment and analysis of an organization's cybersecurity posture, allowing for real-time detection of vulnerabilities, threats, and non-compliance issues. By implementing or continuously monitoring the right tools and processes, organizations can proactively identify and address risks, maintain continuous compliance, and respond quickly to evolving cybersecurity challenges. Let's explore the key tools and techniques for continuous monitoring and maintaining CMMC 2.0 compliance.

1. Security Information and Event Management (SIEM):

- Implement an SIEM solution to collect, aggregate, and analyze security logs and events from various sources across the organization's network, systems, and applications.
- Configure the SIEM to monitor for specific CMMC 2.0 compliance indicators, such as unauthorized access attempts, configuration changes, or suspicious user activities.
- Establish real-time rules and alerts to notify security teams of potential compliance violations or security incidents.
- Use the SIEM's reporting and dashboard capabilities to generate compliance reports, track key performance indicators (KPIs), and demonstrate adherence to CMMC 2.0 requirements.

2. Vulnerability Management:

- Deploy a vulnerability management tool to regularly scan the organization's network, systems, and applications for known vulnerabilities and misconfigurations.
- Integrate the vulnerability management tool with the organization's asset inventory to ensure comprehensive coverage of all relevant systems and devices.
- Prioritize vulnerabilities based on their severity, exploitability, and potential impact on CMMC 2.0 compliance.
- Establish a process for triaging, remediating, and tracking vulnerabilities, ensuring that critical issues are addressed promptly.
- Regular vulnerability assessments and penetration testing should be conducted to validate the effectiveness of security controls and identify potential weaknesses.

3. Configuration Management and Change Monitoring:

- Implement a configuration management database (CMDB) to maintain an accurate inventory of all hardware, software, and network assets relevant to CMMC 2.0 compliance.
- Establish baseline configurations for systems, applications, and network devices that align with CMMC 2.0 requirements and industry best practices.
- Use configuration management tools to monitor for unauthorized changes to system configurations, security settings, or access controls.
- Implement change management processes to ensure all modifications to critical systems and configurations are properly reviewed, approved, and documented.

- Conduct regular configuration audits and reviews to identify and remediate any deviations from the approved baselines.

4. Security Orchestration, Automation, and Response (SOAR):

- Leverage SOAR tools to automate and streamline the incident response and compliance management processes.
- Integrate SOAR with the organization's SIEM, vulnerability management, and other security tools to enable rapid detection, investigation, and response to potential compliance violations or security incidents.
- Define and implement automated playbooks and workflows that align with CMMC 2.0 requirements and the organization's incident response procedures.
- Use SOAR to automate compliance-related tasks, such as generating audit trails, updating asset inventories, or triggering notifications to relevant stakeholders.

5. Endpoint Detection and Response (EDR):

- Implement an EDR solution to monitor and protect endpoints, such as workstations, servers, and mobile devices, against advanced threats and malicious activities.
- Configure the EDR to detect and alert on indicators of compromise (IoCs), suspicious behaviors, or deviations from the organization's security policies.
- Use the EDR's investigation and forensic capabilities to analyze and respond to potential security incidents or compliance breaches.

- Integrate EDR with the organization's SIEM and other security tools to provide a comprehensive view of the endpoint security posture and enable coordinated response efforts.

6. Data Loss Prevention (DLP):

- Deploy DLP tools to monitor and protect sensitive information, such as Controlled Unclassified Information (CUI), from unauthorized access, exfiltration, or misuse.
- Configure DLP policies and rules to align with CMMC 2.0 requirements for data protection, access controls, and information handling.
- Monitor data flows across the organization's network, endpoints, and cloud services to detect and prevent potential data leaks or compliance violations.
- Use DLP's reporting and auditing capabilities to demonstrate compliance with CMMC 2.0 data protection requirements and identify areas for improvement.

7. Identity and Access Management (IAM):

- Implement an IAM solution to centrally manage user identities, access rights, and authentication processes across the organization's systems and applications.
- Enforce strong authentication mechanisms, such as multi-factor authentication (MFA), for all user accounts, especially those with privileged access.
- Use IAM to automate the provisioning and de-provisioning of user accounts, ensuring access rights are granted based on the

principle of least privilege and revoked promptly.

- Monitor and audit user activities, access attempts, and permission changes to detect and investigate potential compliance violations or unauthorized access.

8. Continuous Compliance Monitoring:

- Implement a continuous compliance monitoring tool that maps the organization's security controls and processes to the specific CMMC 2.0 requirements.
- Automate the collection and analysis of evidence, such as system logs, configuration settings, and audit trails, to assess the organization's compliance posture in real time.
- Use the tool's dashboards, reports, and alerts to identify compliance gaps, track remediation efforts, and demonstrate adherence to CMMC 2.0 requirements.
- Integrate the continuous compliance monitoring tool with other security tools, such as SIEM, vulnerability management, and IAM, to provide a holistic view of the organization's compliance posture.

9. Third-Party Risk Management:

- Implement tools and processes to continuously monitor and assess the cybersecurity and compliance posture of third-party vendors, suppliers, and partners.
- Use vendor risk assessment questionnaires, security ratings, and continuous monitoring solutions to identify potential risks and compliance gaps in the third-party ecosystem.

- Establish contractual requirements and service level agreements (SLAs) that mandate adherence to CMMC 2.0 requirements and regular reporting on compliance status.
- Conduct periodic audits and assessments of third-party security controls and processes to validate compliance with CMMC 2.0 standards.

10. Training and Awareness:

- Implement a comprehensive training and awareness program to educate employees, contractors, and third-party personnel on CMMC 2.0 requirements, cybersecurity best practices, and their roles and responsibilities in maintaining compliance.
- Use learning management systems (LMS) and other training tools to deliver interactive, role-based training modules and track completion rates.
- Conduct regular phishing simulations and social engineering exercises to assess and improve employees' security awareness and compliance with policies.
- Monitor and analyze training metrics, such as completion rates, quiz scores, and feedback, to identify areas for improvement and demonstrate the training program's effectiveness.

When implementing tools for continuous monitoring and maintaining CMMC 2.0 compliance, consider the following best practices:

- **Integrate and automate:** Ensure the various monitoring tools and technologies are integrated and can exchange data seamlessly to provide a comprehensive view of the organization's compliance posture. Automate processes wherever possible to reduce manual effort and minimize the risk of errors.

- **Prioritize based on risk:** Focus monitoring efforts on the most critical assets, systems, and processes that have the greatest impact on CMMC 2.0 compliance and the organization's overall cybersecurity posture. Use risk assessments to prioritize remediation efforts and allocate resources effectively.

- **Establish clear roles and responsibilities:** Define clear roles and responsibilities for the teams and individuals involved in continuous monitoring and compliance management. Ensure adequate expertise, resources, and oversight to implement and maintain the monitoring tools and processes effectively.

- **Develop actionable insights:** Use the data and insights generated by monitoring tools to drive meaningful actions and improvements. Establish processes for analyzing and reporting on compliance metrics, identifying trends and patterns, and communicating the results to relevant stakeholders.

- **Continuously review and improve:** Regularly assess the effectiveness and efficiency of the monitoring tools and processes and make necessary adjustments based on changes in the threat landscape, regulatory requirements, and organizational needs. Encourage feedback and suggestions from stakeholders to identify opportunities for improvement and optimization.

Implementing effective tools for continuous monitoring and maintaining CMMC 2.0 compliance requires combining technology, processes, and people. Organizations should carefully evaluate their specific needs, existing infrastructure, and resources when selecting and deploying monitoring tools. Adequate training and support for the teams responsible for managing and using these tools are also essential to ensure their effective utilization.

Continuous monitoring is not a one-time effort but an ongoing process that requires dedication, vigilance, and continuous improvement. By leveraging the right tools and techniques, organizations can proactively identify and address compliance gaps, strengthen their cybersecurity posture, and maintain a state of continuous compliance with CMMC 2.0 requirements.

Ultimately, the investment in robust continuous monitoring capabilities helps organizations meet CMMC 2.0 standards and enables them to detect and respond to cyber threats more effectively, protect sensitive information, and build trust with their customers, partners, and stakeholders in the defense industrial base.

Handling non-compliance and corrective actions

When conducting internal audits and continuous monitoring as part of a CMMC 2.0 compliance program, organizations may identify non-compliance or areas requiring corrective actions. Effectively handling non-compliance and implementing timely corrective actions are critical to maintaining the integrity of the compliance program, mitigating risks, and demonstrating a commitment to continuous improvement. Let's explore the key steps and best practices for handling non-compliance and corrective actions in the context of CMMC 2.0.

1. Establish a non-compliance and corrective action policy:

- Develop a comprehensive policy outlining the organization's approach to handling non-compliance and implementing corrective actions.
- Define the roles and responsibilities of individuals and teams involved in the non-compliance and corrective action process, including the internal audit team, compliance officers, and business unit owners.
- Establish guidelines for classifying and prioritizing non-compliance findings based on their severity, impact, and potential risks to the organization.
- Document the procedures for reporting, investigating, and resolving non-compliance issues, including timelines, documentation requirements, and approval processes.

2. Identify and document non-compliance:

- During internal audits and continuous monitoring activities, thoroughly document any non-compliance with CMMC 2.0 requirements or the organization's cybersecurity policies and procedures.
- Capture relevant details, such as the specific CMMC 2.0 practice or control that was violated, the date and time of the non-compliance, the systems or assets involved, and any evidence or observations supporting the finding.
- Classify the non-compliance based on its severity and potential impact, using a risk-based approach aligned with the organization's risk management framework.
- Assign a unique identifier to each non-compliance finding to facilitate tracking, reporting, and follow-up activities.

3. Investigate and determine root causes:

- Conduct a thorough investigation to determine the root causes of the non-compliance, looking beyond the immediate symptoms to identify underlying issues or gaps in processes, controls, or human behavior.
- Engage relevant stakeholders, such as system owners, business process owners, and subject matter experts, to gather additional information and insights.
- Use techniques such as root cause analysis, fishbone diagrams, or 5 Whys to systematically analyze the contributing factors and identify the fundamental reasons for the non-compliance.
- Document the investigation findings, including the identified root causes, any mitigating factors, and potential systemic issues that may require broader corrective actions.

4. Develop and implement corrective action plans:

- Based on the investigation findings and root cause analysis, develop a comprehensive corrective action plan (CAP) to address the non-compliance and prevent recurrence.
- Identify the specific actions required to remediate the non-compliance, such as updating policies and procedures, implementing technical controls, or providing additional training to personnel.
- Assign clear ownership and accountability for each corrective action, specifying the responsible individuals or teams and realistic timelines for completion.
- Allocate necessary resources, including budget, personnel, and tools, to ensure the effective implementation of the corrective

actions.

- Obtain approval from relevant stakeholders, such as senior management or the compliance steering committee, for the proposed corrective action plan.

5. Monitor and track corrective action progress:

- Establish a system for monitoring and tracking the progress of corrective actions using tools such as project management software, spreadsheets, or governance, risk, and compliance (GRC) platforms.
- Regularly review the status of each corrective action, assessing progress against the defined timelines and milestones.
- Conduct periodic meetings with the responsible individuals or teams to discuss challenges, roadblocks, and any additional support needed to complete the corrective actions.
- Provide regular updates to senior management and relevant stakeholders on the progress of corrective actions, highlighting any significant delays or issues that may impact the overall compliance posture.

6. Verify and validate corrective actions:

- Once the corrective actions have been implemented, thorough verification and validation activities will be conducted to ensure their effectiveness in addressing the non-compliance.
- Perform follow-up audits or assessments to confirm that the corrective actions have been properly implemented and are operating as intended.

- Test the updated controls, processes, or procedures to vali-date their effectiveness in preventing or detecting similar non-compliance.
- Document the results of the verification and validation activities, including any evidence or artifacts demonstrating the successful implementation of the corrective actions.

7. Communicate and report on non-compliance and corrective actions:

- Develop clear and concise reports that summarize the non-compliance findings, corrective action plans, and the status of their implementation.
- As appropriate, communicate the reports to relevant stakeholders, including senior management, the compliance steering commit-tee, and external auditors or assessors.
- Highlight the significance of the non-compliance issues, the potential risks they pose to the organization, and the steps taken to address them.
- Emphasize the lessons learned from the non-compliance and corrective action process, and share any insights or best practices that can help prevent similar issues.

8. Incorporate lessons learned and continuous improvement:

- Use the non-compliance and corrective action process as an opportunity for organizational learning and continuous improve-ment.
- Analyze the root causes and contributing factors identified during

the investigation to identify potential systemic issues or weaknesses in the compliance program.
· Incorporate the lessons learned into the organization's policies, procedures, and training programs to enhance the overall effectiveness of the compliance efforts.
· Encourage open communication and feedback from employees and stakeholders to identify areas for improvement and foster a culture of compliance and accountability.

9. Maintain documentation and audit trails:

· Maintain comprehensive documentation of all non-compliance findings, corrective action plans, and related activities.
· Ensure the documentation is accurate, complete, and easily accessible for future reference or audits.
· Establish a centralized repository or system for storing and managing non-compliance and corrective action documentation, with appropriate access controls and backup procedures.
· Retain documentation following the organization's record retention policies and applicable legal and regulatory requirements.

10. Continuously monitor and reassess:

· Establish a process for continuous monitoring and reassessment of the compliance posture, even after implementing corrective actions.
· Review the effectiveness of the corrective actions regularly and assess whether they continue to mitigate the identified risks and prevent non-compliance.

- Monitor for any changes in the CMMC 2.0 requirements, industry best practices, or the organization's business environment that may necessitate updates to the corrective actions or compliance controls.
- Conduct periodic risk assessments and internal audits to identify potential non-compliance areas and proactively initiate preventive measures.

When handling non-compliance and corrective actions, consider the following best practices:

- **Prioritize based on risk:** First, focus on addressing the most critical and high-risk instances of non-compliance, using a risk-based approach to prioritize corrective actions and allocate resources effectively.
- **Engage stakeholders:** Involve relevant stakeholders, such as business unit owners, system owners, and subject matter experts, throughout the non-compliance and corrective action process to ensure a comprehensive understanding of the issues and buy-in for the proposed solutions.
- **Foster a culture of compliance:** Encourage a culture of openness, transparency, and accountability, where employees feel comfortable reporting potential non-compliance issues and are encouraged to participate in the corrective action process.
- **Communicate effectively:** Develop clear and concise communication plans to inform stakeholders about non-compliance findings, corrective action progress, and the organization's overall compliance posture.
- **Learn and improve continuously:** Treat each instance of non-compliance as an opportunity for learning and improvement,

using the insights gained to strengthen the overall compliance program and prevent future occurrences.

Handling non-compliance and corrective actions is essential to maintaining an effective CMMC 2.0 compliance program. By establishing clear policies and procedures, conducting thorough investigations, implementing robust corrective action plans, and fostering a culture of continuous improvement, organizations can proactively identify and address compliance gaps, mitigate risks, and demonstrate their commitment to cybersecurity excellence.

It is important to approach non-compliance and corrective actions with a systematic, risk-based, and collaborative mindset, engaging stakeholders across the organization to ensure a comprehensive and sustainable resolution. Regular communication, documentation, and monitoring are also critical to maintaining the integrity and effectiveness of the compliance program over time.

Ultimately, effectively handling non-compliance and implementing timely corrective actions is a hallmark of a mature and resilient CMMC 2.0 compliance program. By dedicating the necessary resources, expertise, and leadership support to this process, organizations can not only meet the requirements of CMMC 2.0 but also strengthen their overall cybersecurity posture and build trust with their customers, partners, and stakeholders in the defense industrial base.

Best Practices: Establish a routine schedule for internal audits and continuous monitoring, using automated tools to assist in regular checks.

Establishing a routine schedule for internal audits and continuous monitoring is a crucial best practice for maintaining an effective CMMC 2.0 compliance program. Organizations can proactively identify potential vulnerabilities, control gaps, and non-compliance issues by conducting regular assessments and leveraging automated tools, enabling timely remediation and risk mitigation. Let's explore the key considerations and strategies for implementing a robust internal audit and continuous monitoring schedule.

1. Determine the audit and monitoring frequency:

- Assess the organization's risk profile, considering factors such as the sensitivity of the information handled, the complexity of the IT environment, and the criticality of the systems and processes.
- Establish an appropriate frequency for internal audits based on the risk assessment results and the organization's compliance requirements. Common frequencies include quarterly, semi-annually, or annually.
- Determine the frequency of continuous monitoring activities, such as vulnerability scans, log reviews, and configuration checks, based on the organization's risk appetite and the dynamic nature of the threat landscape. Continuous monitoring should occur on an ongoing basis, with some activities performed daily, weekly, or monthly.
- Consider any regulatory or contractual obligations that may

dictate specific audit and monitoring frequencies, such as those required by CMMC 2.0 or other industry standards.

2. Develop an audit and monitoring plan:

- Create a comprehensive plan that outlines the scope, objectives, and timelines for internal audits and continuous monitoring activities.
- Identify the specific systems, processes, and controls subject to audits and monitoring, prioritizing those most critical to CMMC 2.0 compliance and the organization's cybersecurity posture.
- Define the audit and monitoring procedures, including the tools, techniques, and methodologies to be used and the roles and responsibilities of the individuals involved.
- Establish clear criteria and thresholds for identifying potential issues, vulnerabilities, or non-compliance findings during audits and monitoring activities.
- Incorporate risk-based sampling and testing approaches to ensure adequate coverage of the organization's systems and controls while optimizing resource utilization.

3. Leverage automated tools and technologies:

- Identify and implement automated tools and technologies to streamline and enhance the efficiency of internal audits and continuous monitoring processes.
- Use vulnerability scanning tools to automatically assess systems and applications for known vulnerabilities, misconfigurations, and weaknesses. These tools can help identify potential security

gaps and prioritize remediation efforts.

- Employ security information and event management (SIEM) solutions to collect, aggregate, and analyze log data from various sources across the organization's network. SIEM tools can help detect potential security incidents, anomalies, or non-compliance events in real time.
- Implement configuration management tools to automatically monitor and assess the configuration settings of systems, applications, and network devices against established baselines and best practices. These tools can help identify unauthorized changes or deviations from the approved configurations.
- Utilize data loss prevention (DLP) tools to monitor and protect sensitive information, such as controlled unclassified information (CUI), from unauthorized access, exfiltration, or misuse. DLP tools can help detect data leakage and ensure compliance with CMMC 2.0 requirements.
- Leverage automated compliance management platforms that map the organization's controls and processes to specific CMMC 2.0 requirements, enabling continuous assessment and reporting of compliance status.

4. Establish an audit and monitoring team:

- Assign dedicated personnel or a team responsible for conducting internal audits and overseeing continuous monitoring activities.
- Ensure the team members have the necessary skills, expertise, and certifications relevant to CMMC 2.0 compliance and cybersecurity auditing.
- Provide the team with adequate resources, including tools, training, and access to relevant systems and data, to perform their

roles effectively.

- Foster a culture of independence and objectivity within the audit and monitoring team, ensuring they can conduct assessments without undue influence or bias.
- To facilitate a holistic approach to compliance, encourage collaboration and communication between the audit and monitoring team and other relevant stakeholders, such as IT, security, and compliance personnel.

5. Implement a risk-based approach:

- Prioritize audit and monitoring activities based on the organization's risk assessment results, focusing on the highest-risk areas and potential impacts on CMMC 2.0 compliance.
- Use risk scoring or rating methodologies to assess the criticality and sensitivity of systems, processes, and data and allocate audit and monitoring resources accordingly.
- Continuously reassess and update the risk profile based on changes in the organization's environment, threat landscape, or compliance requirements, and adjust the audit and monitoring schedule as needed.
- Communicate the risk-based approach to stakeholders, emphasizing the importance of prioritizing efforts based on the potential impact on the organization's cybersecurity posture and compliance status.

6. Develop and maintain audit and monitoring procedures:

- Establish clear and documented internal audits and continuous monitoring procedures aligned with CMMC 2.0 requirements and industry best practices.

- Define the specific steps, tools, and techniques for audits and monitoring, including testing methodologies, sampling approaches, and evidence-collection protocols.
- Develop standardized templates, checklists, and workpapers to ensure consistency and completeness of audit and monitoring activities across different systems and processes.
- Review and update the procedures regularly to incorporate changes in CMMC 2.0 requirements, technological advancements, or lessons learned from previous audits and monitoring efforts.

7. Conduct training and awareness:

- Provide regular training and awareness sessions to the audit and monitoring team and other relevant personnel on CMMC 2.0 requirements, auditing techniques, and the use of automated tools.
- Ensure the training covers the latest cybersecurity threats, vulnerabilities, and best practices relevant to the organization's industry and compliance obligations.
- Encourage the audit and monitoring team to participate in professional development activities like conferences, workshops, or certification programs to stay up-to-date with the evolving compliance landscape.
- Foster a culture of continuous learning and knowledge sharing within the organization, promoting the importance of cybersecurity and compliance awareness at all levels.

8. Communicate and report findings:

- Establish clear communication channels and reporting mechanisms for sharing the results of internal audits and continuous monitoring activities with relevant stakeholders.
- Develop concise and actionable reports highlighting key findings, risks, and improvement recommendations tailored to different audiences' needs and understanding.
- Report the audit and monitoring results regularly to senior management, the compliance steering committee, and other relevant stakeholders, emphasizing their impact on the organization's CMMC 2.0 compliance posture.
- Use data visualization techniques, such as dashboards and trend analyses, to present the findings clearly and meaningfully. This will enable informed decision-making and prioritize remediation efforts.

9. Implement continuous improvement:

- Treat internal audits and continuous monitoring as opportunities for continuous improvement, identifying areas for optimization and enhancement in the organization's cybersecurity and compliance practices.
- Analyze the audit and monitoring findings to identify trends, patterns, or systemic issues requiring broader organizational changes or process improvements.
- Encourage open communication and feedback from stakeholders, soliciting input on improving the effectiveness and efficiency of audit and monitoring activities.
- Assess the performance and impact of the audit and monitoring

program regularly, using metrics and key performance indicators (KPIs) to measure its effectiveness and identify areas for improvement.

· Continuously refine and adapt the audit and monitoring schedule, procedures, and tools based on the lessons learned, changes in the compliance landscape, and the organization's evolving needs and priorities.

10. Maintain documentation and records:

· Establish a robust documentation and record-keeping process to maintain an accurate audit trail of internal audits and continuous monitoring activities.
· Document each audit and monitoring activity's scope, objectives, procedures, findings, and recommendations, ensuring the records are easily accessible and retrievable for future reference or regulatory audits.
· Maintain version control and access controls on audit and monitoring documentation to ensure the integrity and confidentiality of the information.
· Retain the audit and monitoring records following the organization's record retention policies and applicable legal and regulatory requirements, such as CMMC 2.0 documentation retention guidelines.

Establishing a routine schedule for internal audits and continuous monitoring can help organizations proactively identify and address potential compliance gaps and vulnerabilities and control weaknesses. Automated tools and technologies can significantly enhance the efficiency and effectiveness of these activities, enabling organizations to cover a wider range of systems and processes while optimizing resource utilization.

It is important to approach internal audits and continuous monitoring as ongoing processes rather than one-time events. Regular assessments and monitoring activities help organizations maintain a constant state of compliance readiness, adapt to changes in the threat landscape, and foster a culture of continuous improvement.

To ensure the success of the internal audit and continuous monitoring program, organizations should prioritize risk-based approaches, invest in skilled personnel and advanced tools, and foster collaboration and communication among stakeholders. Regular training and awareness initiatives are also critical to ensure that the audit and monitoring team and the broader organization stay current with the latest CMMC 2.0 requirements and cybersecurity best practices.

Establishing a robust and routine internal audit and continuous monitoring schedule, supported by automated tools and technologies, is a fundamental best practice for achieving and maintaining CMMC 2.0 compliance. By dedicating the necessary resources, expertise, and leadership support to these activities, organizations can strengthen their cybersecurity posture, proactively mitigate risks, and demonstrate their commitment to protecting sensitive information and safeguarding national security interests.

Chapter 9: Navigating the CMMC 2.0 Assessment Process

Understanding the CMMC 2.0 assessment process for each level

The CMMC 2.0 assessment process is critical to demonstrating an organization's compliance with the required cybersecurity practices and controls. The process varies depending on the CMMC level an organization seeks to achieve. Understanding each level's assessment requirements and procedures is essential for successfully navigating the CMMC 2.0 compliance journey. Let's explore the assessment process for CMMC Levels 1, 2, and 3.

CMMC Level 1 Assessment Process:

1. Self-assessment:

- For CMMC Level 1, organizations are required to self-assess their cybersecurity practices against the 17 controls specified in the CMMC 2.0 Model.

- The organization performs the self-assessment internally with-out the involvement of an external assessor or certification body.
- The organization reviews its policies, procedures, and technical controls to determine whether they meet the Level 1 requirements.

2. Documentation and evidence:

- The organization should gather and maintain documentation and evidence demonstrating compliance with the Level 1 controls during the self-assessment.
- This documentation may include policies, procedures, system configurations, training records, and other relevant artifacts.
- The organization should ensure that the documentation is com-plete, accurate, and up to date and reflects the current state of its cybersecurity practices.

3. Assertion of compliance:

- Once the self-assessment is complete and the organization is confident in its compliance with Level 1 requirements, it can assert its compliance to the Department of Defense (DoD) or the relevant contracting authority.
- Compliance is typically asserted through a formal statement or representation indicating that the organization has met the Level 1 requirements based on its self-assessment.
- The organization may be required to provide the self-assessment results and supporting documentation to the DoD or the contract-ing authority upon request.

4. Monitoring and continuous improvement:

- After asserting compliance, the organization should continue to monitor its cybersecurity practices and controls to ensure ongoing adherence to the Level 1 requirements.
- The organization should regularly review and update its policies, procedures, and technical controls to address any changes in the threat landscape or the CMMC 2.0 Model.
- Continuous improvement efforts should be undertaken to enhance the organization's cybersecurity posture and maintain its Level 1 compliance status.

CMMC Level 2 Assessment Process:

1. Preparation for third-party assessment:

- For CMMC Level 2, organizations must undergo a third-party assessment conducted by a CMMC Third-Party Assessment Organization (C3PAO).
- The organization should begin by selecting an authorized C3PAO to perform the assessment.
- Before the assessment, the organization should conduct a self-assessment against the 110 practices specified in the CMMC 2.0 Model for Level 2, identifying any gaps or areas for improvement.
- The organization should gather and organize all relevant documentation, evidence, and artifacts required to demonstrate compliance with the Level 2 practices.

2. Scoping and assessment planning:

- The organization and the C3PAO collaborate to define the scope of the assessment, identifying the systems, networks, and assets that will be evaluated for compliance.
- The C3PAO develops an assessment plan outlining the objectives, timeline, and methodology for conducting the assessment.
- The organization and the C3PAO review and agree upon the assessment plan, ensuring a clear understanding of the assessment process and expectations.

3. On-site or remote assessment:

- Depending on the specific circumstances and requirements, the C3PAO conducts the assessment, which may be performed on-site at the organization's facilities or remotely.
- The assessment typically involves interviews with key personnel, documentation, evidence review, technical controls, and testing configurations.
- The C3PAO assesses the organization's compliance with the 110 practices, evaluating the effectiveness and maturity of the implemented controls.

4. Reporting and remediation:

- Upon completion of the assessment, the C3PAO provides a detailed assessment report outlining the findings, observations, and any identified non-conformities or gaps in compliance.
- The report includes recommendations for remediation and

improvement, prioritizing the areas of highest risk or non-compliance.

- The organization reviews the assessment report and develops a corrective action plan (CAP) to address the identified non-conformities and improve cybersecurity practices.
- The CAP should include specific actions, timelines, and responsible parties for each remediation item.

5. Certification decision:

- Based on the assessment report and the organization's CAP, the C3PAO recommends that the organization comply with CMMC Level 2 requirements.
- If the organization has demonstrated satisfactory compliance and has a robust plan for addressing any identified gaps, the C3PAO may recommend certification at Level 2.
- The CMMC Accreditation Body (CMMC-AB) makes the final certification decision after reviewing the assessment report and the C3PAO's recommendation.
- If approved, the organization is awarded a CMMC Level 2 certification, valid for a specified period (typically three years).

6. Continuous monitoring and renewal:

- After achieving CMMC Level 2 certification, the organization must maintain compliance through continuous monitoring and improvement efforts.
- The organization should regularly assess its cybersecurity practices, address any changes in the threat landscape, and ensure

ongoing adherence to the Level 2 requirements.

· Before the expiration of the certification, the organization should engage with a C3PAO to undergo a recertification assessment, demonstrating its continued compliance with the Level 2 practices.

CMMC Level 3 Assessment Process:

1. Preparation for government-led assessment:

· For CMMC Level 3, organizations must undergo a government-led assessment, typically conducted by the Defense Industrial Base Cybersecurity Assessment Center (DIBCAC) or another authorized government entity.

· The organization should begin with the appropriate government agency to initiate the assessment process.

· Like Level 2, the organization should conduct a thorough self-assessment against the additional practices required for Level 3, identifying any gaps or areas for improvement.

· The organization should gather and organize all relevant documentation, evidence, and artifacts required to demonstrate compliance with the Level 3 practices.

2. Scoping and assessment planning:

· The organization collaborates with the government assessment team to define the scope of the assessment, identifying the systems, networks, and assets that will be evaluated for compliance.

- The government assessment team develops an assessment plan outlining the objectives, timeline, and methodology for conducting the assessment.
- The organization and the government assessment team review and agree upon the assessment plan, ensuring a clear understanding of the assessment process and expectations.

3. On-site assessment:

- The government assessment team conducts the assessment on-site at the organization's facilities.
- The assessment involves a comprehensive evaluation of the organization's cybersecurity practices, including interviews with key personnel, review of documentation and evidence, and testing of technical controls and configurations.
- The assessment team assesses the organization's compliance with the additional practices required for Level 3 and the practices inherited from Levels 1 and 2.

4. Reporting and remediation:

- Upon completion of the assessment, the government assessment team provides a detailed assessment report outlining the findings, observations, and any identified non-conformities or gaps in compliance.
- The report includes recommendations for remediation and improvement, prioritizing the areas of highest risk or non-compliance.
- The organization reviews the assessment report and develops

a corrective action plan (CAP) to address the identified non-conformities and improve cybersecurity practices.

- The CAP should include specific actions, timelines, and responsible parties for each remediation item.

5. Certification decision:

- The government assessment team determines the organization's compliance with CMMC Level 3 requirements based on the assessment report and its CAP.
- If the organization has demonstrated satisfactory compliance and has a robust plan for addressing any identified gaps, the government assessment team may recommend certification at Level 3.
- The appropriate government authority makes the final certification decision after reviewing the assessment report and the team's recommendation.
- If approved, the organization is awarded a CMMC Level 3 certification, valid for a specified period (typically three years).

6. Continuous monitoring and renewal:

- After achieving CMMC Level 3 certification, the organization must maintain compliance through rigorous, continuous monitoring and improvement efforts.
- The organization should regularly assess its cybersecurity practices, address any changes in the threat landscape, and ensure ongoing adherence to the Level 3 requirements.
- Before the certification expires, the organization should engage

with the appropriate government agency to undergo a recertifica-tion assessment, demonstrating its continued compliance with the Level 3 practices.

Understanding each level's CMMC 2.0 assessment process is crucial for organizations seeking to achieve and maintain compliance. The assessment process becomes more rigorous and comprehensive as organizations progress from Level 1 to Level 3, reflecting the increasing sensitivity of the protected information and the maturity of the required cybersecurity practices.

Organizations should approach the assessment process proactively, conducting thorough self-assessments, gathering necessary evidence and documentation, and engaging with the appropriate entities (C3PAOs for Level 2 and government assessment teams for Level 3). Effective preparation, open communication, and a commitment to continuous improvement are key to successfully navigating the CMMC 2.0 assessment process and achieving the desired level of certification.

It is important to note that the CMMC 2.0 assessment process is subject to ongoing refinement and updates as the framework evolves. Organizations should stay informed about the latest guidance, requirements, and best practices related to CMMC assessments. They should work closely with their assessment partners and the CMMC-AB to ensure a smooth and successful assessment experience.

Preparing for self-assessments (Level 1) and third-party assessments (Levels 2 and 3)

Effective preparation is crucial for successfully navigating the CMMC 2.0 assessment process, whether it involves a self-assessment for Level 1 or third-party assessments for Levels 2 and 3. By proactively preparing for the assessments, organizations can ensure a smooth and efficient evaluation of their cybersecurity practices, identify gaps and areas for improvement, and increase the likelihood of achieving the desired level of certification. Let's explore the key steps and considerations for preparing for self-assessments and third-party assessments.

Preparing for Self-Assessments (Level 1):

1. Understand the Level 1 requirements:

- Thoroughly review and understand the 17 cybersecurity practices and controls specified in the CMMC 2.0 Model for Level 1.
- Familiarize yourself with the associated documentation, guidance, and templates provided by the CMMC Accreditation Body (CMMC-AB) and the Department of Defense (DoD).
- Ensure that all relevant personnel, including management, IT staff, and security teams, clearly understand the Level 1 requirements and their roles in achieving compliance.

2. Conduct a gap analysis:

- Perform a comprehensive gap analysis to assess your organization's current cybersecurity posture against the Level 1 requirements.
- Identify gaps or areas where your current practices, policies, and technical controls do not meet the specified requirements.
- Document the gap analysis findings, prioritizing the areas that require attention and improvement.

3. Develop and implement a remediation plan:

- Based on the results of the gap analysis, develop a remediation plan to address the identified gaps and bring your organization into compliance with the Level 1 requirements.
- Assign responsibilities, allocate resources, and set realistic timelines for implementing changes and improvements.
- Update policies, procedures, and technical controls to align with the Level 1 practices.
- Provide training and guidance to personnel on the updated practices and their roles in maintaining compliance.

4. Gather evidence and documentation:

- Collect and organize the evidence and documentation required to demonstrate compliance with the Level 1 practices during the self-assessment.
- This may include policies, procedures, system configurations, training records, and other relevant artifacts.
- Ensure that the documentation is complete, accurate, and up to date and reflects the current state of your organization's

cybersecurity practices.

5. Conduct the self-assessment:

- Follow the self-assessment guidance the CMMC-AB and the DoD provided to evaluate your organization's compliance with the Level 1 requirements.
- Use self-assessment tools, checklists, or templates to assess each of the 17 practices systematically.
- Involve relevant personnel in self-assessment, gathering input and evidence from different departments and functions as needed.
- Document the self-assessment results, noting any areas of compliance, non-compliance, or partial compliance.

6. Address any identified gaps:

- Based on the self-assessment results, identify any remaining gaps or areas of non-compliance.
- Develop and implement a plan to address these gaps promptly, assigning responsibilities and setting timelines for completion.
- Update the relevant documentation, policies, and procedures to reflect the changes made.

7. Assert compliance:

- Once you have completed the self-assessment and addressed any identified gaps, you can assert your organization's compliance with the Level 1 requirements.

- Prepare a formal statement or representation indicating that your organization has met the Level 1 requirements based on the self-assessment.
- Be prepared to provide the self-assessment results and supporting documentation to the DoD or the relevant contracting authority upon request.

Preparing for Third-Party Assessments (Levels 2 and 3):

1. Understand the assessment requirements:

- Familiarize yourself with the specific assessment requirements for CMMC Levels 2 and 3, as outlined in the CMMC 2.0 Model and associated guidance.
- Review the assessment objectives, methodologies, and procedures that will be followed by the CMMC Third-Party Assessment Organizations (C3PAOs) for Level 2 or the government assessment teams for Level 3.
- Ensure that all relevant personnel understand the assessment process, their roles and responsibilities, and the expectations for demonstrating compliance.

2. Conduct a readiness assessment:

- Perform a thorough readiness assessment to evaluate your organization's preparedness for the third-party evaluation.
- Use the CMMC 2.0 assessment guides, practice descriptions, and

other reference materials to assess your compliance with each of the required practices for the target level (110 practices for Level 2, additional practices for Level 3).

- Identify any gaps, weaknesses, or areas for improvement in your cybersecurity practices, policies, and technical controls.
- Document the findings of the readiness assessment and prioritize the areas that require remediation or enhancement.

3. Implement necessary improvements:

- Based on the readiness assessment results, develop and execute a plan to address the identified gaps and improve your cybersecurity posture.
- Assign responsibilities, allocate resources, and set realistic timelines for implementing changes and enhancements.
- Update policies, procedures, and technical controls to align with the CMMC 2.0 practices and assessment requirements.
- Provide personnel with training and guidance on the updated practices, their roles in maintaining compliance, and the expectations for the third-party assessment.

4. Gather and organize evidence:

- Collect and organize the evidence and documentation required to demonstrate compliance with the CMMC practices during the third-party assessment.
- This may include policies, procedures, system configurations, logs, training records, incident response plans, and other relevant artifacts.

- Ensure that the evidence is comprehensive, accurate, and up to date, reflecting the current state of your organization's cybersecurity practices.
- Organize the evidence logically and easily navigably, aligning it with the specific CMMC practices and assessment objectives.

5. Conduct internal assessments and audits:

- Conduct internal assessments and audits to validate your organization's compliance with CMMC practices prior to the third-party assessment.
- Use the CMMC assessment guides and methodologies as a reference to assess each practice thoroughly.
- Involve relevant personnel, including IT staff, security teams, and process owners, in the internal assessments to gather input and verify compliance.
- Document the results of the internal assessments, noting any areas of strength, weakness, or non-compliance.

6. Remediate identified gaps:

- Based on the internal assessments and audits, identify any remaining gaps or areas of non-compliance.
- Develop and implement a remediation plan to address these gaps promptly, assigning responsibilities and setting timelines for completion.
- Update the relevant documentation, policies, and procedures to reflect the changes made.
- Retest and validate the effectiveness of the remediation efforts

through follow-up internal assessments.

7. Prepare for the assessment logistics:

- Engage with the selected C3PAO (for Level 2) or the government assessment team (for Level 3) to plan and coordinate the assessment logistics.
- Determine the scope of the assessment, including the systems, networks, and facilities that will be evaluated.
- Agree on the assessment timeline, duration, and specific requirements or arrangements.
- Ensure that the necessary resources, including personnel, facilities, and access to systems and documentation, are available and prepared for the assessment.

8. Communicate and coordinate with the assessment team:

- Establish open and effective communication channels with the assessment team, whether it's a C3PAO or a government assessment team.
- As requested, provide the assessment team with the necessary information, documentation, and access to systems and personnel.
- Be responsive to the assessment team's inquiries, clarifications, and requests for additional evidence or documentation.
- Foster a collaborative and transparent relationship with the assessment team, working together to ensure a smooth and efficient assessment process.

9. Participate actively in the assessment:

- Actively participate in the assessment process, providing the assessment team with the necessary support, information, and access to systems and personnel.
- Be prepared to answer questions, provide explanations, and demonstrate the effectiveness of your cybersecurity practices and controls.
- Proactively address any concerns or findings the assessment team raises, providing additional evidence or clarifications as needed.
- Use the assessment process as an opportunity for continuous improvement, gathering insights and feedback from the assessment team to enhance your cybersecurity posture.

10. Address findings and achieve certification:

- After completing the assessment, review the report provided by the C3PAO or the government assessment team.
- Carefully analyze the findings, observations, and recommendations outlined in the report.
- Develop a corrective action plan to address any identified non-conformities, gaps, or areas for improvement.
- Assign responsibilities, allocate resources, and set timelines for implementing the necessary corrective actions.
- Work closely with the assessment team and the CMMC-AB to resolve any outstanding issues and achieve the desired level of certification.

Effective preparation is key to successfully navigating the CMMC 2.0

assessment process, whether it involves a self-assessment for Level 1 or third-party assessments for Levels 2 and 3. By proactively assessing your organization's cybersecurity posture, gathering necessary evidence and documentation, and addressing identified gaps, you can demonstrate your commitment to cybersecurity and increase the likelihood of achieving certification.

It is important to approach the assessment process as an opportunity for continuous improvement rather than a one-time event. Regularly reviewing and enhancing your cybersecurity practices, staying updated with the latest CMMC requirements and guidance, and fostering a culture of cybersecurity awareness and responsibility throughout your organization are essential for maintaining compliance and safeguarding sensitive information.

By investing time and resources in thorough preparation, engaging collaboratively with the assessment teams, and demonstrating a proactive approach to cybersecurity, you can navigate the CMMC 2.0 assessment process with confidence and position your organization for success in the evolving landscape of cybersecurity and defense contracting.

What to expect during and after the assessment

Understanding what to expect during and after the CMMC 2.0 assessment process is crucial for organizations preparing for certification. The assessment experience may vary depending on the CMMC level being pursued, but there are common elements and considerations that apply across all levels. Let's explore what organizations can anticipate during and after the assessment process.

During the Assessment:

1. Assessment kickoff meeting:

- The assessment typically begins with a kickoff meeting between the organization and the assessment team (C3PAO for Level 2, government assessment team for Level 3).
- The kickoff meeting aims to establish a common understanding of the assessment objectives, scope, timeline, and expectations.
- The assessment team will provide an overview of the assessment process, the activities to be conducted, and the roles and responsibilities of the involved parties.
- The organization can ask questions, clarify concerns, and ensure alignment with the assessment plan.

2. Documentation review:

- The assessment team will review the organization's policies, procedures, and documentation related to cybersecurity practices and CMMC requirements.
- The organization should provide the assessment team with access to the necessary documentation, including system security plans, incident response plans, training records, and other relevant artifacts.
- The assessment team will evaluate the documentation's completeness, accuracy, and effectiveness in meeting the CMMC practices and controls.

· The organization may be asked to provide additional documentation or clarifications during the review process.

3. Interviews and discussions:

· The assessment team will conduct interviews and discussions
with key personnel involved in the organization's cybersecurity
practices and CMMC implementation.
· These interviews may include senior management, IT staff, security teams, process owners, and other relevant individuals.
· The interviews aim to gather information, validate the implementation of CMMC practices, and assess personnel's knowledge and
awareness of cybersecurity and CMMC requirements.
· The organization should ensure that the designated personnel are
available, prepared, and can respond accurately and comprehensively to the assessment team's questions.

4. Technical testing and verification:

· The assessment team will perform technical testing and verification of the organization's systems, networks, and security
controls.
· This may involve vulnerability scans, penetration testing, configuration reviews, and other technical assessments to validate the
effectiveness of the implemented controls.
· The organization should provide the necessary access and support
to the assessment team to facilitate the technical testing activities.
· The assessment team will document the technical testing results,
including any identified vulnerabilities, misconfigurations, or

weaknesses.

5. Evidence collection and validation:

- Throughout the assessment, the assessment team will collect and validate evidence to support the organization's compliance with the CMMC practices and controls.
- The organization should be prepared to provide the necessary evidence, such as system logs, audit trails, screenshots, and other artifacts, to demonstrate the implementation and effectiveness of the required practices.
- The assessment team will review and verify the provided evidence, ensuring that it aligns with the CMMC requirements and supports the organization's compliance assertions.

6. Ongoing communication and collaboration:

- During the assessment, it is essential to maintain open and collaborative communication between the organization and the assessment team.
- The organization should promptly address requests for information, clarifications, or additional evidence from the assessment team.
- Regular status updates and progress meetings may be held to discuss the assessment findings, address any concerns or challenges, and ensure a smooth and efficient assessment process.
- The organization should view the assessment as an opportunity for continuous improvement and actively seek feedback and guidance from the assessment team to enhance its cybersecurity

posture.

After the Assessment:

1. Assessment report:

- Upon completion of the assessment, the assessment team will generate a comprehensive assessment report.
- The report will outline the assessment findings, including areas of compliance and non-compliance and any identified gaps or weaknesses.
- The report may also include recommendations for remediation and improvement, prioritizing the areas of highest risk or non-compliance.
- The organization will receive a copy of the assessment report for review and analysis.

2. Remediation planning:

- Based on the assessment report findings, the organization should develop a remediation plan to address any identified non-conformities, gaps, or areas for improvement.
- The remediation plan should include specific actions, timelines, and responsible parties for each item requiring attention.
- The organization should prioritize the remediation efforts based on the criticality and potential impact of the identified issues.
- The remediation plan should be comprehensive, realistic, and aligned with the organization's resources and timelines.

3. Corrective actions and implementation:

- The organization should promptly implement the corrective actions outlined in the remediation plan.
- This may involve updating policies, procedures, and technical controls, providing additional training to personnel, or implementing new security measures.
- The organization should allocate the necessary resources, including personnel, budget, and tools, to execute corrective actions effectively.
- Regular progress monitoring and tracking should be performed to ensure that the remediation efforts are on track and meeting the established timelines.

4. Evidence of remediation:

- As the organization implements the corrective actions, it should gather and maintain evidence to demonstrate the effectiveness of the remediation efforts.
- This evidence may include updated documentation, system configurations, logs, or other artifacts showcasing improvements.
- The organization should be prepared to provide this evidence to the assessment team or the CMMC-AB as part of the follow-up or closure process.

5. Certification decision:

- The assessment report, remediation efforts, and evidence provided will inform the certification decision of the CMMC-AB or the designated authority.

· If the organization has demonstrated satisfactory compliance with the CMMC requirements and has effectively addressed any identified issues, it may be granted certification at the assessed level.

· The certification decision and any additional feedback or recommendations will be communicated to the organization.

6. Continuous monitoring and improvement:

· Achieving CMMC certification is not a one-time event but an ongoing continuous monitoring and improvement journey.

· After certification, the organization should establish a robust continuous monitoring program to assess its cybersecurity posture regularly, identify potential risks or gaps, and proactively address them.

· The organization should stay informed about updates to the CMMC model, industry best practices, and emerging cybersecurity threats and adapt its practices accordingly.

· Regular internal audits, vulnerability assessments, and risk assessments should be conducted to ensure the ongoing effectiveness of the controls and practices implemented.

7. Certification maintenance and renewal:

· CMMC certifications are typically valid for a specified period, usually three years.

· During the certification validity period, the organization should maintain compliance with the CMMC requirements and demonstrate continuous improvement in cybersecurity practices.

- Before the certification expires, the organization should engage with the appropriate assessment body (C3PAO for Level 2, government assessment team for Level 3) to schedule a recertification assessment.
- The recertification assessment process will be similar to the initial assessment, focusing on verifying the organization's continued compliance with the CMMC practices and controls.

8. Collaboration and communication:

- After the assessment, it is important to maintain open communication and collaboration with the assessment team, the CMMC-AB, and other relevant stakeholders.
- The organization should actively seek guidance, clarifications, and support to address any challenges or concerns related to CMMC compliance and continuous improvement.
- Participation in CMMC-related forums, working groups, or industry associations can provide valuable insights, best practices, and peer learning opportunities.

9. Continual improvement and maturity:

- The organization should view the CMMC assessment process as a catalyst for continual improvement and maturity in its cybersecurity practices.
- Lessons learned from the assessment should be incorporated into the organization's cybersecurity strategy, processes, and training programs.

- The organization should continually assess its cybersecurity posture against the evolving threat landscape and the latest CMMC requirements, making necessary adjustments and enhancements.
- Pursuing higher levels of CMMC certification over time can demonstrate the organization's commitment to cybersecurity excellence and position it for new business opportunities.

Understanding what to expect during and after the CMMC assessment process helps organizations prepare effectively, navigate the assessment smoothly, and achieve their desired certification goals. It is crucial to approach the assessment with a proactive, collaborative, and improvement-oriented mindset, leveraging the insights and guidance provided by the assessment team to strengthen the organization's cybersecurity posture.

By actively engaging in the assessment process, promptly addressing identified gaps, and establishing a robust continuous monitoring and improvement program, organizations can achieve CMMC certification and cultivate a culture of cybersecurity excellence. This, in turn, enhances their ability to protect sensitive information, maintain the trust of their customers and partners, and compete effectively in the evolving landscape of defense contracting.

Best Practices: Start early, be proactive, and maintain open communication throughout the assessment process.

Navigating the CMMC 2.0 assessment process successfully requires a proactive approach, early preparation, and open communication throughout the entire journey. By adopting these best practices, organizations can streamline their efforts, minimize challenges, and increase the likelihood of achieving the desired level of certification. Let's explore these best practices in detail.

1. Start early:

- Begin preparing for the CMMC assessment well in advance of the target certification date.
- Allocate sufficient time and resources to thoroughly assess your organization's current cybersecurity posture, identify gaps, and implement necessary improvements.
- Conduct a comprehensive gap analysis against the CMMC requirements for your target level (Level 1, 2, or 3) to understand the scope of work required.
- Develop a detailed project plan outlining the tasks, timelines, and responsibilities for achieving CMMC compliance.
- Engage with key stakeholders, including senior management, IT teams, and process owners, to ensure buy-in and support for the CMMC initiative from the outset.

2. Be proactive:

- Take a proactive approach to cybersecurity and CMMC compliance rather than waiting for the assessment to uncover gaps or weaknesses.
- Conduct regular internal assessments, audits, and vulnerability scans to identify and address potential issues before the formal CMMC assessment.
- Implement a robust risk management program to assess and mitigate cybersecurity risks across your organization continuously.
- Stay informed about the latest CMMC requirements, guidance, and best practices, and proactively adapt your practices accordingly.
- Foster a cybersecurity awareness and responsibility culture throughout your organization, encouraging proactive identification and reporting of potential vulnerabilities or non-compliance issues.

3. Maintain open communication:

- Establish and maintain open communication channels with all relevant stakeholders throughout the CMMC assessment process.
- Engage with your chosen CMMC Third-Party Assessment Organization (C3PAO) for Level 2 or the government assessment team for Level 3 early in the process.
- Clearly communicate your organization's goals, timelines, and expectations for the assessment, and seek guidance and clarification as needed.
- Provide the assessment team with timely access to the necessary documentation, systems, and personnel to facilitate a smooth assessment process.
- Regularly update internal stakeholders, including senior manage-

ment and employees, on the progress of the CMMC assessment and any key milestones or challenges.

4. Assign dedicated resources:

- Allocate dedicated resources, including personnel, budget, and tools, to support the CMMC assessment process.
- Identify a CMMC project team or steering committee responsible for overseeing the assessment preparation, coordination, and remediation efforts.
- Ensure that the assigned resources have the necessary skills, knowledge, and authority to manage the CMMC assessment process effectively.
- Provide the project team with the necessary support, training, and resources to fulfill their responsibilities effectively.

5. Collaborate with the assessment team:

- Foster a collaborative and transparent relationship with the C3PAO or government assessment team throughout the assessment process.
- Provide the assessment team with comprehensive and accurate information about your organization's cybersecurity practices, systems, and controls.
- Be responsive to the assessment team's requests for documentation, evidence, or clarifications, and promptly address any identified gaps or non-conformities.
- View the assessment team as a valuable resource for guidance, best practices, and continuous improvement opportunities, and

actively seek their input and feedback.

6. Prioritize and remediate gaps:

- Prioritize identifying and remedying gaps or non-conformities based on their criticality and potential impact on your organization's cybersecurity posture and CMMC compliance.
- Develop a comprehensive remediation plan outlining the specific actions, timelines, and responsible parties for addressing each identified gap.
- Allocate the necessary resources and budget to implement the remediation actions effectively and efficiently.
- Monitor and track the progress of remediation efforts regularly and provide updates to the assessment team and internal stakeholders as needed.

7. Document and maintain evidence:

- Maintain comprehensive and up-to-date documentation of your organization's cybersecurity practices, policies, procedures, and controls.
- Ensure that the documentation aligns with the CMMC requirements and provides clear evidence of compliance.
- Organize and store the documentation in a centralized and easily accessible manner, facilitating efficient retrieval and review during the assessment process.
- Regularly review and update the documentation to reflect changes in your organization's practices or the CMMC requirements.

8. Conduct training and awareness:

- Provide comprehensive training and awareness programs to employees, contractors, and third-party partners on the CMMC requirements, cybersecurity best practices, and their roles and responsibilities in maintaining compliance.
- Tailor the training content to different stakeholders' specific needs and roles, ensuring relevance and applicability.
- Conduct regular refresher training sessions to reinforce key concepts and inform stakeholders of any updates or changes to the CMMC requirements or your organization's practices.
- Foster a culture of continuous learning and improvement, encouraging stakeholders to participate in training and share their knowledge and experiences actively.

9. Leverage automation and tools:

- Utilize automated tools and technologies to streamline and enhance the efficiency of the CMMC assessment process.
- Implement security information and event management (SIEM) solutions, vulnerability scanners, and compliance management platforms to monitor and assess your organization's cybersecurity posture continuously.
- Use automated testing and validation tools to assess the effectiveness of your security controls and identify potential weaknesses or gaps.
- Leverage project management and collaboration tools to track and manage the assessment process, facilitate stakeholder communication, and maintain a centralized repository of documentation and evidence.

10. Continuously monitor and improve:

- Establish a robust continuous monitoring and improvement program to maintain and enhance your organization's cybersecurity posture and CMMC compliance beyond the assessment process.
- Regularly assess and update your cybersecurity practices, policies, and controls based on changes in the threat landscape, regulatory requirements, and industry best practices.
- Conduct periodic internal audits, vulnerability scans, and risk assessments to identify and address potential gaps or weaknesses proactively.
- Engage with industry peers, participate in cybersecurity forums and events, and collaborate with CMMC-focused organizations to stay informed of the latest trends, challenges, and solutions.
- Encourage a culture of continuous improvement, fostering open communication, feedback, and knowledge sharing among stakeholders to drive ongoing enhancements to your cybersecurity posture.

By starting early, being proactive, and maintaining open communication throughout the CMMC assessment process, organizations can effectively prepare for and navigate the assessment journey. These best practices enable organizations to proactively identify and address potential challenges, collaborate effectively with the assessment team, and demonstrate their commitment to cybersecurity excellence.

It is important to recognize that the CMMC assessment process is not a one-time event but an ongoing journey of continuous improvement. By embracing and integrating these best practices into your organization's cybersecurity culture and operations, you can establish a strong foundation for long-term success in achieving and maintaining CMMC compliance.

Remember, the ultimate goal of the CMMC assessment process is to achieve certification and enhance your organization's overall cybersecurity posture, protect sensitive information, and build trust with your customers, partners, and stakeholders in the defense industrial base. By proactively preparing, collaborating openly, and continuously improving, you can confidently navigate the CMMC assessment process and position your organization for success in the evolving landscape of cybersecurity and defense contracting.

Chapter 10: Achieving and Maintaining Certification

The certification process explained for each CMMC 2.0 level.

Achieving CMMC 2.0 certification demonstrates an organization's commitment to implementing and maintaining robust cybersecurity practices to protect sensitive information, including Controlled Unclassified Information (CUI) and Federal Contract Information (FCI). The certification process varies depending on the CMMC level an organization seeks to attain. Let's explore the certification process for each CMMC 2.0 level in detail.

CMMC Level 1 Certification Process:

1. Self-assessment:

- For Level 1 certification, organizations are required to self-assess their cybersecurity practices against the 17 practices outlined in the CMMC 2.0 Model.

- The self-assessment involves reviewing and evaluating the organization's policies, procedures, and technical controls to ensure alignment with the Level 1 requirements.
- The organization should document the self-assessment results, identifying gaps or areas for improvement.

2. Remediation and documentation:

- Based on the self-assessment results, the organization should develop and implement a remediation plan to address any identified gaps or weaknesses.
- The remediation efforts may involve updating policies and procedures, implementing additional technical controls, or providing necessary training to personnel.
- The organization should maintain documentation and evidence demonstrating the implementation of the required practices and the effectiveness of the remediation efforts.

3. Assertion of compliance:

- Once the organization has completed the self-assessment and implemented the necessary remediation measures, it can assert its compliance with the Level 1 requirements.
- The assertion of compliance involves submitting a formal statement or representation to the Department of Defense (DoD) or the relevant contracting authority, affirming that the organization has met the Level 1 requirements based on its self-assessment.
- The organization should be prepared to provide supporting documentation and evidence of compliance upon request.

4. Maintenance and continuous monitoring:

- After achieving Level 1 certification, the organization must maintain its compliance posture through ongoing monitoring and continuous improvement efforts.
- The organization should regularly review and update its policies, procedures, and technical controls to ensure continued alignment with the Level 1 requirements.
- Continuous monitoring activities, such as vulnerability scans, log reviews, and incident response exercises, should be conducted to proactively identify and address any potential security risks or non-compliance issues.

CMMC Level 2 Certification Process:

1. Preparation and self-assessment:

- For Level 2 certification, organizations must conduct a thorough self-assessment against the 110 practices outlined in the CMMC 2.0 Model.
- The self-assessment involves evaluating the organization's current cybersecurity posture, identifying gaps or weaknesses, and implementing necessary remediation measures.
- The organization should gather and organize all relevant documentation, evidence, and artifacts required to demonstrate compliance with the Level 2 practices.

2. Engagement with a C3PAO:

- To pursue Level 2 certification, organizations must engage with a CMMC Third-Party Assessment Organization (C3PAO) authorized by the CMMC Accreditation Body (CMMC-AB).
- The organization should select an appropriate C3PAO based on experience, expertise, and availability.
- The organization and the C3PAO will collaborate to define the scope of the assessment, establish timelines, and coordinate logistics.

3. Assessment by the C3PAO:

- The C3PAO will comprehensively assess the organization's cyber-security practices and controls against the Level 2 requirements.
- The assessment may involve interviews with key personnel, documentation, evidence review, technical controls, and testing configurations.
- The C3PAO will evaluate the organization's compliance with the 110 practices, noting any gaps, weaknesses, or areas for improvement.

4. Remediation and corrective actions:

- Based on the assessment findings, the C3PAO will provide the organization with a detailed report highlighting any non-conformities or areas requiring remediation.
- The organization should develop a corrective action plan (CAP) to address the identified issues, assigning responsibilities and timelines for each remediation task.
- The organization should work collaboratively with the C3PAO to

resolve outstanding issues and implement corrective actions.

5. Certification recommendation and decision:

- Once the organization has successfully addressed the identified non-conformities and implemented the required corrective actions, the C3PAO will recommend certification to the CMMC-AB.
- The CMMC-AB will review the assessment report, the CAP, and supporting documentation to determine if the organization has met the Level 2 certification requirements.
- If the CMMC-AB approves the recommendation, the organization will be granted a Level 2 certification, valid for a specified period (typically three years).

6. Continuous monitoring and recertification:

- After achieving Level 2 certification, the organization must maintain compliance through ongoing monitoring, risk assessments, and continuous improvement efforts.
- The organization should regularly review and update its policies, procedures, and technical controls to ensure continued alignment with the Level 2 requirements and evolving cybersecurity best practices.
- Before the certification expires, the organization should engage with a C3PAO to undergo a recertification assessment, demonstrating its ongoing compliance with the Level 2 practices.

CMMC Level 3 Certification Process:

1. Preparation and readiness assessment:

- For Level 3 certification, organizations must first conduct a comprehensive readiness assessment against the additional practices beyond Level 2, as outlined in the CMMC 2.0 Model.
- The readiness assessment involves evaluating the organization's cybersecurity posture against the enhanced requirements, identifying gaps or weaknesses, and implementing necessary improvements.
- The organization should gather and organize all relevant documentation, evidence, and artifacts required to demonstrate compliance with the Level 3 practices.

2. Engagement with the government assessment team:

- To pursue Level 3 certification, organizations must engage with the appropriate government assessment team, typically from the Defense Industrial Base Cybersecurity Assessment Center (DIBCAC) or another authorized entity.
- The organization should coordinate with the government assessment team to define the scope of the assessment, establish timelines, and plan logistics.

3. Assessment by the government assessment team:

- The government assessment team will rigorously assess the organization's cybersecurity practices and controls against the

Level 3 requirements.
- The assessment may involve in-depth interviews with key personnel, a detailed review of documentation and evidence, and comprehensive testing of technical controls and configurations.
- The government assessment team will evaluate the organization's compliance with the additional practices beyond Level 2 and the practices inherited from Levels 1 and 2.

4. Remediation and corrective actions:

- Based on the assessment findings, the organization will receive a detailed report from the government assessment team, highlighting any non-conformities or areas requiring remediation.
- The organization should develop a corrective action plan (CAP) to address the identified issues, assigning responsibilities and timelines for each remediation task.
- The organization should work collaboratively with the government assessment team to resolve outstanding issues and implement corrective actions.

5. Certification decision:

- Once the organization has successfully addressed the identified non-conformities and implemented the required corrective actions, the government assessment team will decide regarding certification.
- The appropriate government authority will review the assessment report, the CAP, and supporting documentation to determine if the organization has met the Level 3 certification requirements.

- If the government authority approves the certification, the organization will be granted a Level 3 certification, valid for a specified period (typically three years).

6. Continuous monitoring and recertification:

- After achieving Level 3 certification, the organization must maintain compliance through rigorous ongoing monitoring, risk assessments, and continuous improvement efforts.
- The organization should regularly review and update its policies, procedures, and technical controls to ensure continued alignment with the Level 3 requirements and evolving cybersecurity best practices.
- Before the certification expires, the organization should engage with the government assessment team to undergo a recertification assessment, demonstrating its ongoing compliance with the Level 3 practices.

Regardless of the CMMC level pursued, achieving and maintaining certification requires a strong commitment to cybersecurity excellence, proactive risk management, and continuous improvement. Organizations should approach the certification process as an opportunity to strengthen their cybersecurity posture, protect sensitive information, and build trust with their customers, partners, and stakeholders in the defense industrial base.

It is important to note that the certification process may evolve as the CMMC 2.0 Model and its associated requirements are refined and updated. Organizations should stay informed about the latest developments, guidance, and best practices related to CMMC certification and work closely with the appropriate assessment entities and accreditation bodies to ensure a smooth and successful certification journey.

Tips for a successful CMMC 2.0 assessment

Preparing for and undergoing a CMMC 2.0 assessment can be a complex and demanding process. However, by following some essential tips and best practices, organizations can increase their chances of a successful assessment and achieve their desired level of certification. Let's explore these tips in detail.

1. Start early and allocate sufficient time:

- Begin preparing for the CMMC assessment well in advance of the target certification date.
- Allocate ample time to thoroughly assess your organization's current cybersecurity posture, identify gaps, and implement necessary improvements.
- Develop a detailed project plan with realistic timelines, considering the scope of work required and the resources available.
- Ensure that all stakeholders, including senior management, IT teams, and process owners, know the assessment timeline and their roles and responsibilities.

2. Conduct a comprehensive gap analysis:

- Perform a thorough gap analysis to assess your organization's alignment with the CMMC requirements for your target level.
- Use the CMMC 2.0 Model, assessment guides, and other relevant resources to evaluate your current policies, procedures, and technical controls against the required practices.
- Identify gaps, weaknesses, or areas for improvement and prioritize them based on their criticality and potential impact on your cybersecurity posture.
- Document the gap analysis findings and use them to develop a targeted remediation plan.

3. Develop and implement a remediation plan:

- Create a comprehensive remediation plan to address the identified gaps and weaknesses based on the gap analysis results.
- Break down the remediation tasks into manageable actions, assigning clear ownership, timelines, and resources to each task.
- Prioritize the remediation efforts based on the gaps' criticality and alignment with the CMMC requirements.
- Regularly monitor and track the progress of the remediation plan, adjusting course as needed to ensure timely completion.

4. Engage with the appropriate assessment entity:

- For Level 2 assessments, select and engage with a CMMC Third-Party Assessment Organization (C3PAO) authorized by the CMMC Accreditation Body (CMMC-AB).
- For Level 3 assessments, coordinate with the appropriate government assessment team, typically from the Defense Industrial Base

Cybersecurity Assessment Center (DIBCAC) or another authorized entity.

- Establish clear communication channels and maintain an open dialogue with the assessment entity throughout the assessment process.
- Seek guidance and clarification from the assessment entity on any questions or concerns related to the CMMC requirements or the assessment process.

5. Gather and organize evidence and documentation:

- Compile comprehensive proof and documentation to demonstrate your organization's compliance with the CMMC practices.
- Ensure the documentation is well-organized, up-to-date, and easily accessible to the assessment team.
- Use a centralized repository or document management system to store and manage the evidence and documentation.
- Review and update the documentation regularly to reflect any changes in your organization's policies, procedures, or technical controls.

6. Conduct internal assessments and mock audits:

- Perform internal assessments and mock audits to evaluate your organization's readiness for the CMMC assessment.
- Use the CMMC assessment guides and tools to simulate the actual assessment process and identify potential gaps or improvement areas.
- To gather diverse perspectives and insights, key personnel, in-

cluding IT staff, security teams, and process owners, should be involved in the internal assessments.

- Document the findings of the internal assessments and use them to refine your remediation efforts and strengthen your overall cybersecurity posture.

7. Provide comprehensive training and awareness:

- Educate and train all relevant personnel on the CMMC requirements, their roles and responsibilities, and the importance of cybersecurity best practices.
- Conduct targeted training sessions for individuals directly involved in the assessment process, such as IT staff, security teams, and key stakeholders.
- Ensure that all employees understand the significance of the CMMC assessment and their contributions to the organization's cybersecurity posture.
- Foster a continuous learning and improvement culture, encouraging employees to stay updated on the latest cybersecurity trends and best practices.

8. Collaborate and communicate effectively:

- Foster a collaborative and transparent relationship with the assessment entity and all relevant stakeholders throughout the assessment process.
- Maintain open and timely communication with the assessment team, providing them with the necessary information, access, and support to facilitate a smooth assessment.

- Update senior management, employees, and other stakeholders regularly on the progress of the assessment and any key milestones or challenges.
- Encourage open dialogue and feedback among team members to proactively identify and address any concerns or potential roadblocks.

9. Leverage automation and tools:

- Utilize automated tools and technologies to streamline and enhance the efficiency of the assessment process.
- Implement security information and event management (SIEM) solutions, vulnerability scanners, and compliance management platforms to monitor and assess your organization's cybersecurity posture continuously.
- Use automated testing and validation tools to assess the effectiveness of your security controls and identify potential weaknesses or gaps.
- Leverage project management and collaboration tools to track and manage the assessment process, facilitate stakeholder communication, and maintain a centralized repository of documentation and evidence.

10. Treat the assessment as an ongoing process:

- Approach the CMMC assessment as an ongoing process rather than a one-time event.
- Continuously monitor and assess your organization's cybersecurity posture, even after achieving certification, to identify and

address any emerging risks or gaps.

- Review and update your policies, procedures, and technical controls regularly to ensure ongoing alignment with the CMMC requirements and evolving cybersecurity best practices.
- Foster a culture of continuous improvement, encouraging employees to identify and report potential vulnerabilities or areas for enhancement proactively.

11. Be proactive and responsive during the assessment:

- Actively participate in the assessment process, providing the assessment team with the necessary information, access, and support.
- Be prepared to answer questions, provide explanations, and clarify any concerns the assessment team raises.
- Promptly address any findings or non-conformities identified during the assessment, demonstrating a commitment to remediation and continuous improvement.
- Maintain a positive and collaborative attitude throughout the assessment, viewing it as an opportunity for growth and learning.

12. Celebrate successes and learn from the experience:

- Recognize and celebrate the achievements and milestones reached during the CMMC assessment process.
- Acknowledge the efforts and contributions of the assessment team, employees, and stakeholders who played a vital role in the success of the assessment.
- Conduct a post-assessment review to identify lessons learned,

best practices, and areas for continuous improvement.
- Share the insights and experiences gained from the assessment with the broader organization to foster a culture of cybersecurity awareness and excellence.

By following these tips and best practices, organizations can enhance their chances of a successful CMMC 2.0 assessment and demonstrate their commitment to cybersecurity maturity. It is crucial to approach the assessment process with a proactive, collaborative, and improvement-oriented mindset, leveraging the expertise and guidance of the assessment entity and all relevant stakeholders.

Remember, the ultimate goal of the CMMC assessment is not just to achieve certification but to strengthen your organization's overall cybersecurity posture, protect sensitive information, and build trust with your customers, partners, and stakeholders in the defense industrial base. By investing time, resources, and effort in thorough preparation, effective collaboration, and continuous improvement, you can confidently navigate the assessment process and position your organization for long-term success in the evolving landscape of cybersecurity and defense contracting.

Maintaining compliance and preparing for recertification

Achieving CMMC certification is a significant milestone, but it is not the journey's end. Maintaining compliance and preparing for recertification are equally important to ensure the ongoing protection of sensitive information and demonstrate a strong commitment to cybersecurity maturity. Let's explore the key aspects of maintaining compliance and preparing for recertification in the context of CMMC 2.0.

1. Establish a continuous monitoring program:

- Develop and implement a robust continuous monitoring program to proactively assess and maintain your organization's cybersecurity posture.
- Review and update your policies, procedures, and technical controls regularly to ensure ongoing alignment with the CMMC requirements and evolving cybersecurity best practices.
- Conduct periodic risk assessments to identify and address any new or emerging threats, vulnerabilities, or gaps in your security controls.
- Monitor system logs, security events, and user activities to detect and respond promptly to potential security incidents or anomalies.

2. Conduct regular internal audits:

- Perform regular internal audits to assess your organization's ongoing compliance with the CMMC requirements.

- Use the CMMC assessment guides and tools to evaluate the effectiveness of your security controls, policies, and procedures.
- Identify any deviations from the CMMC practices or areas for improvement and develop corrective action plans to address them.
- Document the internal audits' findings and use them to inform continuous improvement efforts and prepare for future recertification assessments.

3. Maintain comprehensive documentation:

- Maintain detailed and up-to-date documentation of your organization's cybersecurity practices, policies, procedures, and technical controls.
- Ensure the documentation aligns with the CMMC requirements and provides clear evidence of ongoing compliance.
- Review and update the documentation regularly to reflect any changes in your organization's practices, systems, or personnel.
- A centralized repository or document management system stores and manages the documentation, making it easily accessible for internal reference and external assessments.

4. Provide ongoing training and awareness:

- Implement a comprehensive training and awareness program to ensure all employees, contractors, and stakeholders understand their roles and responsibilities in maintaining CMMC compliance.
- Conduct regular training sessions to reinforce cybersecurity best practices, update personnel on changes to the CMMC require-

ments or your organization's policies, and address emerging threats and vulnerabilities.

- Tailor the training content to different stakeholders' specific needs and roles, ensuring relevance and applicability.
- Foster a culture of continuous learning and improvement, encouraging employees to participate in training and share their knowledge and experiences actively.

5. Monitor and manage third-party risks:

- Regularly assess and monitor the cybersecurity practices and compliance of your third-party vendors, suppliers, and partners.
- Ensure that contracts and service-level agreements (SLAs) with third parties include provisions for compliance with the CMMC requirements and regular reporting on their security posture.
- Conduct periodic audits or assessments of third-party security controls and practices to verify their ongoing compliance and identify potential risks or gaps.
- Establish clear communication channels and incident response procedures with third parties to effectively collaborate and address security incidents or compliance issues.

6. Stay informed and adapt to changes:

- Stay informed about updates, clarifications, and guidance related to the CMMC requirements, assessment processes, and best practices.
- Regularly engage with the CMMC Accreditation Body (CMMC-AB), the Department of Defense (DoD), and other relevant authorities

to receive timely information and support.
- Participate in industry forums, webinars, and conferences to learn from the experiences and insights of other organizations and cybersecurity experts.
- Adapt your organization's practices, policies, and controls to align with evolving CMMC requirements, regulatory changes, or emerging industry standards.

7. Plan for recertification:

- Understand the recertification requirements and timelines for your organization's CMMC level.
- Typically, CMMC certifications are valid for three years, after which organizations need to undergo a recertification assessment to maintain their certification status.
- Develop a detailed plan for the recertification process, including the necessary preparations, resources, and timelines.
- Assign responsibilities and allocate adequate resources to ensure a smooth and successful recertification assessment.

8. Conduct pre-recertification assessments:

- Well in advance of the recertification deadline, conduct thorough pre-recertification assessments to evaluate your organization's readiness.
- Use the CMMC assessment guides and tools to assess your compliance with the latest CMMC requirements and identify any gaps or areas for improvement.
- Engage key personnel, including IT staff, security teams, and

process owners, in the pre-recertification assessments to gather diverse perspectives and insights.

- Document the findings of the pre-recertification assessments and use them to develop targeted remediation plans and strengthen your overall cybersecurity posture.

9. Address identified gaps and improvements:

- Based on the pre-recertification assessment results, prioritize and address any identified gaps, weaknesses, or areas for improvement.
- Develop and implement corrective action plans, assigning clear ownership, timelines, and resources to each remediation task.
- Regularly monitor and track the progress of the remediation efforts, ensuring that all necessary improvements are completed well before the recertification assessment.
- Validate the effectiveness of the remediation actions through follow-up assessments and testing.

10. Engage with the assessment entity:

- For Level 2 recertification, engage with an authorized CMMC Third-Party Assessment Organization (C3PAO) to schedule and plan the recertification assessment.
- For Level 3 recertification, coordinate with the appropriate government assessment team, typically from the Defense Industrial Base Cybersecurity Assessment Center (DIBCAC) or another authorized entity.
- Establish clear communication channels and maintain an open di-

alogue with the assessment entity throughout the recertification process.

- Provide the assessment entity with information, access, and support to facilitate a smooth and efficient recertification assessment.

11. Demonstrate continuous improvement:

- During the recertification assessment, emphasize your organization's continuous improvement efforts since the initial certification.
- Highlight enhancements to your cybersecurity practices, policies, and controls based on lessons learned, industry best practices, and evolving CMMC requirements.
- Provide evidence of regular internal audits, risk assessments, and remediation activities to demonstrate your organization's ongoing commitment to cybersecurity maturity.
- Showcase the impact of your continuous improvement efforts on strengthening your overall cybersecurity posture and protecting sensitive information.

12. Celebrate and communicate recertification success:

- Celebrate the achievement with your employees, stakeholders, and partners upon completing the assessment of the recertifica.
- Recognize the efforts and contributions of the individuals and teams who played a vital role in maintaining compliance and achieving recertification.
- Communicate the successful recertification to relevant stake-

holders, including customers, suppliers, and regulatory bodies, to reinforce your organization's commitment to cybersecurity excellence.
- Leverage the recertification success to build trust, credibility, and competitive advantage in the marketplace.

Maintaining compliance and preparing for recertification are ongoing processes that require sustained effort, resources, and commitment from the entire organization. By establishing a robust continuous monitoring program, conducting regular internal audits, providing ongoing training and awareness, and staying informed about evolving CMMC requirements and best practices, organizations can maintain a strong cybersecurity posture and position themselves for successful recertification.

Recertification is an opportunity to showcase continuous improvement and maturity in cybersecurity practices. By proactively identifying and addressing gaps, engaging with assessment entities, and demonstrating a commitment to ongoing enhancement, organizations can confidently navigate the recertification process and reaffirm their dedication to protecting sensitive information.

Ultimately, maintaining compliance and achieving recertification are vital to safeguarding the integrity of the defense industrial base and building long-term trust with customers, partners, and stakeholders. By embracing a mindset of continuous improvement and investing in the necessary resources and expertise, organizations can successfully maintain their CMMC certification and contribute to the overall security and resilience of the national defense ecosystem.

Best Practices: Develop a culture of continuous improvement and regular compliance review to simplify the recertification process.

Developing a culture of continuous improvement and conducting regular compliance reviews are essential best practices for simplifying the CMMC recertification process and maintaining a robust cybersecurity posture. By embedding these practices into the organization's DNA, companies can proactively identify and address gaps, stay aligned with evolving requirements, and foster a mindset of ongoing enhancement. Let's explore these best practices in detail.

1. Establish a continuous improvement framework:

- Develop a formal continuous improvement framework that outlines the processes, roles, and responsibilities for ongoing cybersecurity enhancement.
- Define clear objectives and metrics to measure cybersecurity practices' effectiveness and identify areas for improvement.
- To drive continuous improvement efforts, encourage a culture of open communication, collaboration, and knowledge sharing across the organization.
- Regularly review and update the continuous improvement framework to ensure alignment with changing business needs, technologies, and cybersecurity best practices.

2. Conduct regular compliance reviews:

- Establish a schedule for regular compliance reviews to assess the organization's adherence to CMMC requirements and identify potential gaps or areas for improvement.
- Develop standardized assessment templates and checklists based on the CMMC framework to ensure consistent and comprehensive reviews.
- Assign dedicated personnel or teams to conduct the compliance reviews and provide them with the necessary resources, training, and authority.
- Document the findings of each compliance review, including identified strengths, weaknesses, and recommendations for improvement.

3. Prioritize and address identified gaps:

- Analyze the results of the compliance reviews to prioritize the identified gaps based on their potential impact on cybersecurity and CMMC compliance.
- Develop action plans to address the prioritized gaps, assigning clear ownership, timelines, and resources to each remediation task.
- Regularly monitor and track the progress of remediation efforts, ensuring that identified issues are promptly resolved and improvements are effectively implemented.
- Validate the effectiveness of remediation actions through follow-up assessments and testing.

4. Foster a culture of continuous learning:

- Promote a culture of continuous learning and professional development within the organization to keep personnel updated on the latest cybersecurity trends, threats, and best practices.
- Provide regular training and awareness programs to educate employees about CMMC requirements, their roles in maintaining compliance, and the importance of continuous improvement.
- Encourage employees to pursue relevant certifications, attend industry conferences, and participate in cybersecurity communities of practice to expand their knowledge and skills.
- Recognize and reward individuals and teams who demonstrate exceptional commitment to continuous learning and drive impactful improvements in cybersecurity practices.

5. Leverage automation and tools:

- Implement automated tools and technologies to streamline compliance monitoring, assessment, and reporting processes.
- Utilize security information and event management (SIEM) solutions, vulnerability scanners, and compliance management platforms to monitor the organization's cybersecurity posture continuously.
- Leverage data analytics and visualization tools to identify trends, patterns, and insights from compliance data, enabling data-driven decision-making and improvement initiatives.
- Automate routine compliance tasks, such as system configuration checks, access reviews, and policy attestations, to reduce manual effort and ensure consistency.

6. Collaborate with internal and external stakeholders:

- Foster collaboration and communication among internal stakeholders, including IT, security, compliance, and business units, to ensure a shared understanding of CMMC requirements and continuous improvement goals.
- Engage with external stakeholders, such as customers, partners, and industry associations, to exchange best practices, lessons learned, and insights on CMMC compliance and cybersecurity trends.
- Participate in CMMC-focused forums, working groups, and communities to stay informed about evolving requirements, interpretations, and guidance.
- Collaborate with third-party assessors and consultants, as well as managed security service providers (MSSPs), to leverage their expertise and support in continuous improvement efforts.

7. Integrate compliance into business processes:

- Embed CMMC compliance and cybersecurity considerations into the organization's core business processes, such as product development, vendor management, and project management.
- Develop and implement security-by-design principles, ensuring cybersecurity is integrated into the early stages of product and system development lifecycles.
- Incorporate compliance checks and security reviews into project milestones and gate reviews to proactively identify and address potential issues.
- Establish governance structures and oversight mechanisms to ensure compliance and cybersecurity are regularly discussed and prioritized at the leadership level.

8. Conduct regular risk assessments:

- Perform regular risk assessments to identify and evaluate the organization's exposure to cybersecurity risks, including those related to CMMC compliance.
- Use established risk assessment methodologies and frameworks, such as NIST SP 800-30 or ISO 27005, to ensure a structured and comprehensive approach.
- Involve cross-functional teams in the risk assessment process to gather diverse perspectives and ensure a holistic view of the organization's risk landscape.
- Use the results of the risk assessments to prioritize continuous improvement efforts and allocate resources effectively.

9. Establish metrics and key performance indicators (KPIs):

- Define a set of metrics and KPIs to measure the effectiveness of the organization's cybersecurity practices and track progress towards continuous improvement goals.
- To ensure relevance and comparability, align the metrics and KPIs with CMMC requirements, business objectives, and industry benchmarks.
- Collect, analyze, and report on the defined metrics and KPIs regularly to provide visibility into the organization's cybersecurity performance and identify areas for improvement.
- Use the insights gained from the metrics and KPIs to inform decision-making, prioritize initiatives, and communicate the value of continuous improvement efforts to stakeholders.

10. Celebrate successes and share lessons learned:

- Recognize and celebrate the achievements and milestones in the organization's continuous improvement journey, highlighting the impact on CMMC compliance and overall cybersecurity posture.
- Acknowledge the contributions of individuals and teams who have played a key role in driving continuous improvement initiatives and achieving significant results.
- Share success stories, best practices, and lessons learned across the organization to foster a culture of knowledge sharing and inspire further improvement efforts.
- Communicate the benefits and value of continuous improvement to external stakeholders, such as customers, partners, and regulatory bodies, to build trust and demonstrate the organization's commitment to cybersecurity excellence.

11. Continuously monitor and adapt:

- Establish processes for continuous monitoring and adaptation of the organization's cybersecurity practices, policies, and controls.
- Review and update documentation, such as policies, procedures, and system security plans, regularly to ensure alignment with evolving CMMC requirements and industry best practices.
- Monitor the external environment for changes in the threat landscape, regulatory requirements, and emerging technologies, and adapt the organization's cybersecurity strategies and practices accordingly.
- Foster a culture of agility and responsiveness, enabling the organization to quickly identify and address new risks, opportunities,

and challenges related to CMMC compliance and cybersecurity.

12. Seek external validation and feedback:

- Engage with external assessors, auditors, or consultants to provide independent validation of the organization's cybersecurity practices and CMMC compliance posture.
- Participate in third-party assessments, such as penetration testing or vulnerability assessments, to identify potential weaknesses and areas for improvement.
- Seek feedback and benchmarking data from industry peers, customers, and partners to gain insights into best practices and comparative performance.
- Use the external validation and feedback to validate the effectiveness of continuous improvement efforts, identify blind spots, and drive further enhancements.

By developing a culture of continuous improvement and conducting regular compliance reviews, organizations can proactively identify and address gaps, ensure ongoing alignment with CMMC requirements, and simplify the recertification process. These best practices foster a mindset of ongoing enhancement, enabling organizations to stay ahead of evolving cybersecurity challenges and maintain a robust security posture.

Implementing these best practices requires leadership commitment, employee engagement, and allocating sufficient resources and expertise. Organizations should prioritize continuous improvement as a strategic imperative, embedding it into their core values, processes, and performance metrics.

By embracing a culture of continuous improvement and regular compliance review, organizations can streamline the CMMC recertification process and elevate their overall cybersecurity maturity, build trust with stakeholders, and establish a competitive advantage in the marketplace. Ultimately, these practices contribute to the collective security and resilience of the defense industrial base, safeguarding sensitive information and supporting national security objectives.

Chapter 11: Advanced Topics and Future Trends

Integrating CMMC 2.0 with other compliance frameworks (e.g., NIST, ISO)

As organizations navigate the complex landscape of cybersecurity compliance, it is increasingly important to understand how CMMC 2.0 aligns and integrates with other widely recognized compliance frameworks. By harmonizing CMMC 2.0 with frameworks such as NIST and ISO, organizations can streamline their compliance efforts, reduce duplication, and enhance their overall cybersecurity posture. Let's explore the integration of CMMC 2.0 with NIST and ISO frameworks in detail.

1. CMMC 2.0 and NIST Frameworks:

a. NIST Cybersecurity Framework (CSF):

- The NIST CSF provides a comprehensive framework for managing cybersecurity risks and aligning cybersecurity practices with business objectives.

- CMMC 2.0 aligns with the core functions of the NIST CSF, including Identifying, Protecting, Detecting, Responding, and Recovering.
- Organizations can map CMMC 2.0 practices to the corresponding NIST CSF subcategories to demonstrate alignment and identify areas for improvement.
- Integrating CMMC 2.0 with the NIST CSF enables organizations to take a holistic approach to cybersecurity risk management and compliance.

b. NIST Special Publication 800-171:

- NIST SP 800-171 provides a set of security controls for protecting Controlled Unclassified Information (CUI) in nonfederal systems and organizations.
- CMMC 2.0 Level 2 is closely aligned with NIST SP 800-171, requiring organizations to implement the 110 security controls outlined in the publication.
- Organizations already implementing NIST SP 800-171 controls have a solid foundation for achieving CMMC 2.0 Level 2 compliance.
- Mapping CMMC 2.0 practices to NIST SP 800-171 controls helps organizations identify gaps, prioritize efforts, and leverage existing compliance initiatives.

c. NIST Special Publication 800-53:

- NIST SP 800-53 provides a comprehensive set of security and privacy controls for federal information systems and organizations.
- While CMMC 2.0 does not directly map to NIST SP 800-53, the frameworks share many common security practices and principles.
- Organizations can use NIST SP 800-53 as a reference to enhance their cybersecurity practices beyond the specific requirements of CMMC 2.0.
- Aligning CMMC 2.0 with NIST SP 800-53 controls can help organizations demonstrate a higher level of cybersecurity maturity and meet additional regulatory requirements.

2. CMMC 2.0 and ISO Frameworks:

a. ISO/IEC 27001:

- ISO/IEC 27001 is an international information security management system (ISMS) standard.
- While CMMC 2.0 and ISO/IEC 27001 have different focuses and requirements, they share common principles of risk management, continuous improvement, and the implementation of security controls.
- Organizations can map CMMC 2.0 practices to the corresponding ISO/IEC 27001 controls to identify alignment and gaps.
- Achieving ISO/IEC 27001 certification can complement CMMC 2.0 compliance efforts and demonstrate a commitment to internationally recognized cybersecurity best practices.

b. ISO/IEC 27002:

- ISO/IEC 27002 provides a code of practice for information security controls, supporting the implementation of ISO/IEC 27001.
- Many security practices outlined in CMMC 2.0 align with the controls and guidelines provided in ISO/IEC 27002.
- Organizations can use ISO/IEC 27002 as a reference to inform the implementation of CMMC 2.0 practices and enhance their overall cybersecurity posture.
- Mapping CMMC 2.0 practices to ISO/IEC 27002 controls can help organizations identify additional security measures and best practices to consider.

c. ISO/IEC 27032:

- ISO/IEC 27032 provides guidelines for improving cybersecurity and managing cybersecurity risks.
- While not directly aligned with CMMC 2.0, ISO/IEC 27032 offers valuable cybersecurity principles, techniques, and control guidance.
- Organizations can leverage ISO/IEC 27032 to inform their cybersecurity strategies, incident management processes, and risk assessment methodologies.
- Aligning CMMC 2.0 efforts with ISO/IEC 27032 guidelines can help organizations enhance cybersecurity resilience and preparedness.

3. Benefits of Integrating CMMC 2.0 with Other Frameworks:

a. Holistic Approach to Cybersecurity:

- Integrating CMMC 2.0 with other frameworks allows organizations to take a holistic and comprehensive approach to cybersecurity.
- By aligning CMMC 2.0 with NIST and ISO frameworks, organizations can address a wider range of cybersecurity risks and best practices.
- A holistic approach helps organizations build a more robust and resilient cybersecurity posture beyond the specific requirements of CMMC 2.0.

b. Reduced Duplication and Increased Efficiency:

- Many organizations already have existing compliance initiatives based on NIST or ISO frameworks.
- Organizations can identify overlaps by mapping CMMC 2.0 practices to these frameworks and streamline their compliance efforts.
- Integrating CMMC 2.0 with other frameworks reduces duplication of effort, saves resources, and increases the efficiency of compliance activities.

c. Enhanced Risk Management:

- NIST and ISO frameworks provide additional guidance and best practices for managing cybersecurity risks.

- By integrating CMMC 2.0 with these frameworks, organizations can enhance their risk management processes and make informed decisions based on a broader understanding of cybersecurity risks.
- Aligning CMMC 2.0 with risk management frameworks helps organizations prioritize their efforts, allocate resources effectively, and mitigate risks more comprehensively.

d. Improved Communication and Collaboration:

- Integrating CMMC 2.0 with widely recognized frameworks like NIST and ISO facilitates better stakeholder communication and collaboration.
- Common frameworks provide a shared language and understanding of cybersecurity practices, enabling effective dialogue between technical teams, business leaders, and external partners.
- Harmonizing CMMC 2.0 with other frameworks promotes consistency and interoperability, making sharing information, best practices, and lessons learned across organizations and industries easier.

4. Challenges and Considerations:

a. Complexity and Resource Requirements:

- Integrating CMMC 2.0 with multiple frameworks can introduce additional complexity and resource requirements.

- Organizations must invest time and effort in understanding the mappings, identifying gaps, and aligning their practices across different frameworks.
- Adequate resources, including skilled personnel, tools, and budget, are necessary to manage the integration and effectively maintain compliance with multiple frameworks.

b. Prioritization and Scope:

- Organizations must carefully prioritize their compliance efforts based on their specific business needs, risk profile, and regulatory requirements.
- Attempting to integrate CMMC 2.0 with too many frameworks simultaneously may strain resources and lead to a lack of focus.
- Organizations should assess the relevance and applicability of each framework to their specific context and prioritize the most critical integrations.

c. Ongoing Maintenance and Updates:

- Compliance frameworks, including CMMC 2.0, NIST, and ISO, are subject to periodic updates and revisions.
- Organizations must stay informed about the latest changes and updates to each framework and assess the impact on their integrated compliance efforts.
- Maintaining alignment and compliance with multiple frameworks requires ongoing monitoring, assessment, and adjustment of practices and controls.

d. Seeking Expert Guidance:

- Integrating CMMC 2.0 with other frameworks can be a complex undertaking, requiring specialized knowledge and expertise.
- Organizations may benefit from seeking guidance from experienced cybersecurity professionals, consultants, or managed security service providers (MSSPs) who have expertise in multiple frameworks.
- Expert guidance can help organizations navigate the complexities of integration, identify the most effective approaches, and ensure a smooth and successful implementation.

Integrating CMMC 2.0 with other compliance frameworks, such as NIST and ISO, significantly benefits organizations seeking to enhance their cybersecurity posture and streamline their compliance efforts. By aligning CMMC 2.0 with widely recognized frameworks, organizations can take a holistic approach to cybersecurity, reduce duplication, improve risk management, and facilitate better communication and collaboration.

However, organizations must also be aware of the challenges and considerations associated with integrating multiple frameworks. Careful planning, prioritization, and resource allocation are essential to manage the complexity and ensure the effectiveness of the integration efforts.

Ultimately, the decision to integrate CMMC 2.0 with other frameworks should be based on a thorough understanding of the organization's specific needs, risk profile, and regulatory landscape. By strategically aligning CMMC 2.0 with relevant frameworks and seeking expert guidance when needed, organizations can strengthen their cybersecurity posture, demonstrate compliance with multiple standards, and build trust with their customers, partners, and stakeholders in the defense industrial base.

Future developments in CMMC

As the cybersecurity landscape continues to evolve and new threats emerge, the Cybersecurity Maturity Model Certification (CMMC) framework is expected to undergo future developments to keep pace with the changing dynamics. These developments will focus on enhancing the framework's effectiveness, addressing emerging challenges, and ensuring the continued protection of sensitive information within the defense industrial base. Let's explore some of the anticipated future developments in CMMC.

1. Continuous Refinement and Updating of CMMC Requirements:

- The CMMC Accreditation Body (CMMC-AB) and the Department of Defense (DoD) will continuously review and update the CMMC requirements based on stakeholder feedback, lessons learned from assessments, and evolving cybersecurity best practices.
- Future versions of CMMC may introduce new or modified practices, controls, and maturity levels to address emerging threats and align with the latest industry standards.
- The framework will likely incorporate more granular and prescriptive requirements for specific technologies, such as cloud computing, the Internet of Things (IoT), and artificial intelligence (AI), to ensure comprehensive coverage of cybersecurity risks.

2. Expanded Scope and Applicability:

- While CMMC initially focuses on the defense industrial base, future developments may expand its scope and applicability to other critical sectors and industries.
- The success and effectiveness of CMMC in improving cybersecurity practices within the DoD supply chain may lead to its adoption by other government agencies, such as the Department of Homeland Security (DHS) or the General Services Administration (GSA).
- The framework may also be adapted and applied to international defense contracts and collaborations, promoting a consistent approach to cybersecurity across global supply chains.

3. Integration with Other Frameworks and Standards:

- Future developments in CMMC will likely emphasize greater alignment and integration with other widely recognized cybersecurity frameworks and standards, such as NIST, ISO, and CIS Controls.
- Efforts will be made to map CMMC practices and controls to corresponding requirements in these frameworks, facilitating a more streamlined and harmonized approach to compliance.
- The integration will enable organizations to leverage their existing compliance efforts and reduce duplication while benefiting from multiple frameworks' collective wisdom and best practices.

4. Automation and Continuous Monitoring:

- As the volume and complexity of cybersecurity data continue to grow, future developments in CMMC will focus on leveraging automation and continuous monitoring technologies.

- Automated tools and platforms will be developed to assess, monitor, and report on CMMC compliance in real time, reducing manual effort and increasing the efficiency of assessment processes.
- Continuous monitoring solutions will enable organizations to proactively identify and respond to cybersecurity risks, ensuring ongoing compliance with CMMC requirements.
- Integrating machine learning and AI techniques will enhance the accuracy and effectiveness of threat detection, risk assessment, and incident response capabilities within the CMMC framework.

5. Emphasis on Supply Chain Risk Management:

- Future developments in CMMC will emphasize supply chain risk management, recognizing the interdependencies and potential vulnerabilities introduced by third-party vendors and partners.
- The framework will likely incorporate more robust requirements for vendor risk assessment, due diligence, and monitoring of continuous supply chain security practices.
- Organizations will be expected to establish comprehensive vendor management programs, including contractual obligations, security assessments, and incident response protocols, to ensure the security and resilience of their supply chains.

6. Increased Focus on Incident Response and Resilience:

- As cyber threats continue to evolve and become more sophisticated, future developments in CMMC will prioritize incident response and resilience capabilities.

- The framework will provide more detailed guidance on establishing effective incident response plans, conducting regular exercises and simulations, and maintaining business continuity during cyber incidents.
- Organizations will be required to demonstrate their ability to detect, respond to, and recover from cybersecurity incidents promptly and effectively, minimizing the impact on operations and sensitive information.

7. Workforce Development and Cybersecurity Education:

- Future developments in CMMC will emphasize the importance of workforce development and cybersecurity education to address the growing skills gap in the cybersecurity industry.
- The framework will likely require organizations to implement robust training and awareness programs, ensuring that personnel at all levels possess the necessary knowledge and skills to support CMMC compliance.
- Collaboration between the CMMC-AB, educational institutions, and industry partners will be encouraged to develop standardized curricula, certifications, and career pathways aligned with CMMC requirements.

8. International Collaboration and Harmonization:

- As the global nature of cybersecurity threats becomes more apparent, future developments in CMMC will focus on fostering international collaboration and harmonization.
- Efforts will be made to align CMMC with international cybersecu-

rity frameworks and standards, promoting a consistent approach to cybersecurity across borders.
- The CMMC-AB may establish partnerships and agreements with foreign governments, regulatory bodies, and industry associations to facilitate the adoption and recognition of CMMC in international markets.
- International collaboration will enable the sharing of threat intelligence, best practices, and lessons learned, strengthening the collective defense against cyber threats.

9. Integration with Emerging Technologies:

- Future developments in CMMC will need to keep pace with the rapid advancement of emerging technologies, such as blockchain, quantum computing, and 5G networks.
- The framework will likely incorporate specific requirements and guidance for securing these technologies and mitigating the unique risks they introduce.
- Organizations will be expected to assess the impact of emerging technologies on their cybersecurity posture and adapt their CMMC compliance efforts accordingly.
- The CMMC-AB will collaborate with technology experts, industry leaders, and academic institutions to develop best practices and standards for securing emerging technologies within the CMMC framework.

10. Continuous Improvement and Maturity Progression:

- Future developments in CMMC will emphasize the importance

of continuous improvement and progression towards higher cybersecurity maturity levels.

- The framework will provide more guidance and resources to help organizations assess their current maturity level, identify gaps, and develop roadmaps for advancing to higher levels of CMMC certification.
- The CMMC-AB will encourage sharing success stories, best practices, and lessons learned among certified organizations to foster a culture of continuous improvement and knowledge sharing.
- Organizations will be expected to demonstrate their commitment to continuously improving their cybersecurity practices even after achieving the desired level of CMMC certification.

As the cybersecurity landscape continues to evolve, future developments in CMMC will focus on adapting the framework to address emerging threats, align with industry best practices, and support the ongoing protection of sensitive information within the defense industrial base. These developments will require close collaboration among the CMMC-AB, DoD, industry stakeholders, and cybersecurity experts to ensure the framework remains relevant, effective, and responsive to the changing dynamics of cybersecurity.

Organizations should stay informed about the latest developments in CMMC and proactively engage with the CMMC-AB and other relevant stakeholders to provide input, feedback, and insights. By actively participating in the ongoing evolution of CMMC, organizations can help shape the framework's future direction and ensure it remains a valuable tool for enhancing cybersecurity practices and safeguarding national security interests.

Ultimately, CMMC's future lies in its ability to adapt, innovate, and drive continuous improvement in cybersecurity across the defense industrial base. By embracing these future developments and committing to the ongoing advancement of their cybersecurity posture, organizations can position themselves as leaders, build trust with their customers and partners, and contribute to the collective defense against ever-evolving cyber threats.

The role of CMMC in enhancing national security

The Cybersecurity Maturity Model Certification (CMMC) framework plays a crucial role in enhancing national security by strengthening the cybersecurity posture of the defense industrial base and protecting sensitive information from adversaries. As the threat landscape continues to evolve and nation-state actors increasingly target the defense supply chain, CMMC serves as a critical line of defense in safeguarding national security interests. Let's explore the multifaceted role of CMMC in enhancing national security.

1. Protecting Controlled Unclassified Information (CUI):

- CMMC helps protect Controlled Unclassified Information (CUI) by ensuring that defense contractors and subcontractors implement adequate cybersecurity practices and controls.
- While not classified, CUI still requires safeguarding and dissemination controls to prevent unauthorized access, modification, or disclosure.
- By mandating compliance with CMMC requirements, the framework reduces the risk of CUI falling into the hands of adversaries

who could exploit it for malicious purposes, such as intellectual property theft, espionage, or sabotage.

- Protecting CUI is essential for maintaining the confidentiality, integrity, and availability of sensitive information related to national defense, military operations, and critical technologies.

2. Securing the Defense Supply Chain:

- CMMC plays a vital role in securing the defense supply chain by establishing a consistent and rigorous approach to cybersecurity across all levels of contractors and subcontractors.
- The defense supply chain is a complex ecosystem involving numerous entities, including prime contractors, suppliers, and service providers, each posing potential cybersecurity risks.
- CMMC helps mitigate supply chain risks by requiring all participants to implement appropriate cybersecurity practices based on the sensitivity of the information they handle and the scope of their involvement in defense contracts.
- By strengthening the cybersecurity posture of the entire supply chain, CMMC reduces the likelihood of successful cyberattacks, minimizes the impact of breaches, and ensures the integrity and reliability of defense systems and technologies.

3. Countering Nation-State Threats:

- CMMC is critical in countering nation-state threats targeting the defense industrial base.
- Nation-state adversaries, such as China, Russia, and Iran, actively seek to exploit vulnerabilities in the defense supply chain to gain

unauthorized access to sensitive information, steal intellectual property, and undermine U.S. military advantages.

· By requiring defense contractors to implement robust cyber-security practices and controls, CMMC helps thwart nation-state actors' attempts to infiltrate defense networks, exfiltrate sensitive data, or introduce malicious code into defense systems.

· CMMC's emphasis on continuous monitoring, incident response, and threat intelligence sharing enables defense contractors to detect and respond more effectively to nation-state threats, reducing the risk of successful cyberattacks.

4. Protecting Critical Technologies and Innovation:

· CMMC protects critical technologies and innovation within the defense industrial base.

· The U.S. defense sector relies on advanced technologies, such as artificial intelligence, autonomous systems, and quantum computing, to maintain military superiority and national security.

· CMMC helps safeguard these critical technologies by requiring defense contractors to implement stringent cybersecurity measures, including access controls, encryption, and secure development practices.

· By protecting intellectual property and preventing the unauthorized disclosure of sensitive technical information, CMMC ensures that the U.S. maintains its technological edge and prevents adversaries from gaining access to cutting-edge defense innovations.

5. Enhancing Collaboration and Information Sharing:

- CMMC promotes collaboration and information sharing among defense contractors, government agencies, and cybersecurity stakeholders to enhance collective defense against cyber threats.
- The framework establishes a common language and expectations for cybersecurity practices, facilitating more effective communication and coordination among defense industrial base participants.
- CMMC encourages sharing threat intelligence, best practices, and lessons learned, enabling defense contractors to stay informed about the latest cybersecurity threats and mitigation strategies.
- Enhanced collaboration and information sharing fostered by CMMC contribute to a more resilient and responsive defense industrial base better equipped to detect, prevent, and respond to cyber incidents that could impact national security.

6. Boosting Confidence and Trust in Defense Capabilities:

- CMMC helps boost confidence and trust in U.S. defense capabilities by demonstrating a strong commitment to cybersecurity and protecting sensitive information.
- By requiring defense contractors to meet rigorous cybersecurity standards, CMMC assures stakeholders, including Congress, allies, and the public, that the defense industrial base is taking proactive measures to safeguard national security interests.
- CMMC certification serves as a mark of trust, signaling to customers and partners that a defense contractor has implemented the necessary cybersecurity practices to protect sensitive information and maintain the integrity of defense systems.
- Enhanced confidence and trust in defense capabilities strengthen the U.S. military's ability to deter adversaries, maintain alliances,

and project power to support national security objectives.

7. Supporting International Cooperation and Interoperability:

- CMMC supports international cooperation and interoperability in cybersecurity by providing a framework for consistent and verifiable cybersecurity practices across global defense supply chains.
- Many U.S. defense programs involve collaboration with international partners, requiring the secure sharing of sensitive information and technologies.
- CMMC helps ensure that international defense contractors and subcontractors adhere to the same high cybersecurity standards, reducing the risk of compromises and enabling more seamless and secure collaboration.
- By aligning with international cybersecurity frameworks and standards, CMMC facilitates interoperability and trust among allies and partners, strengthening collective defense against global cyber threats.

8. Enabling Rapid Response and Resilience:

- CMMC enhances national security by enabling rapid response and resilience in the face of cyber incidents or attacks.
- The framework requires defense contractors to establish incident response plans, conduct regular exercises and simulations, and maintain business continuity capabilities.
- By ensuring that defense contractors are prepared to detect, respond to, and recover from cybersecurity incidents promptly

and effectively, CMMC minimizes the potential impact on defense operations and national security.

- CMMC's emphasis on continuous monitoring and real-time threat detection enables defense contractors to identify and mitigate cyber risks before they escalate into full-scale incidents, enhancing the overall resilience of the defense industrial base.

9. Driving Cybersecurity Innovation and Workforce Development:

- CMMC contributes to national security by driving cybersecurity innovation and workforce development within the defense industrial base.
- The framework's rigorous requirements and certification process incentivize defense contractors to invest in advanced cybersecurity technologies, tools, and practices to meet the evolving threat landscape.
- CMMC encourages the development of a skilled cybersecurity workforce by requiring defense contractors to implement comprehensive training and awareness programs aligned with the framework's practices.
- By fostering a cybersecurity excellence and continuous improvement culture, CMMC helps attract and retain top cybersecurity talent within the defense sector, strengthening the nation's ability to defend against cyber threats.

10. Enabling Effective Oversight and Accountability:

- CMMC enhances national security by enabling effective oversight and accountability of defense contractors' cybersecurity practices.

- The framework establishes clear expectations and requirements for cybersecurity, providing a standardized approach for assessing and certifying the maturity of defense contractors' practices.
- CMMC assessments and certifications conducted by accredited third-party assessment organizations (C3PAOs) validate defense contractors' compliance with the framework's requirements.
- CMMC's oversight and accountability help ensure that defense contractors are held to the highest cybersecurity standards, reducing the risk of non-compliance and potential harm to national security interests.

In conclusion, CMMC plays a vital role in enhancing national security by strengthening the cybersecurity posture of the defense industrial base, protecting sensitive information, and countering nation-state threats. By establishing a consistent and rigorous approach to cybersecurity across all defense contractors and subcontractors levels, CMMC helps secure the defense supply chain, safeguard critical technologies, and enable effective collaboration and information sharing.

Moreover, CMMC contributes to national security by boosting confidence and trust in defense capabilities, supporting international cooperation and interoperability, enabling rapid response and resilience, driving cybersecurity innovation and workforce development, and ensuring effective oversight and accountability.

As the cybersecurity landscape continues to evolve and new threats emerge, the role of CMMC in enhancing national security will become increasingly critical. Defense contractors must embrace the framework's requirements and actively participate in its ongoing development and implementation to ensure the continued protection of sensitive information and the resilience of the defense industrial base.

Ultimately, the success of CMMC in enhancing national security depends on the collective efforts of the Department of Defense, the CMMC Accreditation Body, defense contractors, and cybersecurity stakeholders. By working together to improve and adapt the framework continuously, these entities can create a more secure and resilient defense ecosystem, better equipped to defend against cyber threats and safeguard the nation's most sensitive information and assets.

Best Practices: Stay informed on cybersecurity trends and CMMC updates to adjust your security strategy proactively.

In the rapidly evolving cybersecurity landscape and the ongoing development of the Cybersecurity Maturity Model Certification (CMMC) framework, it is crucial for organizations to stay informed about the latest trends, threats, and updates. By proactively monitoring the cybersecurity landscape and adapting their security strategies accordingly, organizations can maintain a robust security posture, ensure continued compliance with CMMC requirements, and effectively protect sensitive information. Let's explore the best practices for staying informed and proactively adjusting your security strategy.

1. Engage with the CMMC Ecosystem:

- Actively engage with the CMMC Accreditation Body (CMMC-AB), the Department of Defense (DoD), and other relevant stakeholders in the CMMC ecosystem.
- Visit the official CMMC-AB website regularly and subscribe to their newsletter or alerts to stay informed about the latest updates, guidance, and resources related to CMMC.
- Participate in CMMC-related webinars, workshops, and events organized by the CMMC-AB or other industry associations to gain insights into the framework's development and best practices for implementation.
- Join CMMC-focused online communities, forums, or social media groups to engage with peers, share experiences, and learn from the collective knowledge of the CMMC community.

2. Monitor Cybersecurity News and Publications:

- Stay updated on the latest cybersecurity news, trends, and emerging threats by regularly monitoring reputable industry publications, blogs, and news outlets.
- Subscribe to cybersecurity newsletters from the Cybersecurity and Infrastructure Security Agency (CISA), the National Institute of Standards and Technology (NIST), or leading cybersecurity vendors and research firms.
- Follow cybersecurity thought leaders, experts, and influencers on social media platforms to gain insights into the latest developments, best practices, and opinions in the field.
- Attend cybersecurity conferences, webinars, and seminars to learn about the latest trends, technologies, and strategies from industry experts and practitioners.

3. Leverage Threat Intelligence:

- Incorporate threat intelligence into your security strategy to stay informed about the latest cyber threats, attack vectors, and vulnerabilities relevant to your organization and industry.
- Subscribe to threat intelligence feeds and services from reputable providers, such as government agencies, cybersecurity vendors, or information sharing and analysis centers (ISACs).
- Review and analyze threat intelligence reports regularly to understand adversaries' tactics, techniques, and procedures (TTPs) and assess their potential impact on your organization.
- Use threat intelligence to prioritize security investments, refine your defense mechanisms, and proactively address vulnerabilities before they can be exploited.

4. Collaborate with Industry Peers:

- Engage in collaborative efforts with industry peers, including other defense contractors, suppliers, and partners, to share information, best practices, and lessons learned related to CMMC and cybersecurity.
- Participate in industry-specific forums, working groups, or consortia focused on cybersecurity and CMMC implementation.
- Establish regular communication channels with your supply chain partners to exchange insights, discuss common challenges, and coordinate efforts to enhance collective cybersecurity resilience.
- Collaborate with academic institutions, research organizations, or cybersecurity centers of excellence to gain access to cutting-edge research, tools, and expertise.

5. Conduct Regular Risk Assessments:

- Perform regular risk assessments to identify and prioritize your organization's cybersecurity risks, considering the evolving threat landscape and changes in your business environment.
- Use industry-standard risk assessment methodologies, such as NIST SP 800-30 or ISO 27005, to ensure a comprehensive and structured risk identification and evaluation approach.
- Assess the potential impact of emerging threats, vulnerabilities, and regulatory changes on your organization's cybersecurity posture and CMMC compliance.
- Use the risk assessment results to inform decision-making, prioritize security investments, and adapt your security strategy to mitigate the most critical risks.

6. Monitor Regulatory and Compliance Landscape:

- Stay informed about updates and changes to relevant cybersecurity regulations, standards, and frameworks, including CMMC, NIST, ISO, and industry-specific requirements.
- Regularly review guidance documents, publications, and updates issued by regulatory bodies and standard-setting organizations to understand the implications for your organization.
- Engage with legal and compliance experts to interpret regulatory changes and assess their impact on your cybersecurity practices and CMMC compliance efforts.
- Adapt your security policies, procedures, and controls to ensure alignment with the latest regulatory requirements and best practices.

7. Invest in Continuous Learning and Skills Development:

- Foster a culture of continuous learning and skills development within your organization to keep your cybersecurity workforce updated with the latest knowledge and skills.
- Encourage your team members to pursue relevant certifications, such as CMMC Certified Professional (CCP), Certified Information Systems Security Professional (CISSP), or Certified Ethical Hacker (CEH), to enhance their expertise and stay current with industry standards.
- Provide regular training and awareness programs to educate employees about emerging cybersecurity trends, best practices, and their roles in maintaining a strong security posture.
- Allocate resources for your cybersecurity team to attend conferences, workshops, and training sessions, where they can expand

their knowledge and network with industry experts.

8. Leverage Automation and Intelligence:

- Harness the power of automation and artificial intelligence (AI) to proactively monitor, detect, and respond to cybersecurity threats and anomalies.
- Implement security information and event management (SIEM) solutions, security orchestration, automation, and response (SOAR) platforms, and other intelligent tools to streamline security operations and improve threat detection and response capabilities.
- Use machine learning algorithms and behavioral analytics to identify patterns, anomalies, and potential indicators of compromise (IoCs) in real time.
- Continuously refine and update your automated security controls and incident response playbooks based on the latest threat intelligence and best practices.

9. Conduct Regular Security Assessments and Audits:

- Perform regular security assessments and audits to evaluate the effectiveness of your cybersecurity controls, identify gaps or weaknesses, and ensure compliance with CMMC requirements.
- Engage with independent third-party assessment organizations (C3PAOs) or cybersecurity experts to conduct objective assessments and provide recommendations for improvement.
- Use automated vulnerability scanning and penetration testing tools to identify and prioritize vulnerabilities in your systems,

networks, and applications.

- Review and update your security assessment and audit processes regularly to ensure compliance with the latest CMMC guidelines and industry best practices.

10. Establish a Continuous Improvement Mindset:

- Cultivate a mindset of continuous improvement within your organization, recognizing that cybersecurity and CMMC compliance are ongoing journeys rather than one-time achievements.
- Review and update your cybersecurity policies, procedures, and controls regularly based on the latest trends, threats, and best practices.
- Encourage a culture of open communication, knowledge sharing, and lessons learned to foster continuous learning and improvement across your organization.
- Establish metrics and key performance indicators (KPIs) to measure the effectiveness of your cybersecurity program and track progress over time.
- Celebrate successes and milestones in your cybersecurity journey while acknowledging areas for improvement and committing to ongoing enhancement.

By staying informed about cybersecurity trends and CMMC updates and proactively adjusting your security strategy, you can position your organization to effectively navigate the evolving threat landscape and maintain a robust security posture. Staying ahead of emerging threats and ensuring ongoing compliance with CMMC requirements requires a combination of continuous learning, collaboration, and adaptation.

Remember, cybersecurity is a shared responsibility that requires the active engagement and commitment of everyone within your organization. By fostering a culture of cybersecurity awareness, investing in the necessary resources and expertise, and staying vigilant in the face of evolving threats, you can strengthen your organization's resilience and contribute to the overall security of the defense industrial base.

Proactively staying informed and adapting your security strategy is a best practice for CMMC compliance and a critical component of effective risk management and business continuity. By embracing this proactive approach, you can safeguard your organization's sensitive information, protect your reputation, and maintain the trust of your customers, partners, and stakeholders in the face of ever-evolving cybersecurity challenges.

Appendix A: Glossary of Terms

Assessment: The process of evaluating an organization's cyberse-curity practices against the requirements of the CMMC framework. Assessments are conducted by authorized C3PAOs for Level 2 and by government assessors for Level 3.

Assessor: An individual who is trained and certified to conduct CMMC assessments. Assessors are employed by C3PAOs for Level 2 assessments and by the government for Level 3 assessments.

C3PAO (CMMC Third-Party Assessment Organization): An indepen-dent entity authorized by the CMMC-AB to conduct CMMC Level 2 assessments. C3PAOs must meet rigorous requirements for certifica-tion, including having certified assessors, maintaining appropriate insurance, and following strict assessment protocols.

Certification: The formal recognition that an organization has met the requirements of a specific CMMC level. The CMMC-AB grants certification based on the results of an assessment conducted by a C3PAO (for Level 2) or a government assessor (for Level 3).

CIO (Chief Information Officer): The senior executive responsible for an organization's information technology and computer systems. The

CIO is critical in implementing and overseeing cybersecurity practices, including CMMC's requirements.

CISO (Chief Information Security Officer): The senior executive responsible for an organization's information security program. The CISO is responsible for developing and implementing cybersecurity policies, procedures, and controls, including those required by CMMC.

CMMC (Cybersecurity Maturity Model Certification): A comprehensive framework that assesses and enhances organizations' cybersecurity posture in the Defense Industrial Base (DIB). CMMC consists of three levels of certification, each with progressively more stringent requirements.

CMMC-AB (CMMC Accreditation Body): The entity responsible for overseeing the CMMC ecosystem, including training, accreditation, and certification. The CMMC-AB establishes and maintains the standards, policies, and procedures for CMMC assessments and certifications.

Continuous Monitoring: The ongoing process of monitoring, assessing, and reporting on an organization's cybersecurity posture. Continuous monitoring is required to maintain CMMC certification and ensure that an organization's cybersecurity practices remain effective over time.

CUI (Controlled Unclassified Information): Information that requires safeguarding or dissemination controls according to and consistent with laws, regulations, and government-wide policies. CUI is a key focus of the CMMC framework, particularly at Level 2 and above.

Domain: A grouping of cybersecurity best practices in the CMMC framework, such as Access Control, Incident Response, or Risk Management. The CMMC framework consists of 17 domains, each with its own set of practices and processes.

ERP (Enterprise Resource Planning): A software system that integrates and manages critical business processes, such as accounting, procurement, and human resources. ERP systems often contain sensitive data and are subject to CMMC requirements.

FCI (Federal Contract Information): Information provided by or generated for the government under a contract to develop or deliver a product or service to the government. FCI is not intended for public release and is subject to CMMC Level 1 requirements.

Maturity Level: A benchmark in the CMMC framework that indicates an organization's cybersecurity capabilities and institutionalization of processes. CMMC consists of three maturity levels, each with progressively more stringent requirements.

MFA (Multi-Factor Authentication): An authentication method that requires users to provide two or more forms of identification to access a system or resource. MFA is a key requirement of CMMC Level 2 and above.

NIST (National Institute of Standards and Technology): A non-regulatory agency of the United States Department of Commerce that develops cybersecurity standards and guidelines. NIST standards, particularly NIST SP 800-171, align closely with CMMC requirements.

OSC (Organization Seeking Certification): An organization pursuing

CMMC certification. To achieve certification, OSCs must undergo an assessment by a C3PAO (for Level 2) or a government assessor (for Level 3).

POA&M (Plan of Action and Milestones): A document that identifies tasks needing to be accomplished to remediate gaps or deficiencies in an organization's cybersecurity practices. POA&Ms are a key tool for tracking and managing remediation efforts in the CMMC framework.

Practice: A specific cybersecurity activity or control required by the CMMC framework. The CMMC framework comprises 171 practices organized into 17 domains and three maturity levels.

Remediation: The act of correcting identified gaps or deficiencies in an organization's cybersecurity practices to meet CMMC requirements. Remediation is a critical step in achieving and maintaining CMMC certification.

RPO (Registered Provider Organization): An organization that the CMMC-AB authorizes to provide CMMC consulting, training, and other support services to OSCs. RPOs must meet specific certification requirements and be listed on the CMMC Marketplace.

Scope: The systems, networks, and assets relevant to an organization's CMMC assessment and certification. The scope is determined based on the sensitivity of the information processed, stored, or transmitted by the organization and the specific contracts or agreements that the organization has with the DoD.

Security Control: A safeguard or countermeasure prescribed for an information system or organization to protect its information's confidentiality, integrity, and availability. Security controls are a key component of the CMMC framework and are organized into 17 domains.

SSP (System Security Plan): A document that describes the security requirements for a system and how those requirements are implemented. SSPs are a key artifact in the CMMC assessment process and must be maintained and updated regularly.

These key terms and concepts are associated with the CMMC framework and its implementation. Understanding these terms is essential for organizations seeking to achieve and maintain CMMC certification and for cybersecurity professionals who support those efforts. The CMMC-AB and other authoritative sources provide more detailed definitions and explanations of these and other relevant terms.

Appendix B: List of CMMC 2.0 Resources and Tools

1. CMMC 2.0 Model: This is the official document that outlines the requirements and practices for each CMMC level. It is the foundational resource for understanding the framework and its implementation. It describes the 17 domains, 171 practices, and 3 maturity levels that comprise the CMMC framework. Organizations seeking certification should thoroughly review the CMMC 2.0 Model to understand the specific requirements and expectations for their desired level of certification.

2. CMMC Assessment Guides: Detailed guides provided by the CMMC-AB that describe the assessment process, objectives, and procedures for each CMMC level. The Assessment Guides are essential resources for organizations preparing for a CMMC assessment and C3PAOs and assessors conducting the assessments. The guides provide step-by-step instructions for evaluating an organization's cybersecurity practices against the CMMC requirements, including document reviews, interviews, and technical testing.

3. CMMC Assessment Scope Guides: Documents that help organizations determine the scope of their CMMC assessment based on the specific contracts and information they handle. The Assessment

Scope Guides provide guidance on identifying the systems, networks, and assets subject to CMMC requirements based on factors such as the sensitivity of the information processed, stored, or transmitted and the specific contract requirements. Organizations should use the Assessment Scope Guides to ensure their CMMC assessment covers all relevant business areas.

4. CMMC Self-Assessment Handbook: This resource provides guidance for organizations conducting self-assessments against CMMC requirements. It is a valuable tool for organizations that want to evaluate their cybersecurity posture and identify areas for improvement prior to undergoing a formal CMMC assessment. The handbook provides a step-by-step self-assessment process, including identifying relevant systems and assets, reviewing policies and procedures, and testing technical controls.

5. CMMC Marketplace: An online platform provided by the CMMC-AB that connects organizations with CMMC ecosystem partners, including C3PAOs, training providers, and consultants. The CMMC Marketplace is a one-stop shop for organizations seeking CMMC-related services and support. It provides a directory of authorized C3PAOs, training providers, and consultants and a platform for requesting proposals and comparing service offerings. The Marketplace also provides resources and guidance for organizations navigating the CMMC certification process.

6. NIST SP 800-171 DoD Assessment Methodology: A tool used to assess an organization's implementation of NIST SP 800-171 controls closely aligned with CMMC Level 2 requirements. The NIST SP 800-171 DoD Assessment Methodology is a valuable resource for organizations that have already implemented NIST SP 800-171 controls and are seeking to transition to CMMC certification. The methodology provides a standardized approach for evaluating an organization's implementation of the NIST controls and identifying areas for improvement.

7. CMMC Companion Guide for NIST SP 800-171: A document that maps NIST SP 800-171 controls to CMMC practices, helping organizations leverage their existing compliance efforts. The CMMC Companion Guide for NIST SP 800-171 is a valuable resource for organizations that have already implemented NIST SP 800-171 controls and are seeking to transition to CMMC certification. The guide provides a detailed mapping of the NIST controls to the corresponding CMMC practices, allowing organizations to identify areas where they may already comply with CMMC requirements.

8. Cybersecurity Maturity Model Certification (CMMC) FAQ: This official resource answers frequently asked questions about the CMMC framework and its implementation. It is a valuable resource for organizations seeking to understand the CMMC framework and its requirements. It answers common questions about the certification process, the roles and responsibilities of different stakeholders, and the technical specifications for each CMMC level. The CMMC-AB regularly updates the FAQ to address emerging issues and concerns.

9. CMMC 2.0 Appendices: Additional resources, such as glossaries, acronyms, and mappings, support the understanding and implementation of CMMC 2.0. The CMMC 2.0 Appendices provide supplementary information and guidance to help organizations navigate the CMMC framework. The appendices include a glossary of key terms and definitions, a list of acronyms and abbreviations, and mappings of CMMC practices to other cybersecurity frameworks and standards, such as NIST SP 800-53 and ISO 27001.

10. CMMC Approved Training Providers: A list of training providers authorized by the CMMC-AB to deliver CMMC-related training and certification programs. CMMC Approved Training Providers are organizations vetted and authorized by the CMMC-AB to provide training and certification programs for individuals and organizations seeking to understand and implement the CMMC framework. These providers offer a range of training options, including online courses, in-person workshops, and certification programs for CMMC professionals, such as Certified CMMC Professionals (CCP) and Certified CMMC Assessors (CCA).

In addition to these official resources, many other tools and resources are available to support organizations in their CMMC implementation efforts. These include:

11. Cybersecurity risk assessment tools: Software tools that help organizations identify and assess the cybersecurity risks associated with their systems, networks, and data. These tools can support the risk management practices required by CMMC, such as conducting periodic risk assessments and implementing risk-based security controls.

12. Vulnerability scanning tools: Software tools automatically scan an organization's systems and networks for known vulnerabilities and misconfigurations. These tools can support the vulnerability management practices required by CMMC, such as regularly scanning for and remediating vulnerabilities.

13. Security information and event management (SIEM) tools:

Software tools that collect and analyze log data from various sources across an organization's network to detect and respond to cybersecurity threats and anomalies. SIEM tools can be used to support the incident detection and response practices required by CMMC.

14. Backup and disaster recovery tools: Software and hardware tools enable organizations to regularly back up their data and systems and quickly recover from cybersecurity incidents or disasters. These tools can support the recovery practices required by CMMC.

15. Cybersecurity training and awareness platforms: These are online platforms that provide cybersecurity training and awareness content for employees and other stakeholders. These platforms can support the awareness and training practices required by CMMC, such as providing regular cybersecurity awareness training to all users.

16. Third-party risk management platforms: Software tools that help organizations assess and manage the cybersecurity risks associated with their vendors, suppliers, and other third-party partners. These platforms can support the supply chain risk management practices required by CMMC.

17. Compliance management platforms: Software tools that help organizations manage and track compliance with various cybersecurity frameworks and standards, including CMMC. These platforms can automate compliance tasks such as conducting self-assessments, generating compliance reports, and managing remediation efforts.

18. Incident response platforms: Software tools that help organizations plan for, detect, and respond to cybersecurity incidents. These platforms can be used to support the incident response practices required by CMMC, such as developing and testing incident response plans and procedures.

19. Penetration testing tools: Software tools that simulate cyber attacks to identify vulnerabilities and weaknesses in an organization's cybersecurity defenses. C3PAOs and other assessors can use these tools to conduct the penetration testing required for CMMC Level 3 assessments.

20. Governance, risk, and compliance (GRC) platforms: Software tools that provide an integrated view of an organization's governance, risk management, and compliance processes. GRC platforms can support the various cybersecurity practices required by CMMC, such as risk management, incident response, and continuous monitoring.

These are just a few examples of the many tools and resources available to support organizations in their CMMC implementation efforts. The tools and resources an organization uses will depend on factors such as its size, industry, and the CMMC practices and processes it is implementing. Organizations should carefully evaluate their needs and select appropriate tools and resources for their specific context and requirements.

Appendix C: List of CMMC Controls Ordered by Domain and Maturity Level

Access Control (AC)

Level 1

- **AC.1.001:** Limit information system access to authorized users, processes acting on behalf of authorized users, or devices (including other information systems). This practice ensures that only authorized individuals, processes, and devices can access the organization's systems and data.
- **AC.1.002:** Limit information system access to the types of transactions and functions authorized users can execute. This practice restricts user access to only the specific functions and transactions necessary for their role or job responsibilities.

Level 2

- **AC.2.001:** Provide privacy and security notices consistent with applicable CUI rules. This practice ensures users know the organization's privacy and security policies for handling Controlled

Unclassified Information (CUI).

- **AC.2.002:** Prevent non-privileged users from executing privileged functions and capture the execution of such functions in audit logs. This practice restricts privileged functions to authorized users and ensures all privileged actions are logged for auditing purposes.

- **AC.2.003:** Enforce a minimum password complexity and change of characters when new passwords are created. This practice ensures that user passwords meet minimum complexity requirements to enhance security.

- **AC.2.004:** Prohibit password reuse for a specified number of generations. This practice prevents users from reusing previous passwords to reduce the risk of unauthorized access.

- **AC.2.005:** Allow temporary password use for system logons with an immediate change to a permanent password. This practice enables temporary passwords for initial system access but requires users to change them immediately to a permanent password.

- **AC.2.006:** Use multifactor authentication for local and network access to privileged accounts and network access to non-privileged accounts. This practice requires users to provide two or more forms of authentication to access privileged and non-privileged accounts, enhancing security.

- **AC.2.007:** Employ replay-resistant authentication mechanisms for network access to privileged and non-privileged accounts. This practice uses authentication mechanisms, such as one-time passwords or cryptographic keys, that prevent capturing and reusing authentication data.

- **AC.2.008:** Prevent reuse of identifiers for a defined period. This practice prevents unauthorized access by preventing the reuse of user identifiers for a specified time period.

- **AC.2.009:** Disable identifiers after a defined period of inactivity. This practice automatically disables user identifiers that have been inactive for a specified period to prevent unauthorized access.
- **AC.2.010:** Use encrypted sessions to transmit authentication and authenticator data. This practice ensures that authentication data is encrypted during transmission to prevent interception and unauthorized access.

Level 3

- **AC.3.001:** Protect wireless access using authentication, encryption, and a Wireless Intrusion Detection System (WIDS) to identify rogue wireless devices and detect attack attempts and potential compromises. This practice enhances wireless security through authentication, encryption, and monitoring for unauthorized wireless devices and attacks.
- **AC.3.002:** Protect internal network communications traffic through network segmentation and encryption. This practice enhances the security of internal communications by separating network segments and encrypting traffic between them.
- **AC.3.003:** Create separate network segments for Internet-facing systems and internally-facing systems to limit access to CUI. This practice isolates CUI systems from Internet-facing systems to reduce the risk of unauthorized access from external sources.
- **AC.3.004:** Disable all workstation-to-workstation communication to limit an attacker's ability to spread malware or laterally move across the network. This practice restricts direct communication between workstations to prevent attackers' spread of malware and lateral movement.

- **AC.3.005:** Control mobile device connection. This practice establishes controls for mobile device connection to the organization's network to prevent unauthorized access and data exfiltration.
- **AC.3.006:** Prohibit the use of unencrypted USB drives. This practice ensures that all USB drives used within the organization are encrypted to protect sensitive data.
- **AC.3.007:** Restrict remote network access based on organizationally defined risk factors such as time of day, location of access, physical location, network connection state, and measured properties of the current user and role. This practice establishes granular controls for remote network access based on various risk factors to enhance security.
- **AC.3.008:** Route remote access via managed access control points. This practice ensures that all remote access to the organization's network is routed through managed access control points for monitoring and control.
- **AC.3.009:** Authorize remote execution of privileged commands and remote access to security-relevant information. This practice establishes a process for authorizing and logging the remote execution of privileged commands and access to security-relevant information.
- **AC.3.010:** Employ cryptographic mechanisms to protect the confidentiality of remote access sessions. This practice ensures that remote access sessions are encrypted to protect the confidentiality of transmitted data.
- **AC.3.011:** Terminate network connections associated with communications sessions at the end of the sessions or after an organizationally defined period of inactivity. This practice automatically terminates network connections after a specified period of inactivity to prevent unauthorized access.
- **AC.3.012:** Establish and manage cryptographic keys for cryptog-

raphy employed in organizational systems. This practice ensures that cryptographic keys are properly managed and protected to maintain the effectiveness of cryptographic controls.

- **AC.3.013:** Employ cryptography following applicable federal laws, executive orders, directives, regulations, policies, standards, and guidance. This practice ensures that cryptographic controls comply with applicable federal requirements.
- **AC.3.014:** Disable and remove or isolate mission-critical systems and components of high-value assets in the case of an imminent threat. This practice enables the rapid disabling, removal, or isolation of critical systems and assets to minimize potential damage in response to imminent threats.

Asset Management (AM)

Level 2

- **AM.2.001:** Develop, document, and maintain an inventory of organizational assets. This practice establishes a comprehensive inventory of all organizational assets, including systems, devices, and data.
- **AM.2.002:** Establish a process for managing inventory that addresses asset ownership and associated responsibilities. This practice ensures that asset ownership and responsibilities are clearly defined and managed.

Level 3

- **AM.3.001:** Employ automated mechanisms where safe and feasible to maintain an up-to-date, complete, accurate, and readily available inventory of organizational assets. This practice uses automated tools to maintain a current and accurate inventory of assets where safe and feasible.

Audit and Accountability (AU)

Level 2

- **AU.2.001:** Ensure that the actions of individual system users can be uniquely traced to those users so they can be held accountable for their actions. This practice ensures that user actions are logged and can be traced back to individual users for accountability purposes.
- **AU.2.002:** Create and retain system audit logs and records to the extent needed to enable the monitoring, analysis, investigation, and reporting of unlawful or unauthorized system activity. This practice ensures that system audit logs and records are created and retained to support monitoring, analysis, investigation, and reporting of unauthorized activity.
- **AU.2.003:** Provide a system capability that compares and synchronizes internal system clocks with an authoritative source to generate time stamps for audit records. This practice ensures that system clocks are synchronized with an authoritative time source to generate accurate time stamps for audit records.
- **AU.2.004:** Review audit logs. This practice ensures audit logs are regularly reviewed to identify unauthorized activity or anomalies.

Level 3

- **AU.3.001:** Employ an audit reduction and report generation capability that supports on-demand audit review, analysis, and reporting requirements; does not alter original content or time ordering of audit records; and maintains the integrity of original audit records. This practice uses specialized tools to generate audit reports and support on-demand analysis without altering the original audit records.
- **AU.3.002:** Centrally manage the content of audit records generated by different components throughout the system. This practice centralizes the management of audit records generated by various system components to facilitate analysis and reporting.
- **AU.3.003:** Automate analysis of audit logs to identify and act on critical indicators (TTPs) and organizationally defined suspicious activity. This practice uses automated tools to analyze audit logs and identify suspicious activity or indicators of compromise.
- **AU.3.004:** Alert appropriate staff if an audit logging process fails. This practice ensures that proper personnel are alerted during an audit logging process failure.
- **AU.3.005:** Implement cryptographic mechanisms to protect the integrity of audit information and tools. This practice uses cryptographic controls to prevent tampering or unauthorized modification.
- **AU.3.006:** Protect against an individual (or process acting on behalf of an individual) falsely denying having performed a particular action. This practice ensures that individuals cannot falsely deny performing specific actions by maintaining secure audit trails.
- **AU.3.007:** Retain audit records following organizational, state, and federal retention requirements. This practice ensures that

audit records are retained following applicable retention require-ments for legal or regulatory purposes.

Awareness and Training (AT)

Level 2

- **AT.2.001:** Ensure that managers, systems administrators, and users of organizational systems are made aware of the security risks associated with their activities and of the applicable policies, standards, and procedures related to the security of those systems. This practice ensures that all personnel know security risks and policies related to their activities.
- **AT.2.002:** Ensure personnel are trained to carry out their assigned information security-related duties and responsibilities. This practice ensures that personnel are properly trained to perform their assigned security duties and responsibilities.
- **AT.2.003:** Provide security awareness training on recognizing and reporting potential indicators of insider threat. This practice provides training to personnel on recognizing and reporting indicators of insider threats.

Configuration Management (CM)

Level 2

- **CM.2.001:** Establish and maintain baseline configurations and inventories of organizational systems (including hardware, software, firmware, and documentation) throughout the respective system development life cycles. This practice establishes baseline configurations and inventories of systems and maintains them throughout the system development life cycle.

· **CM.2.002:** Employ the principle of least functionality by configuring organizational systems to provide only essential capabilities. This practice configures systems to provide only the minimum operational functionality, reducing the attack surface.

· **CM.2.003:** Control and monitor user-installed software. This practice establishes controls and monitoring for user-installed software to prevent unauthorized or malicious software.

· **CM.2.004:** Establish and enforce security configuration settings for information technology products employed in organizational systems. This practice establishes and enforces secure configuration settings for IT products used in the organization's systems.

· **CM.2.005:** Track, review, approve/disapprove, and log changes to organizational systems. This practice establishes a process for tracking, reviewing, approving, and logging system changes.

· **CM.2.006:** Analyze the security impact of changes before implementation. This practice requires a security impact analysis of changes before implementation to identify potential risks.

· **CM.2.007:** Restrict, disable, or prevent the use of nonessential programs, functions, ports, protocols, and services. This practice restricts or disables unnecessary programs, functions, ports, protocols, and services to reduce the attack surface.

· **CM.2.008:** Apply a deny-by-exception (blacklisting) policy to prevent the use of unauthorized software or a deny-all permit-by-exception (whitelisting) policy to allow the execution of authorized software. This practice uses blacklisting or whitelisting policies to control the execution of software on systems.

Level 3

- **CM.3.001:** Employ automated mechanisms to maintain an up-to-date, complete, accurate, and readily available baseline configuration of organizational systems. This practice uses automated tools to maintain a current and accurate baseline configuration of systems.
- **CM.3.002:** Maintain an up-to-date list of components (hardware inventory) using automated methods to identify and prevent unauthorized components. This practice uses automated methods to maintain an up-to-date hardware inventory and prevent the use of unauthorized components.
- **CM.3.003:** Employ automated mechanisms to detect unauthorized hardware, firmware, and software. This practice uses automated tools to detect the presence of unauthorized hardware, firmware, and software on systems.
- **CM.3.004:** Employ application whitelisting and an application vetting process for systems identified by the organization. This practice uses application whitelisting and vetting processes for systems the organization identifies requiring additional security controls.

Identification and Authentication (IA)

Level 1

- **IA.1.001:** Identify organizational users, processes acting on behalf of organizational users, or devices. This practice requires identifying users, processes, and devices accessing the organization's systems.

- **IA.1.002:** Authenticate (or verify) the identities of those users, processes, or devices as a prerequisite to allowing access to organizational information systems. This practice requires authentication of identified users, processes, or devices before granting access to systems.

Level 2

- **IA.2.001:** Enforce minimum password complexity and character changes when creating new passwords. This practice establishes minimum requirements for password complexity, and character changes when creating new passwords.
- **IA.2.002:** Prohibit password reuse for a specified number of generations. This practice prevents users from reusing previous passwords for several generations.
- **IA.2.003:** Allow temporary passwords for system logons with an immediate change to a permanent password. This practice enables temporary passwords for initial system access but requires users to change them immediately to a permanent password.
- **IA.2.004:** Store and transmit only cryptographically protected passwords. This practice ensures that passwords are encrypted during storage and transmission.
- **IA.2.005:** Obscure feedback of authentication information. This practice ensures that authentication feedback, such as displaying passwords on the screen, is obscured to prevent unauthorized disclosure.
- **IA.2.006:** Use multifactor authentication for local and network access to privileged and non-privileged accounts. This practice requires users to provide two or more forms of authentication to

access privileged and non-privileged accounts.

- **IA.2.007:** Employ replay-resistant authentication mechanisms for network access to privileged and non-privileged accounts. This practice uses authentication mechanisms that prevent capturing and reusing authentication data, such as one-time passwords or cryptographic keys.

Level 3

- **IA.3.001:** Employ automated mechanisms to prohibit system access for users without valid authentication credentials. This practice uses automated tools to prevent system access by users without valid authentication credentials.
- **IA.3.002:** Uniquely identify and authenticate organizational users (or processes acting on behalf of organizational users). This practice establishes the requirement to uniquely identify and authenticate users or processes acting on behalf of users.
- **IA.3.003:** Use multifactor authentication for remote access to privileged and non-privileged accounts such that one of the factors is provided by a device separate from the system gaining access. This practice requires using a separate device, such as a hardware token, as one of the factors for multifactor authentication for remote access.
- **IA.3.004:** Employ replay-resistant authentication mechanisms for network access to privileged accounts. This practice uses authentication mechanisms that prevent capturing and reusing authentication data for privileged accounts.
- **IA.3.005:** Prevent the reuse of identifiers for a defined period. This practice ensures that user identifiers cannot be reused for a specified time period to prevent unauthorized access.

- **IA.3.006:** Disable identifiers after a defined period of inactivity. This practice automatically disables user identifiers that have been inactive for a specified period to prevent unauthorized access.
- **IA.3.007:** Enforce minimum password complexity and character changes when creating new passwords. This practice establishes minimum requirements for password complexity, and character changes when creating new passwords.
- **IA.3.008:** Prohibit password reuse for a specified number of generations. This practice prevents users from reusing previous passwords for several generations.
- **IA.3.009:** Allow temporary password use for system logons with an immediate change to a permanent password. This practice enables temporary passwords for initial system access but requires users to change them immediately to a permanent password.
- **IA.3.010:** Store and transmit only cryptographically protected passwords. This practice ensures that passwords are encrypted during storage and transmission.
- **IA.3.011:** Obscure feedback of authentication information. This practice ensures that authentication feedback, such as displaying passwords on the screen, is obscured to prevent unauthorized disclosure.
- **IA.3.012:** Require a minimum number of digital certificates per person. This practice establishes a minimum requirement for the number of digital certificates each user must have for authentication purposes.
- **IA.3.013:** Use external certificating authorities to issue digital certificates. This practice requires external certification authorities to issue digital certificates used for authentication.

Incident Response (IR)

Level 2

- **IR.2.001:** Establish an operational incident-handling capability for organizational systems that includes adequate preparation, detection, analysis, containment, recovery, and user response activities. This practice establishes an incident handling capability consisting of all necessary incident response phases.
- **IR.2.002:** Detect and report events. This practice requires the detection and reporting of security events.
- **IR.2.003:** Analyze and triage events to support event resolution and incident declaration. This practice requires analyzing and triaging detected events to determine appropriate resolution and incident declaration.
- **IR.2.004:** Develop and implement responses to declared incidents according to pre-defined procedures. This practice requires developing and implementing incident response procedures for declared incidents.
- **IR.2.005:** Perform root cause analysis on incidents to determine underlying causes. This practice requires conducting root cause analysis on incidents to identify and address underlying causes.
- **IR.2.006:** Track, document, and report incidents to designated officials and authorities, both internal and external to the organization. This practice requires tracking, documenting, and reporting incidents to designated internal and external officials and authorities.
- **IR.2.007:** Test the organizational incident response capability. This practice requires regular testing of the organization's incident response capability to ensure effectiveness.

Level 3

- **IR.3.001:** Use automated mechanisms to assist in reporting security incidents. This practice requires automated tools to facilitate the reporting of security incidents.
- **IR.3.002:** Employ automated mechanisms to support the incident handling process. This practice requires automated tools to support various phases of the incident-handling process.
- **IR.3.003:** Correlate incident information and individual incident responses to achieve an organization-wide perspective on incident awareness and response. This practice requires correlating incident information and responses to provide an organization-wide view of incident awareness and response.
- **IR.3.004:** Employ automated mechanisms to support the incident response process. This practice requires automated tools to support the overall incident response process.
- **IR.3.005:** Automatically disable system access for non-compliant individuals with security requirements. This practice requires automatically disabling system access for users who fail to comply with security requirements.
- **IR.3.006:** Establish and maintain a security operations center capability that facilitates a 24/7 response capability. This practice requires establishing and maintaining a security operations center with 24/7 response capabilities.
- **IR.3.007:** Publish information about cyber threat intelligence, incident reporting, and incident response in an organization-defined forum accessible to personnel with an organization-defined frequency. This practice requires regularly publishing information about cyber threats, incident reporting, and incident response in a forum accessible to personnel.

Maintenance (MA)

Level 2

- **MA.2.001:** Perform maintenance on organizational systems. This practice requires regular maintenance of organizational systems.
- **MA.2.002:** Control the tools, techniques, mechanisms, and personnel used for system maintenance. This practice requires establishing controls on these elements.
- **MA.2.003:** Ensure equipment removed for off-site maintenance is sanitized of any CUI. This practice requires sanitizing any CUI equipment before removing it for off-site maintenance.
- **MA.2.004:** Check media containing diagnostic and test programs for malicious code before the media are used in organizational systems. This practice requires checking media containing diagnostic and test programs for malicious code before using them in organizational systems.
- **MA.2.005:** Require multifactor authentication to establish nonlocal maintenance sessions via external network connections and terminate such connections when nonlocal maintenance is complete. This practice requires using multifactor authentication for nonlocal maintenance sessions via external networks and terminating the connections when maintenance is complete.
- **MA.2.006:** Supervise the maintenance activities of maintenance personnel without the required access authorization. This practice requires supervising maintenance personnel without the required access authorization.

Level 3

- **MA.3.001:** Ensure that individuals conducting maintenance on a system processing, storing, or transmitting CUI sign a document acknowledging that they understand and agree to abide by all organizational policies concerning maintenance activities before being granted access authorization. This practice requires maintenance personnel to sign a document acknowledging their understanding and agreement to abide by organizational policies before being granted access authorization.
- **MA.3.002:** Prevent the unauthorized removal of systems or system components from organizational facilities for off-site maintenance, repair, or replacement. This practice requires preventing the unauthorized removal of systems or components from organizational facilities for off-site maintenance, repair, or replacement.
- **MA.3.003:** Maintain and review records for non-local maintenance, diagnostic, and service activities. This practice requires maintaining and reviewing records for non-local maintenance, diagnostic, and service activities.
- **MA.3.004:** Verify security functions following system maintenance or repairs. This practice requires verifying security functions after system maintenance or repairs to ensure they still function properly.

Media Protection (MP)

Level 1

- **MP.1.001:** Protect (i.e., physically control and securely store) system media containing Federal Contract Information (FCI), both paper and digital. This practice requires physically controlling and securely storing system media containing paper or digital FCI.

- **MP.1.002:** Limit access to CUI on system media to authorized users. This practice requires limiting access to CUI on system media to authorized users only.
- **MP.1.003:** Sanitize or destroy system media containing Federal Contract Information before disposal or release for reuse. This practice requires sanitizing or destroying system media containing FCI before disposing or releasing it for reuse.

Level 2

- **MP.2.001:** Protect (i.e., physically control and securely store) system media containing paper and digital CUI. This practice requires physically controlling and securely storing system media containing paper or digital CUI.
- **MP.2.002:** Limit access to CUI on system media to authorized users. This practice requires limiting access to CUI on system media to authorized users only.
- **MP.2.003:** Mark media with necessary CUI markings and distribution limitations. This practice requires marking media containing CUI with the necessary CUI markings and distribution limitations.
- **MP.2.004:** Control access to media containing CUI and maintain accountability for media during transport outside of controlled areas. This practice requires controlling access to media containing CUI and maintaining accountability for it during transport outside of controlled areas.
- **MP.2.005:** Implement cryptographic mechanisms to protect the confidentiality of CUI stored on digital media during transport

unless otherwise protected by alternative physical safeguards. This practice requires using cryptographic mechanisms to protect the confidentiality of CUI stored on digital media during transport unless alternative physical safeguards are used.

Level 3

- **MP.3.001:** Maintain an inventory of all systems and system components to which security controls have been applied. This practice requires maintaining an inventory of all systems and components to which security controls have been applied.
- **MP.3.002:** Protect the confidentiality of backup CUI at storage locations. This practice requires protecting the confidentiality of backup CUI at storage locations.
- **MP.3.003:** Employ automated mechanisms to restrict access to media storage areas and to audit access attempts and access granted. This practice requires automated mechanisms to restrict access to media storage areas, audit access attempts, and access granted.
- **MP.3.004:** Maintain records of information system components throughout the system development life cycle. This practice requires maintaining records of information system components throughout the entire system development life cycle.
- **MP.3.005:** Ensure that organizational personnel are sanitizing or destroying information system media containing CUI or sensitive information when it is no longer needed and following organizational policy and procedures. This practice requires ensuring that personnel properly sanitize or destroy media containing CUI or sensitive information when it is no longer needed, per organizational policy and procedures.

Personnel Security (PS)

Level 2

- **PS.2.001:** Screen individuals before authorizing access to organizational systems containing CUI. This practice requires screening individuals before granting them access to organizational systems containing CUI.
- **PS.2.002:** Ensure that organizational systems containing CUI are protected during and after personnel actions such as terminations and transfers. This practice requires the protection of organizational systems containing CUI during and after personnel actions like terminations and transfers.
- **PS.2.003:** Ensure that individuals requiring access to organizational systems containing CUI sign appropriate access agreements before being granted access. This practice requires individuals to sign appropriate access agreements before being granted access to organizational systems containing CUI.

Level 3

- **PS.3.001:** Ensure that individuals receive security awareness and literacy training before being granted access to CUI and at least annually after that. This practice requires providing security awareness and literacy training to individuals before granting them access to CUI and at least annually after that.

Physical Protection (PE)

Level 1

- **PE.1.001:** Limit physical access to organizational information systems, equipment, and the respective operating environments to authorized individuals. This practice requires limiting physical access to organizational systems, equipment, and operating environments to authorized individuals only.
- **PE.1.002:** Escort visitors and monitor visitor activity. This practice requires escorting visitors and monitoring their activity.
- **PE.1.003:** Maintain audit logs of physical access. This practice requires maintaining audit logs of physical access.
- **PE.1.004:** Control and manage physical access devices. This practice requires controlling and managing physical access devices.

Level 2

- **PE.2.001:** Protect and monitor the physical facility and support infrastructure for organizational systems. This practice requires protecting and monitoring the physical facility and supporting the infrastructure of organizational systems.
- **PE.2.002:** Protect CUI at alternate work sites. This practice requires protecting CUI at alternate work sites.

Level 3

- **PE.3.001:** Employ an automated mechanism to notify appropriate personnel of unauthorized physical access attempts to organizational systems. This practice requires an automated mechanism to notify proper personnel of unauthorized physical access attempts to organizational systems.

- **PE.3.002:** Employ an automated mechanism to detect and alert personnel of potential adverse events or conditions affecting the physical operating environment of organizational systems. This practice requires an automated mechanism to detect and alert personnel of potential adverse events or conditions affecting the physical operating environment of organizational systems.

Recovery (RE)

Level 2

- **RE.2.001:** Ensure the availability of organizational information and systems in the event of a loss of operational capability. This practice requires ensuring the availability of organizational information and systems in the event of a loss of operational capability.
- **RE.2.002:** Regularly perform and test data backup. This practice requires regularly performing and testing data backups.
- **RE.2.003:** Protect the confidentiality of backup CUI at storage locations. This practice requires protecting the confidentiality of backup CUI at storage locations.
- **RE.2.004:** Regularly perform complete, comprehensive, and resilient data backups as organizationally defined. This practice requires regularly performing complete, comprehensive, and resilient data backups as defined by the organization.

Level 3

- **RE.3.001:** Employ an automated capability to restore organizational systems to a known state after a disruption, compromise, or failure. This practice requires an automated capability to restore organizational systems to a known state after a disruption, compromise, or failure.
- **RE.3.002:** Implement transaction recovery for organizational systems. This practice requires implementing transaction recovery for organizational systems.
- **RE.3.003:** Ensure that organizational systems can be recovered and reconstituted to a known state after a disruption, compromise, or failure. This practice requires ensuring that organizational systems can be recovered and reconstituted to a known state after a disruption, compromise, or failure.

Risk Management (RM)

Level 2

- **RM.2.001:** Periodically assess the risk to organizational operations (including mission, functions, image, or reputation), organizational assets, and individuals resulting from operating organizational systems and the associated processing, storage, or transmission of CUI. This practice requires periodically assessing the risk to organizational operations, assets, and individuals resulting from operating organizational systems and the associated processing, storage, or transmission of CUI.
- **RM.2.002:** Scan for vulnerabilities in organizational systems and

applications periodically and when new vulnerabilities affecting those systems and applications are identified. This practice requires periodically scanning for vulnerabilities in organizational systems and applications and when new vulnerabilities are identified.

- **RM.2.003:** Remediate vulnerabilities by risk assessments. This practice requires remediating vulnerabilities by risk assessments.
- **RM.2.004:** Analyze the vulnerability scan reports and results from security control assessments. This practice requires analyzing vulnerability scan reports and results from security control assessments.

Level 3

- **RM.3.001:** Employ an independent assessor or assessment team to monitor the security controls in the information system on an ongoing basis. This practice requires employing an independent assessor or assessment team to continuously monitor the security controls in the informational system.
- **RM.3.002:** Analyze the security impact of system changes. This practice requires analyzing the security impact of system changes.
- **RM.3.003:** Perform periodic penetration testing. This practice requires performing periodic penetration testing.
- **RM.3.004:** Perform risk assessments to identify, prioritize, and estimate risks based on the operation of organizational systems. This practice requires performing risk assessments to identify, prioritize, and estimate risks based on the operation of organizational systems.
- **RM.3.005:** Conduct vulnerability-hunting activities. This practice requires proactively conducting vulnerability-hunting activi-

ties to identify and remediate organizational system vulnerabilities.

Security Assessment (CA)

Level 2

- **CA.2.001:** Develop, document, and periodically update system security plans that describe system boundaries, system environments of operation, how security requirements are implemented, and the relationships with or connections to other systems. This practice requires developing, documenting, and periodically updating system security plans.
- **CA.2.002:** Periodically assess the security controls in organizational systems to determine if they are effective in their application. This practice requires periodically assessing the security controls in organizational systems to determine their effectiveness.
- **CA.2.003:** Monitor security controls on an ongoing basis to ensure the continued effectiveness of the controls. This practice requires continuously monitoring security controls to ensure their ongoing effectiveness.
- **CA.2.004:** Develop and implement action plans designed to correct deficiencies and reduce or eliminate vulnerabilities in organizational systems. This practice requires developing and implementing plans of action to correct deficiencies and reduce or eliminate vulnerabilities in organizational systems.
- **CA.2.005:** Establish and maintain a security assessment and authorization policy and procedures. This practice requires es-

tablishing and maintaining a security assessment, authorization policy, and procedures.

- **CA.2.006:** Conduct penetration testing at least annually, leveraging automated scanning tools and ad hoc tests using subject matter experts. This practice requires conducting penetration testing at least annually, using both automated scanning tools and ad hoc tests by subject matter experts.

Level 3

- **CA.3.001:** Monitor organizational systems, including inbound and outbound communications traffic, to detect attacks and indicators of potential attacks. This practice requires monitoring organizational systems, including inbound and outbound communications traffic, to detect attacks and indicators of potential attacks.
- **CA.3.002:** Employ independent penetration testing in addition to the required annual assessment annually. This practice requires employing independent penetration testing annually in addition to the required yearly assessment.
- **CA.3.003:** Perform periodic Red Team exercises to simulate attempts by adversaries to compromise organizational systems. This practice requires performing periodic Red Team exercises to simulate attempts by adversaries to compromise organizational systems.
- **CA.3.004:** Notify designated stakeholders within 72 hours of discovering a security breach in an organizational system. This practice requires notifying designated stakeholders within 72 hours of discovering a security breach in an organizational system.

Situational Awareness (SA)

Level 2

- **SA.2.001:** Receive and respond to cyber threat intelligence from information-sharing forums and sources and communicate to stakeholders. This practice requires receiving and responding to cyber threat intelligence from information-sharing forums and sources and communicating it to stakeholders.

Level 3

- **SA.3.001:** Employ an automated capability to share threat indicators within the organization and with designated partners. This practice requires an automated capability to share threat indicators within the organization and with designated partners.
- **SA.3.002:** Provide information system protection capabilities to enable authorized users to perform their information security-related duties and responsibilities. This practice requires information system protection capabilities to enable authorized users to perform security-related duties and responsibilities.

System and Communications Protection (SC)

Level 1

- **SC.1.001:** Monitor, control, and protect organizational communications (i.e., information transmitted or received by organizational information systems) at the external boundaries and key internal boundaries of the information systems. This practice requires monitoring, controlling, and protecting organizational communications at information systems' external and key internal boundaries.

- **SC.1.002:** Implement subnetworks for publicly accessible system components physically or logically separated from internal networks. This practice requires implementing subnetworks for publicly accessible system components physically or logically separated from internal networks.

Level 2

- **SC.2.001:** Employ architectural designs, software development techniques, and systems engineering principles that promote effective information security within organizational systems. This practice requires employing architectural designs, software development techniques, and systems engineering principles that promote effective information security within organizational systems.
- **SC.2.002:** Separate user functionality from system management functionality. This practice requires separating user functionality from system management functionality.
- **SC.2.003:** Prevent unauthorized and unintended information transfer via shared system resources. This practice requires preventing unauthorized and unintended information transfer via shared system resources.
- **SC.2.004:** Implement subnetworks for publicly accessible system components physically or logically separated from internal networks. This practice requires implementing subnetworks for

publicly accessible system components physically or logically separated from internal networks.

- **SC.2.005:** Implement cryptographic mechanisms to prevent unauthorized disclosure of CUI during transmission unless otherwise protected by alternative physical safeguards. This practice requires implementing cryptographic mechanisms to prevent unauthorized disclosure of CUI during transmission unless alternative physical safeguards are used.
- **SC.2.006:** Terminate network connections associated with communications sessions at the end of the sessions or after a defined period of inactivity. This practice requires terminating network connections related to communications sessions at the end of the sessions or after a defined period of inactivity.
- **SC.2.007:** Establish and manage cryptographic keys for cryptography employed in organizational systems. This practice requires establishing and managing cryptographic keys for cryptography employed in organizational systems.
- **SC.2.008:** Control and monitor Voice over Internet Protocol (VoIP) technologies. This practice requires controlling and monitoring the use of VoIP technologies.
- **SC.2.009:** Protect the authenticity of communications sessions. This practice requires protecting the authenticity of communication sessions.
- **SC.2.010:** Protect the confidentiality of CUI at rest. This practice requires the protection of the confidentiality of CUI while at rest.

Level 3

- **SC.3.001:** Employ FIPS-validated cryptography when used to protect the confidentiality of CUI. This practice requires employing

FIPS-validated cryptography to protect the confidentiality of CUI.
- **SC.3.002:** Employ automated mechanisms to authenticate and cryptographically protect the integrity of remote access sessions. This practice requires using automated mechanisms to authenticate and cryptographically protect the integrity of remote access sessions.
- **SC.3.003:** Employ automated mechanisms to protect the integrity of network communications sessions cryptographically. This practice requires using automated mechanisms to protect the integrity of network communications sessions cryptographically.
- **SC.3.004:** Employ automated mechanisms to verify the integrity of communications sessions cryptographically. This practice requires using automated mechanisms to verify the integrity of communications sessions cryptographically.
- **SC.3.005:** Protect the confidentiality of transmitted information. This practice requires protecting the confidentiality of transmitted information.
- **SC.3.006:** Protect the integrity of transmitted information. This practice requires protecting the integrity of transmitted information.
- **SC.3.007:** Employ cryptographic mechanisms to prevent unauthorized disclosure of CUI during transmission. This practice requires employing cryptographic mechanisms to prevent unauthorized disclosure of CUI during transmission.
- **SC.3.008:** Implement cryptographic mechanisms to protect the confidentiality and integrity of CUI during storage and transmission. This practice requires implementing cryptographic mechanisms to protect the confidentiality and integrity of CUI during storage and transmission.
- **SC.3.009:** Protect the confidentiality and integrity of CUI at rest. This practice requires protecting the confidentiality and integrity

of CUI at rest.

- **SC.3.010:** Establish and manage cryptographic keys for cryptography employed in the information system in accordance with organizational, state, and federal requirements. This practice requires establishing and managing cryptographic keys for cryptography employed in the information system in accordance with organizational, state, and federal requirements.

- **SC.3.011:** Employ FIPS-compliant key management technology and processes. This practice requires employing FIPS-compliant key management technology and processes.

- **SC.3.012:** Employ automated mechanisms with supporting or manual procedures for cryptographic key establishment and management. This practice requires automated mechanisms with supporting procedures or manual procedures for cryptographic key establishment and management.

- **SC.3.013:** Control and monitor the use of mobile code. This practice requires controlling and monitoring the use of mobile code.

- **SC.3.014:** Control and monitor Voice over Internet Protocol (VoIP) technologies. This practice requires controlling and monitoring the use of VoIP technologies.

- **SC.3.015:** Protect the authenticity of communications sessions. This practice requires protecting the authenticity of communication sessions.

- **SC.3.016:** Protect the confidentiality and integrity of transmitted information. This practice requires protecting the confidentiality and integrity of transmitted information.

- **SC.3.017:** Employ automated mechanisms with supporting procedures or manual procedures for cryptographic key generation, distribution, storage, access, and destruction. This practice requires automated mechanisms with supporting procedures or manual procedures for cryptographic key generation, distribution, storage, access, and destruction.

System and Information Integrity (SI)

Level 1

- **SI.1.001:** Identify, report, and correct information and information system flaws promptly. This practice requires timely identification, reporting, and correction of information and system flaws.
- **SI.1.002:** Protect malicious code at appropriate locations within organizational information systems. This practice requires protecting malicious code at appropriate locations within organizational systems.
- **SI.1.003:** Update malicious code protection mechanisms when new releases are available. This practice requires updating malicious code protection mechanisms when new releases are available.
- **SI.1.004:** Perform periodic scans of the information system and real-time scans of files from external sources as files are downloaded, opened, or executed. This practice requires periodic scans of the information system and real-time scans of files from external sources as they are downloaded, opened, or executed.

Level 2

- **SI.2.001:** Monitor system security alerts and advisories and

344

respond appropriately. This practice requires monitoring system security alerts and advisories and responding appropriately.

- **SI.2.002:** Employ spam protection mechanisms at information system access entry and exit points. This practice requires spam protection mechanisms at system access entry and exit points.
- **SI.2.003:** Implement email forgery protections. This practice requires implementing email forgery protections.
- **SI.2.004:** Utilize sandboxing to detect or block potentially malicious emails. This practice requires utilizing sandboxing to detect or block potentially malicious emails.
- **SI.2.005:** Update malicious code protection mechanisms when new releases are available. This practice requires updating malicious code protection mechanisms when new releases are available.
- **SI.2.006:** Perform periodic scans of the information system and real-time scans of files from external sources as files are downloaded, opened, or executed. This practice requires periodic scans of the information system and real-time scans of files from external sources as they are downloaded, opened, or executed.
- **SI.2.007:** Monitor organizational systems, including inbound and outbound communications traffic, to detect attacks and indicators of potential attacks. This practice requires monitoring organizational systems, including inbound and outbound communications traffic, to detect attacks and indicators of potential attacks.

Level 3

- **SI.3.001:** Employ spam protection mechanisms at information system access entry and exit points to detect and take action on unsolicited messages. This practice requires employing spam

345

protection mechanisms at system access entry and exit points to detect and take action on unsolicited messages.

- **SI.3.002:** Implement email forgery protections. This practice requires implementing email forgery protections.
- **SI.3.003:** Utilize sandboxing to detect or block potentially malicious emails. This practice requires utilizing sandboxing to detect or block potentially malicious emails.
- **SI.3.004:** Update malicious code protection mechanisms when new releases are available. This practice requires updating malicious code protection mechanisms when new releases are available.
- **SI.3.005:** Perform periodic scans of organizational systems and real-time scans of files from external sources as files are downloaded, opened, or executed. This practice requires periodic scans of organizational systems and real-time scans of files from external sources as they are downloaded, opened, or executed.
- **SI.3.006:** Monitor organizational systems, including inbound and outbound communications traffic, to detect attacks and indicators of potential attacks. This practice requires monitoring organizational systems, including inbound and outbound communications traffic, to detect attacks and indicators of potential attacks.
- **SI.3.007:** Employ automated tools that notify appropriate individuals upon discovering discrepancies during integrity verification. This practice requires automated tools that notify appropriate individuals upon discovering discrepancies during integrity verification.
- **SI.3.008:** Automatically update malicious code protection mechanisms. This practice requires automatically updating malicious code protection mechanisms.
- **SI.3.009:** Perform an integrity check of security attributes of files at an organization-defined frequency. This practice requires

performing an integrity check of files' security attributes at an organization-defined frequency.

These CMMC practices provide a comprehensive set of cybersecurity requirements for organizations seeking to protect sensitive information, such as Controlled Unclassified Information (CUI), and strengthen their overall cybersecurity posture. By implementing these practices across various domains, organizations can establish a robust foundation for cybersecurity and demonstrate their commitment to safeguarding critical assets and data.

It is important to note that the specific implementation of these practices may vary based on an organization's unique needs, risk profile, and operational environment. Organizations should carefully assess their current cybersecurity capabilities, identify gaps, and prioritize implementing CMMC practices based on their criticality and potential impact.

Achieving CMMC certification requires implementing the required practices and demonstrating their maturity and institutionalization within the organization. This involves establishing policies, procedures, and processes that support the consistent and effective execution of the practices and continuous monitoring and improvement of the organization's cybersecurity posture.

Organizations should work closely with CMMC-AB accredited assessors, consultants, and training providers to ensure a thorough understanding of the CMMC requirements and to develop a roadmap for successful certification. Regular internal assessments, external audits, and engagement with the CMMC community can help organizations stay informed about evolving threats, best practices, and requirements.

By embracing the CMMC framework and implementing these practices holistically and proactively, organizations can enhance their cybersecurity resilience, protect sensitive information, and contribute to the overall security and integrity of the defense industrial base.

Appendix D: Mapping of CMMC 2.0 Practices to NIST 800-171 Controls

The Cybersecurity Maturity Model Certification (CMMC) framework, particularly Level 2, is closely aligned with the National Institute of Standards and Technology (NIST) Special Publication 800-171. NIST SP 800-171 provides a set of security controls for protecting Controlled Unclassified Information (CUI) in non-federal systems and organizations. Understanding the mapping between CMMC 2.0 practices and NIST 800-171 controls is crucial for organizations that have already implemented NIST 800-171 and are seeking to transition to CMMC 2.0 Level 2 certification.

Here is a detailed mapping of CMMC 2.0 practices to NIST 800-171 controls:

Access Control (AC)

CMMC Practice AC.L2-3.1.1: Limit system access to authorized users, processes acting for authorized users, or devices (including other systems).

- Mapped to NIST 800-171 Control 3.1.1: Limit system access to authorized users and processes acting on behalf of authorized users or devices (including other systems).

CMMC Practice AC.L2-3.1.2: Limit system access to the transactions and functions authorized users can execute.

- Mapped to NIST 800-171 Control 3.1.2: Limit system access to the transactions and functions authorized users can execute.

CMMC Practice AC.L2-3.1.3: Control the flow of CUI following approved authorizations.

- Mapped to NIST 800-171 Control 3.1.3: Control the flow of CUI following approved authorizations.

CMMC Practice AC.L2-3.1.4: Separate the duties of individuals to reduce the risk of malevolent activity without collusion.

- Mapped to NIST 800-171 Control 3.1.4: Separate the duties of individuals to reduce the risk of malevolent activity without collusion.

CMMC Practice AC.L2-3.1.5: Employ the principle of least privilege, including for specific security functions and privileged accounts.

- Mapped to NIST 800-171 Control 3.1.5: Employ the principle of least privilege, including for specific security functions and privileged accounts.

CMMC Practice AC.L2-3.1.6: Use non-privileged accounts or roles when accessing nonsecurity functions.

- Mapped to NIST 800-171 Control 3.1.6: Use non-privileged accounts or roles when accessing nonsecurity functions.

CMMC Practice AC.L2-3.1.7: Prevent non-privileged users from executing privileged functions and capture the execution of such functions in audit logs.

- Mapped to NIST 800-171 Control 3.1.7: Prevent non-privileged users from executing privileged functions and audit the execution of such functions.

CMMC Practice AC.L2-3.1.8: Limit unsuccessful login attempts.

- Mapped to NIST 800-171 Control 3.1.8: Limit unsuccessful logon attempts.

CMMC Practice AC.L2-3.1.9: Provide privacy and security notices consistent with applicable CUI rules.

- Mapped to NIST 800-171 Control 3.1.9: Provide privacy and security notices consistent with applicable CUI rules.

CMMC Practice AC.L2-3.1.10: Use session lock with pattern-hiding displays to prevent access and viewing of data after a period of inactivity.

- Mapped to NIST 800-171 Control 3.1.10: Use session lock with pattern-hiding displays to prevent access and viewing of data after a period of inactivity.

CMMC Practice AC.L2-3.1.11: Terminate (automatically) a user session after a defined condition.

- Mapped to NIST 800-171 Control 3.1.11: Terminate (automatically) a user session after a defined condition.

CMMC Practice AC.L2-3.1.12: Monitor and control remote access sessions.

- Mapped to NIST 800-171 Control 3.1.12: Monitor and control remote access sessions.

CMMC Practice AC.L2-3.1.13: Employ cryptographic mechanisms to protect the confidentiality of remote access sessions.

- Mapped to NIST 800-171 Control 3.1.13: Employ cryptographic mechanisms to protect the confidentiality of remote access sessions.

CMMC Practice AC.L2-3.1.14: Route remote access via managed access control points.

- Mapped to NIST 800-171 Control 3.1.14: Route remote access via managed access control points.

CMMC Practice AC.L2-3.1.15: Authorize remote execution of privileged commands and remote access to security-relevant information.

- Mapped to NIST 800-171 Control 3.1.15: Authorize remote execution of privileged commands and remote access to security-relevant information.

CMMC Practice AC.L2-3.1.16: Authorize wireless access before allowing such connections.

- Mapped to NIST 800-171 Control 3.1.16: Authorize wireless access before allowing such connections.

CMMC Practice AC.L2-3.1.17: Protect wireless access using authentication and encryption.

- Mapped to NIST 800-171 Control 3.1.17: Protect wireless access using authentication and encryption.

CMMC Practice AC.L2-3.1.18: Control connection of mobile devices.

- Mapped to NIST 800-171 Control 3.1.18: Control connection of mobile devices.

CMMC Practice AC.L2-3.1.19: Encrypt CUI on mobile devices and mobile computing platforms.

- Mapped to NIST 800-171 Control 3.1.19: Encrypt CUI on mobile devices and mobile computing platforms.

CMMC Practice AC.L2-3.1.20: Verify and control/limit connections to and use of external systems.

- Mapped to NIST 800-171 Control 3.1.20: Verify and control/limit connections to and use of external information systems.

CMMC Practice AC.L2-3.1.21: Limit use of portable storage devices on external systems.

- Mapped to NIST 800-171 Control 3.1.21: Limit use of organizational portable storage devices on external information systems.

CMMC Practice AC.L2-3.1.22: Control CUI posted or processed on publicly accessible systems.

- Mapped to NIST 800-171 Control 3.1.22: Control information posted or processed on publicly accessible information systems.

Audit and Accountability (AU)

CMMC Practice AU.L2-3.3.1: Create and retain system audit logs and records to the extent needed to enable the monitoring, analysis, investigation, and reporting of unlawful or unauthorized system activity.

- Mapped to NIST 800-171 Control 3.3.1: Create, protect, and retain information system audit records to the extent needed to enable the monitoring, analysis, investigation, and reporting of unlawful, unauthorized, or inappropriate information system activity.

CMMC Practice AU.L2-3.3.2: Ensure that the actions of individual system users can be uniquely traced to those users so they can be held accountable for their actions.

- Mapped to NIST 800-171 Control 3.3.2: Ensure that the actions of individual information system users can be uniquely traced to those users so they can be held accountable for their actions.

CMMC Practice AU.L2-3.3.3: Review and update logged events.

- Mapped to NIST 800-171 Control 3.3.3: Review and update audited events.

CMMC Practice AU.L2-3.3.4: Alert in the event of an audit logging process failure.

- Mapped to NIST 800-171 Control 3.3.4: Alert in the event of an audit processing failure.

CMMC Practice AU.L2-3.3.5: Correlate audit record review, analysis, and reporting processes for investigation and response to indications of unlawful, unauthorized, suspicious, or unusual activity.

- Mapped to NIST 800-171 Control 3.3.5: Correlate audit review, analysis, and reporting processes for investigation and response to indications of inappropriate, suspicious, or unusual activity.

CMMC Practice AU.L2-3.3.6: Provide audit record reduction and report generation to support on-demand analysis and reporting.

- Mapped to NIST 800-171 Control 3.3.6: Provide audit reduction and report generation to support on-demand analysis and reporting.

CMMC Practice AU.L2-3.3.7: Provide a system capability that compares and synchronizes internal system clocks with an authoritative source to generate time stamps for audit records.

- Mapped to NIST 800-171 Control 3.3.7: Provide an information system capability that compares and synchronizes internal system clocks with an authoritative source to generate time stamps for audit records.

CMMC Practice AU.L2-3.3.8: Protect audit information and audit logging tools from unauthorized access, modification, and deletion.

- Mapped to NIST 800-171 Control 3.3.8: Protect audit information and audit tools from unauthorized access, modification, and deletion.

CMMC Practice AU.L2-3.3.9: Limit management of audit logging functionality to a subset of privileged users.

- Mapped to NIST 800-171 Control 3.3.9: Limit management of audit functionality to a subset of privileged users.

Configuration Management (CM)

CMMC Practice CM.L2-3.4.1: Establish and maintain baseline configurations and inventories of organizational systems (including hardware, software, firmware, and documentation) throughout the respective system development life cycles.

- Mapped to NIST 800-171 Control 3.4.1: Establish and maintain baseline configurations and inventories of organizational information systems (including hardware, software, firmware, and documentation) throughout the respective system development life cycles.

CMMC Practice CM.L2-3.4.2: Establish and enforce security config-uration settings for information technology products employed in organizational systems.

- Mapped to NIST 800-171 Control 3.4.2: Establish and enforce se-curity configuration settings for information technology products employed in organizational information systems.

CMMC Practice CM.L2-3.4.3: Track, review, approve/disapprove, and log changes to organizational systems.

- Mapped to NIST 800-171 Control 3.4.3: Track, review, ap-prove/disapprove, and audit changes to information systems.

CMMC Practice CM.L2-3.4.4: Analyze the security impact of changes before implementation.

- Mapped to NIST 800-171 Control 3.4.4: Analyze the security impact of changes before implementation.

CMMC Practice CM.L2-3.4.5: Define, document, approve, and en-force physical and logical access restrictions associated with changes to organizational systems.

- Mapped to NIST 800-171 Control 3.4.5: Define, document, ap-prove, and enforce physical and logical access restrictions associ-ated with changes to the information system.

CMMC Practice CM.L2-3.4.6: Employ the principle of least functionality by configuring organizational systems to provide only essential capabilities.

- Mapped to NIST 800-171 Control 3.4.6: Employ the principle of least functionality by configuring the information system to provide only essential capabilities.

CMMC Practice CM.L2-3.4.7: Restrict, disable, or prevent the use of nonessential programs, functions, ports, protocols, and services.

- Mapped to NIST 800-171 Control 3.4.7: Restrict, disable, and prevent the use of nonessential programs, functions, ports, protocols, and services.

CMMC Practice CM.L2-3.4.8: Apply a deny-by-exception (blacklisting) policy to prevent the use of unauthorized software or a deny-all, permit-by-exception (whitelisting) policy to allow the execution of authorized software.

- Mapped to NIST 800-171 Control 3.4.8: Apply deny-by-exception (blacklist) policy to prevent the use of unauthorized software or deny-all, permit-by-exception (whitelisting) policy to allow the execution of authorized software.

CMMC Practice CM.L2-3.4.9: Control and monitor user-installed software.

- Mapped to NIST 800-171 Control 3.4.9: Control and monitor user-installed software.

Identification and Authentication (IA)

CMMC Practice IA.L2-3.5.1: Identify system users, processes acting on behalf of users, and devices.

- Mapped to NIST 800-171 Control 3.5.1: Identify information system users, processes acting on behalf of users, or devices.

CMMC Practice IA.L2-3.5.2: Authenticate (or verify) the identities of users, processes, or devices as a prerequisite to allowing access to organizational systems.

- Mapped to NIST 800-171 Control 3.5.2: Authenticate (or verify) the identities of those users, processes, or devices as a prerequisite to allowing access to organizational information systems.

CMMC Practice IA.L2-3.5.3: Use multifactor authentication (MFA) for local and network access to privileged accounts and network access to non-privileged accounts.

- Mapped to NIST 800-171 Control 3.5.3: Use multifactor authentication for local and network access to privileged accounts and network access to non-privileged accounts.

CMMC Practice IA.L2-3.5.4: Employ replay-resistant authentication mechanisms for network access to privileged and non-privileged accounts.

- Mapped to NIST 800-171 Control 3.5.4: Employ replay-resistant authentication mechanisms for network access to privileged and non-privileged accounts.

CMMC Practice IA.L2-3.5.5: Prevent reuse of identifiers for a defined period.

- Mapped to NIST 800-171 Control 3.5.5: Prevent reuse of identifiers for a defined period.

CMMC Practice IA.L2-3.5.6: Disable identifiers after a defined period of inactivity.

- Mapped to NIST 800-171 Control 3.5.6: Disable identifiers after a defined period of inactivity.

CMMC Practice IA.L2-3.5.7: Enforce a minimum password complexity and change of characters when new passwords are created.

- Mapped to NIST 800-171 Control 3.5.7: Enforce a minimum password complexity and change of characters when new passwords are created.

CMMC Practice IA.L2-3.5.8: Prohibit password reuse for a specified number of generations.

- Mapped to NIST 800-171 Control 3.5.8: Prohibit password reuse for several generations.

CMMC Practice IA.L2-3.5.9: Allow temporary password use for system logons with an immediate change to a permanent password.

- Mapped to NIST 800-171 Control 3.5.9: Allow temporary password use for system logons with an immediate change to a permanent password.

CMMC Practice IA.L2-3.5.10: Store and transmit only cryptographically protected passwords.

- Mapped to NIST 800-171 Control 3.5.10: Store and transmit only encrypted representations of passwords.

CMMC Practice IA.L2-3.5.11: Obscure feedback of authentication information.

- Mapped to NIST 800-171 Control 3.5.11: Obscure feedback of authentication information.

Incident Response (IR)

CMMC Practice IR.L2-3.6.1: Establish an operational incident-handling capability for organizational systems that includes preparation, detection, analysis, containment, recovery, and user response activities.

- Mapped to NIST 800-171 Control 3.6.1: Establish an operational incident-handling capability for organizational information systems that includes adequate preparation, detection, analysis, containment, recovery, and user response activities.

CMMC Practice IR.L2-3.6.2: Track, document, and report incidents to designated officials and authorities, both internal and external to the organization.

- Mapped to NIST 800-171 Control 3.6.2: Track, document, and report incidents to appropriate organizational officials and authorities.

CMMC Practice IR.L2-3.6.3: Test the organizational incident response capability.

- Mapped to NIST 800-171 Control 3.6.3: Test the organizational incident response capability.

Maintenance (MA)

CMMC Practice MA.L2-3.7.1: Perform maintenance on organizational systems.

- Mapped to NIST 800-171 Control 3.7.1: Perform maintenance on organizational information systems.

CMMC Practice MA.L2-3.7.2: Provide controls on the tools, techniques, mechanisms, and personnel used to conduct system maintenance.

- Mapped to NIST 800-171 Control 3.7.2: Provide effective controls on the tools, techniques, mechanisms, and personnel used to conduct system maintenance.

CMMC Practice MA.L2-3.7.3: Ensure the equipment removed for off-site maintenance is sanitized with any CUI.

- Mapped to NIST 800-171 Control 3.7.3: Ensure equipment removed for off-site maintenance is sanitized of any CUI.

CMMC Practice MA.L2-3.7.4: Check media containing diagnostic and test programs for malicious code before the media are used in organizational systems.

- Mapped to NIST 800-171 Control 3.7.4: Check media containing diagnostic and test programs for malicious code before the media are used in the information system.

CMMC Practice MA.L2-3.7.5: Require multifactor authentication to establish nonlocal maintenance sessions via external network connections and terminate such connections when nonlocal maintenance is complete.

- Mapped to NIST 800-171 Control 3.7.5: Require multifactor authentication to establish nonlocal maintenance sessions via external network connections and terminate such connections when nonlocal maintenance is complete.

CMMC Practice MA.L2-3.7.6: Supervise the maintenance activities of maintenance personnel without required access authorization.

- Mapped to NIST 800-171 Control 3.7.6: Supervise the maintenance activities of personnel without required access authorization.

Media Protection (MP)

CMMC Practice MP.L2-3.8.1: Protect (i.e., physically control and securely store) system media containing paper and digital CUI.

- Mapped to NIST 800-171 Control 3.8.1: Protect (i.e., physically control and securely store) information system media containing paper and digital CUI.

CMMC Practice MP.L2-3.8.2: Limit access to system-media CUI to authorized users.

- Mapped to NIST 800-171 Control 3.8.2: Limit access to CUI on information system media to authorized users.

CMMC Practice MP.L2-3.8.3: Sanitize or destroy system media containing CUI before disposal or release for reuse.

- Mapped to NIST 800-171 Control 3.8.3: Sanitize or destroy information system media containing CUI before disposal or release for reuse.

CMMC Practice MP.L2-3.8.4: Mark media with necessary CUI markings and distribution limitations.

- Mapped to NIST 800-171 Control 3.8.4: Mark media with necessary CUI markings and distribution limitations.

CMMC Practice MP.L2-3.8.5: Control access to media containing CUI and maintain accountability for media during transport outside of controlled areas.

- Mapped to NIST 800-171 Control 3.8.5: Control access to media containing CUI and maintain accountability for media during transport outside of controlled areas.

CMMC Practice MP.L2-3.8.6: Implement cryptographic mechanisms to protect the confidentiality of CUI stored on digital media during transport unless otherwise protected by alternative physical safeguards.

- Mapped to NIST 800-171 Control 3.8.6: Implement cryptographic mechanisms to protect the confidentiality of CUI stored on digital media during transport unless otherwise protected by alternative physical safeguards.

CMMC Practice MP.L2-3.8.7: Control the use of removable media on system components.

- Mapped to NIST 800-171 Control 3.8.7: Control the use of removable media on information system components.

CMMC Practice MP.L2-3.8.8: Prohibit using portable storage devices when such devices have no identifiable owner.

- Mapped to NIST 800-171 Control 3.8.8: Prohibit portable storage devices when such devices have no identifiable owner.

Personnel Security (PS)

CMMC Practice PS.L2-3.9.1: Screen individuals before authorizing access to organizational systems containing CUI.

- Mapped to NIST 800-171 Control 3.9.1: Screen individuals before authorizing access to CUI information systems.

CMMC Practice PS.L2-3.9.2: Ensure that organizational systems containing CUI are protected during and after personnel actions such as terminations and transfers.

- Mapped to NIST 800-171 Control 3.9.2: Ensure that CUI and information systems containing CUI are protected during and after personnel actions such as terminations and transfers.

Physical Protection (PE)

CMMC Practice PE.L2-3.10.1: Authorized individuals are limited to physical access to organizational systems, equipment, and the respective operating environments.

- Mapped to NIST 800-171 Control 3.10.1: Limit physical access to organizational information systems, equipment, and the respective operating environments to authorized individuals.

CMMC Practice PE.L2-3.10.2: Protect and monitor the physical facility and support infrastructure for organizational systems.

- Mapped to NIST 800-171 Control 3.10.2: Protect and monitor the physical facility and support infrastructure for those information systems.

CMMC Practice PE.L2-3.10.3: Escort visitors and monitor visitor activity.

- Mapped to NIST 800-171 Control 3.10.3: Escort visitors and monitor visitor activity.

CMMC Practice PE.L2-3.10.4: Maintain audit logs of physical access.

- Mapped to NIST 800-171 Control 3.10.4: Maintain audit logs of physical access.

CMMC Practice PE.L2-3.10.5: Control and manage physical access devices.

- Mapped to NIST 800-171 Control 3.10.5: Control and manage physical access devices.

CMMC Practice PE.L2-3.10.6: Enforce safeguarding measures for CUI at alternate work sites.

· Mapped to NIST 800-171 Control 3.10.6: Enforce safeguarding measures for CUI at alternate work sites.

Risk Assessment (RA)

CMMC Practice RM.L2-3.11.1: Periodically assess the risk to organizational operations (including mission, functions, image, or reputation), organizational assets, and individuals resulting from operating organizational systems and the associated processing, storage, or transmission of CUI.

· Mapped to NIST 800-171 Control 3.11.1: Periodically assess the risk to organizational operations (including mission, functions, image, or reputation), organizational assets, and individuals resulting from the operation of organizational information systems and the associated processing, storage, or transmission of CUI.

CMMC Practice RM.L2-3.11.2: Scan for vulnerabilities in organizational systems and applications periodically and when new vulnerabilities affecting those systems and applications are identified.

· Mapped to NIST 800-171 Control 3.11.2: Scan for vulnerabilities in the information system and applications periodically and when new system vulnerabilities are identified.

CMMC Practice RM.L2-3.11.3: Remediate vulnerabilities by risk assessments.

- Mapped to NIST 800-171 Control 3.11.3: Remediate vulnerabilities in accordance with assessments of risk.

Security Assessment (CA)

CMMC Practice CA.L2-3.12.1: Periodically assess the security controls in organizational systems to determine if the controls are effective in their application.

- Mapped to NIST 800-171 Control 3.12.1: Periodically assess the security controls in organizational information systems to determine if the controls are effective in their application.

CMMC Practice CA.L2-3.12.2: Develop and implement action plans to correct deficiencies and reduce or eliminate vulnerabilities in organizational systems.

- Mapped to NIST 800-171 Control 3.12.2: Develop and implement action plans to correct deficiencies and reduce or eliminate vulnerabilities in organizational information systems.

CMMC Practice CA.L2-3.12.3: Monitor security controls continuously to ensure the controls' continued effectiveness.

- Mapped to NIST 800-171 Control 3.12.3: Monitor security controls on an ongoing basis to ensure the continued effectiveness of the controls.

CMMC Practice CA.L2-3.12.4: Develop, document, and periodically update system security plans that describe system boundaries, system environments of operation, how security requirements are implemented, and the relationships with or connections to other systems.

- Mapped to NIST 800-171 Control 3.12.4: Develop, document, and periodically update system security plans that describe system boundaries, system environments of operation, how security requirements are implemented, and the relationships with or connections to other systems.

System and Communications Protection (SC)

CMMC Practice SC.L2-3.13.1: Monitor, control, and protect communications (i.e., information transmitted or received by organizational systems) at the external boundaries and key internal boundaries of organizational systems.

- Mapped to NIST 800-171 Control 3.13.1: Monitor, control, and protect organizational communications (i.e., information transmitted or received by organizational information systems) at the external boundaries and key internal boundaries of the information systems.

CMMC Practice SC.L2-3.13.2: Employ architectural designs, software development techniques, and systems engineering principles that promote effective information security within organizational systems.

- Mapped to NIST 800-171 Control 3.13.2: Employ architectural designs, software development techniques, and systems engineering principles that promote effective information security within organizational information systems.

CMMC Practice SC.L2-3.13.3: Separate user functionality from system management functionality.

- Mapped to NIST 800-171 Control 3.13.3: Separate user functionality from information system management functionality.

CMMC Practice SC.L2-3.13.4: Prevent unauthorized and unintended information transfer via shared system resources.

- Mapped to NIST 800-171 Control 3.13.4: Prevent unauthorized and unintended information transfer via shared system resources.

CMMC Practice SC.L2-3.13.5: Implement subnetworks for publicly accessible system components physically or logically separated from internal networks.

- Mapped to NIST 800-171 Control 3.13.5: Implement subnetworks for publicly accessible system components that are physically or logically separated from internal networks.

CMMC Practice SC.L2-3.13.6: Deny network communications traffic by default and allow network communications traffic by exception (i.e., deny all, permit by exception).

- Mapped to NIST 800-171 Control 3.13.6: Deny network communications traffic by default and allow network communications traffic by exception (i.e., deny all, permit by exception).

CMMC Practice SC.L2-3.13.7: Prevent remote devices from simultaneously establishing non-remote connections with organizational systems and communicating via some other connection to resources in external networks (i.e., split tunneling).

- Mapped to NIST 800-171 Control 3.13.7: Prevent remote devices from simultaneously establishing non-remote connections with the information system and communicating via some other connection to resources in external networks.

CMMC Practice SC.L2-3.13.8: Implement cryptographic mechanisms to prevent unauthorized disclosure of CUI during transmission unless otherwise protected by alternative physical safeguards.

- Mapped to NIST 800-171 Control 3.13.8: Implement cryptographic mechanisms to prevent unauthorized disclosure of CUI during transmission unless otherwise protected by alternative physical safeguards.

CMMC Practice SC.L2-3.13.9: Terminate network connections associated with communications sessions at the end of the sessions or after a defined period of inactivity.

- Mapped to NIST 800-171 Control 3.13.9: Terminate network connections associated with communications sessions at the end of the sessions or after a defined period of inactivity.

CMMC Practice SC.L2-3.13.10: Establish and manage cryptographic keys for cryptography employed in organizational systems.

- Mapped to NIST 800-171 Control 3.13.10: Establish and manage cryptographic keys for cryptography employed in the information system.

CMMC Practice SC.L2-3.13.11: Employ FIPS-validated cryptography when used to protect the confidentiality of CUI.

- Mapped to NIST 800-171 Control 3.13.11: Employ FIPS-validated cryptography when used to protect the confidentiality of CUI.

CMMC Practice SC.L2-3.13.12: Prohibit remote activation of collaborative computing devices and indicate to users present at the device that the device is in use.

- Mapped to NIST 800-171 Control 3.13.12: Prohibit remote activation of collaborative computing devices and indicate devices in use to users present at the device.

375

CMMC Practice SC.L2-3.13.13: Control and monitor the use of mobile code.

- Mapped to NIST 800-171 Control 3.13.13: Control and monitor the use of mobile code.

CMMC Practice SC.L2-3.13.14: Control and monitor Voice over Internet Protocol (VoIP) technologies.

- Mapped to NIST 800-171 Control 3.13.14: Control and monitor Voice over Internet Protocol (VoIP) technologies.

CMMC Practice SC.L2-3.13.15: Protect the authenticity of communications sessions.

- Mapped to NIST 800-171 Control 3.13.15: Protect the authenticity of communications sessions.

CMMC Practice SC.L2-3.13.16: Protect the confidentiality of CUI at rest.

- Mapped to NIST 800-171 Control 3.13.16: Protect the confidentiality of CUI at rest.

System and Information Integrity (SI)

CMMC Practice SI.L2-3.14.1: Identify, report, and correct system flaws promptly.

- Mapped to NIST 800-171 Control 3.14.1: Promptly identify, report, and correct information and information system flaws.

CMMC Practice SI.L2-3.14.2: Protect malicious code at designated locations within organizational systems.

- Mapped to NIST 800-171 Control 3.14.2: Protect malicious code at appropriate locations within organizational information systems.

CMMC Practice SI.L2-3.14.3: Monitor system security alerts and advisories and take action in response.

- Mapped to NIST 800-171 Control 3.14.3: Monitor information system security alerts and advisories and respond appropriately.

CMMC Practice SI.L2-3.14.4: Update malicious code protection mechanisms when new releases are available.

- Mapped to NIST 800-171 Control 3.14.4: Update malicious code protection mechanisms when new releases are available.

CMMC Practice SI.L2-3.14.5: Perform periodic scans of organizational systems and real-time scans of files from external sources as files are downloaded, opened, or executed.

- Mapped to NIST 800-171 Control 3.14.5: Perform periodic scans of the information system and real-time scans of files from external sources as files are downloaded, opened, or executed.

CMMC Practice SI.L2-3.14.6: Monitor organizational systems, including inbound and outbound communications traffic, to detect attacks and indicators of potential attacks.

- Mapped to NIST 800-171 Control 3.14.6: Monitor the information system, including inbound and outbound communications traffic, to detect attacks and indicators of potential attacks.

CMMC Practice SI.L2-3.14.7: Identify unauthorized use of organizational systems.

- Mapped to NIST 800-171 Control 3.14.7: Identify unauthorized use of the information system.

This mapping demonstrates the close alignment between CMMC Level 2 practices and NIST 800-171 controls. Organizations already implementing NIST 800-171 controls can leverage their existing efforts to streamline their CMMC Level 2 certification process. By understanding the mapping, organizations can identify areas where they may need to enhance or modify their existing controls to meet the CMMC Level 2 requirements fully.

It is important to note that while the CMMC practices are closely aligned with NIST 800-171 controls, some differences exist in the specific language, scope, and implementation guidance. Organizations should carefully review the CMMC Level 2 requirements and the associated assessment guides to ensure they fully understand and meet the expectations for certification.

Additionally, CMMC Level 2 includes some practices that go beyond the requirements of NIST 800-171, such as implementing a vulnerability management plan, incident response testing, and using automated mechanisms for monitoring and analysis. Organizations should pay close attention to these additional practices and ensure they are properly addressed in their cybersecurity programs.

When preparing for a CMMC Level 2 assessment, organizations should use the mapping as a starting point to identify gaps and prioritize their efforts. They should also ensure that they have comprehensive documentation and evidence to demonstrate the effective implementation of each practice. This may include policies, procedures, system configurations, training records, and other artifacts that support the organization's cybersecurity posture.

Organizations should also engage with authorized CMMC Third-Party Assessment Organizations (C3PAOs) and Registered Provider Organizations (RPOs) to obtain guidance, support, and resources for their CMMC Level 2 certification journey. These organizations can provide valuable insights into the assessment process, help identify areas for improvement, and assist with developing remediation plans.

Ultimately, mapping CMMC Level 2 practices to NIST 800-171 controls provides a valuable tool for organizations seeking to achieve CMMC Level 2 certification. By leveraging their existing NIST 800-171 efforts and focusing on the additional requirements of CMMC Level 2, organizations can streamline their certification process and demonstrate their commitment to protecting sensitive information and supporting national security objectives.

It is important to remember that achieving CMMC Level 2 certification is not a one-time event but an ongoing continuous improvement and maturity process. Organizations should regularly assess their cybersecurity posture, update their policies and procedures, and invest in the training and development of their personnel to maintain a robust and resilient cybersecurity program.

As the cybersecurity landscape evolves and new threats emerge, organizations must remain vigilant and adaptable in protecting sensitive information. The CMMC framework provides a comprehensive and flexible approach to cybersecurity that enables organizations to prioritize their efforts, benchmark their progress, and demonstrate their commitment to safeguarding the nation's critical assets.

By embracing the CMMC Level 2 practices and aligning them with their existing NIST 800-171 efforts, organizations can position themselves as trusted partners in the defense industrial base and contribute to the overall security and resilience of the nation's critical infrastructure.

Appendix E: Templates for Gap Analysis and POA&M

Gap Analysis Template:

A gap analysis is a critical tool for organizations to assess their current cybersecurity posture against the requirements of the CMMC framework. Organizations can prioritize their efforts and develop targeted remediation plans by identifying gaps between their existing practices and the CMMC requirements. Here's a detailed template for conducting a CMMC gap analysis:

1. Overview:

- Purpose: Clearly state the purpose of the gap analysis, which is to assess the organization's current cybersecurity posture against the CMMC requirements and identify areas for improvement.
- Scope: Define the scope of the gap analysis, including the specific systems, networks, and assets that will be assessed, as well as the CMMC level targeted.
- Objectives: Outline the key objectives of the gap analysis, such as identifying gaps, prioritizing remediation efforts, and developing

a roadmap for achieving CMMC compliance.

2. Current State Assessment:

- Cybersecurity Policies and Procedures:
- Review and document the organization's existing cybersecurity policies and procedures.
- Assess these policies and procedures' completeness, effectiveness, and alignment with the CMMC requirements.
- Identify any missing or outdated policies and procedures that must be developed or updated.
- Technical Controls:
- Inventory the organization's existing technical controls, such as firewalls, intrusion detection/prevention systems, and access control mechanisms.
- Assess these controls' configuration, effectiveness, and coverage against the CMMC requirements.
- Identify any gaps or weaknesses in the technical controls that must be addressed.
- Incident Response and Business Continuity:
- Review the organization's incident response and business continuity plans and procedures.
- Assess the adequacy and effectiveness of these plans in addressing the CMMC requirements for incident handling, reporting, and recovery.
- Identify gaps or areas for improvement in the incident response and business continuity capabilities.
- Training and Awareness:
- Assess the organization's current cybersecurity training and awareness programs.

- Evaluate these programs' content, frequency, and effectiveness against the CMMC requirements.
- Identify any gaps in the training and awareness efforts that must be addressed.

3. Gap Identification and Analysis:

- CMMC Domains and Practices:
- Map the organization's current cybersecurity practices and controls to the CMMC domains and practices.
- Identify gaps where the organization's practices do not fully meet the CMMC requirements.
- Document the specific CMMC practices and controls that are missing or inadequate.
- Risk and Impact Assessment:
- Assess the potential risks and impacts associated with each identified gap.
- Consider factors such as the criticality of the affected systems, the sensitivity of the data involved, and the potential consequences of a breach or non-compliance.
- Prioritize the gaps based on their risk levels and potential organizational impacts.
- Root Cause Analysis:
- Investigate the root causes of the identified gaps, such as lack of resources, inadequate processes, or insufficient training.
- Document the findings of the root cause analysis to inform the development of effective remediation strategies.

4. Remediation Planning:

- Gap Closure Strategies:
- Develop specific strategies and actions to close each identified gap.
- Consider the feasibility, resource requirements, and timeline for implementing each remediation action.
- Prioritize the remediation efforts based on the risk levels and impacts of the gaps.
- Resource Allocation:
- Identify the resources (e.g., personnel, budget, tools) needed to implement the remediation actions.
- Allocate the necessary resources and assign responsibilities for each remediation task.
- Establish a timeline for completing the remediation efforts, considering dependencies and constraints.
- Milestones and Metrics:
- Define key milestones and metrics to track the progress and effectiveness of the remediation efforts.
- Establish regular checkpoints to review progress, address challenges, and make necessary adjustments.
- Identify any dependencies or risks that may impact the successful completion of the remediation tasks.

5. Continuous Monitoring and Improvement:

- Ongoing Assessment:
- Establish a process for ongoing assessment and monitoring of the organization's cybersecurity posture.
- Conduct regular internal audits and assessments to identify new gaps or areas for improvement.
- Monitor the effectiveness of the implemented remediation actions

and make necessary adjustments.
- Metrics and Reporting:
- Define metrics to measure the effectiveness of the organization's cybersecurity program and track progress towards CMMC compliance.
- Establish regular reporting mechanisms to communicate the status of the gap analysis and remediation efforts to relevant stakeholders.
- Use the metrics and reporting to inform continuous improvement efforts and decision-making.

6. Conclusion:

- Summary of Findings:
- Provide a high-level summary of the key findings from the gap analysis, including the most critical gaps identified and the organization's overall cybersecurity posture.
- Highlight the prioritized areas for remediation and the expected benefits of closing the identified gaps.
- Next Steps:
- Outline the next steps in the organization's CMMC compliance journey, including developing a detailed Plan of Action and Milestones (POA&M).
- Assign responsibilities and establish timelines for the completion of the next steps.

A comprehensive gap analysis template should accompany supporting documents, such as detailed assessment results, risk assessment matrices, and remediation action plans. The template should be tailored to the organization's specific needs and requirements, considering factors such as size, industry, and the scope of the CMMC assessment.

POA&M Template:

A Plan of Action and Milestones (POA&M) is a critical tool for organizations to prioritize, track, and manage their remediation efforts following a gap analysis. The POA&M template should capture the essential information needed to effectively plan and execute the necessary actions to close the identified gaps and achieve CMMC compliance. Here's a detailed POA&M template:

1. Executive Summary:

- Purpose: Briefly describe the purpose of the POA&M, which is to outline the planned actions and milestones for remediating the gaps identified in the CMMC gap analysis.
- Scope: Define the scope of the POA&M, including the specific systems, networks, and assets covered and the CMMC level targeted.
- Objectives: State the key objectives of the POA&M, such as closing the identified gaps, achieving CMMC compliance, and improving the overall cybersecurity posture of the organization.

2. Gap Summary:

- Gap Identification: Provide a summary of the gaps identified during the gap analysis, including the CMMC domains, practices, and controls affected.

- Risk Assessment: Highlight each gap's risk levels and potential impacts, as determined during the gap analysis.
- Prioritization: Explain the prioritization criteria used to rank the gaps based on their criticality and the urgency of remediation.

3. Remediation Plan:

- Gap Details:
- Provide a detailed description of each gap, including the affected systems, processes, or assets.
- Specify the CMMC domain, practice, and control related to each gap.
- Include any relevant findings or observations from the gap analysis.
- Remediation Actions:
- Outline the specific actions planned to address each gap, including implementing new controls, updating policies and procedures, or enhancing existing practices.
- Break down the remediation actions into specific tasks or steps, assigning responsibility and defining the expected outcomes.
- Identify any dependencies or prerequisites for each remediation action.
- Milestones and Timelines:
- Establish clear milestones for each remediation action, indicating the target completion dates and any intermediate checkpoints.
- Define the overall timeline for the POA&M, considering the prioritization of the gaps and the available resources.
- Identify any critical paths or dependencies that may impact the timeline.

- Resource Allocation:
- Specify the resources (e.g., personnel, budget, tools) required for each remediation action.
- Assign roles and responsibilities for executing each task, ensuring accountability and ownership.
- Identify any resource constraints or limitations that may affect the remediation efforts.

4. Progress Tracking:

- Status Updates:
- Provide regular status updates on each remediation action's progress, indicating the completion percentage, key achievements, and any challenges encountered.
- Use a standardized format for status reporting, such as a color-coded system (e.g., green for on track, yellow for at risk, red for delayed).
- Include comments or notes to provide additional context or explain any deviations from the planned timeline.
- Metrics and Key Performance Indicators (KPIs):
- Define relevant metrics and KPIs to measure the effectiveness and efficiency of the remediation efforts.
- Track and report on these metrics regularly to monitor progress and identify areas for improvement.
- Use the metrics to inform decision-making and adjust the POA&M as needed.

5. Risk Management:

- Risk Identification:
- Identify any risks or potential obstacles that may impact the successful execution of the POA&M.
- Consider risks related to resource availability, technical complexities, or dependencies on external factors.
- Risk Mitigation:
- Develop risk mitigation strategies for each identified risk, outlining the actions to be taken to minimize the potential impact.
- Assign responsibility for implementing and monitoring the risk mitigation measures.
- Contingency Planning:
- Establish contingency plans to address potential delays, setbacks, or unexpected events affecting the POA&M timeline.
- Define trigger points and escalation procedures for invoking the contingency plans.

6. Communication and Reporting:

- Stakeholder Engagement:
- Identify the key stakeholders who need to be informed about the progress and status of the POA&M.
- Establish regular communication channels and reporting mechanisms to keep stakeholders updated and engaged.
- Management Reporting:
- Develop concise and informative management reports summarizing progress, key achievements, and significant challenges or risks.
- Use visualizations, such as dashboards or charts, to present the information clearly and easily digestibly.
- Lessons Learned:

- Document any lessons learned throughout the POA&M execution process, capturing insights and best practices.
- Share the lessons learned with relevant stakeholders to foster continuous improvement and knowledge sharing.

7. Approval and Sign-off:

- Review and Validation:
- Conduct a thorough review of the completed POA&M, ensuring that all planned actions have been executed and the identified gaps have been effectively addressed.
- Validate the effectiveness of the remediation efforts through testing, auditing, or other appropriate means.
- Approval Process:
- Define the approval process for the POA&M, specifying the roles and responsibilities of the individuals involved in reviewing and signing off on the document.
- Obtain the approvals and sign-offs from the designated authorities, such as senior management, the CISO, or the CMMC project sponsor.

The POA&M template should be accompanied by supporting documents, such as detailed task lists, resource allocation plans, and risk registers. The template should be tailored to the organization's specific needs and requirements, considering factors such as the size and complexity of the remediation efforts, the available resources, and the reporting requirements.

Organizations should treat the POA&M as a living document, regularly updating and adjusting it based on progress, new information gathered, or changes in priorities or circumstances. The POA&M should be used as a central tool for tracking, communicating, and managing the remediation efforts, ensuring that all stakeholders are aligned and informed throughout the process.

By leveraging a well-structured POA&M template, organizations can effectively plan, execute, and monitor their remediation efforts, ultimately achieving CMMC compliance and strengthening their overall cybersecurity posture. The POA&M serves as a roadmap for continuous improvement, enabling organizations to prioritize their resources, measure their progress, and demonstrate their commitment to protecting sensitive information and safeguarding national security interests.

About the Author

Edgardo Fernandez Climent, an accomplished IT leader with over two decades of experience, has made significant contributions to the fields of infrastructure, networks, and cybersecurity. His exceptional leadership skills and strategic vision have positioned him as a prominent figure in the industry. After graduating with honors in Computer Information Systems, Edgardo pursued an MBA and a Master's in Management Information Systems degree, further enhancing his expertise. He also holds several industry certifications, such as PMP, ITIL4, and Security+, which demonstrate his commitment to professional development and staying at the forefront of industry standards.

Throughout his career, Edgardo has consistently demonstrated his ability to lead organizations through complex technological transformations. His deep understanding of emerging technologies and industry trends has enabled him to develop and implement innovative strategies that drive business growth and ensure technological resilience. Edgardo's leadership in navigating the ever-changing landscape of cybersecurity has been instrumental in safeguarding organizations against the evolving threats of the digital world.

As a visionary leader, Edgardo is known for his ability to inspire and motivate teams to achieve excellence. He fosters a culture of continuous learning and encourages his team members to embrace new technologies and develop their skills. Edgardo's commitment to mentoring and developing the next generation of IT leaders has had a profound impact on the industry, as he shares his knowledge and experiences to empower others to succeed.

Edgardo's leadership style is characterized by his ability to build strong relationships, promote collaboration, and drive results. He has a proven track record of successfully leading cross-functional teams and aligning IT initiatives with business objectives. His strategic thinking, combined with his technical expertise, has enabled him to develop and execute transformative initiatives that have delivered significant value to the organizations he has served.

Today, as a highly sought-after consultant in the IT industry, Edgardo continues to be at the forefront of shaping the technological landscape. His leadership and expertise are highly valued by organizations seeking to drive innovation, optimize their IT infrastructure, and strengthen their cybersecurity posture. Edgardo's journey is a testament to the power of visionary leadership, continuous learning, and a relentless pursuit of excellence in the ever-evolving field of information technology.

You can connect with me on:
- https://fernandezcliment.com
- https://twitter.com/efernandezclime
- https://www.facebook.com/edgardo.fernandez.climent
- https://amazon.com/author/efernandezcliment

Subscribe to my newsletter:

✉ https://fernandezcliment.com/join-our-mail-list

Also by Edgardo Fernandez Climent

CompTIA Security+ SY0-701 Certification All-in-One Exam Guide: All the resources needed to pass the exam in one comprehensive book

Are you ready to take your cybersecurity career to the next level? Look no further than the "CompTIA Security+ SY0-701 Certification All-in-One Exam Guide"! This comprehensive resource is designed to give you all the knowledge and tools to pass the CompTIA Security+ SY0-701 exam with flying colors.

Written by a renowned cybersecurity expert and educator, this book is the ultimate one-stop-shop for anyone looking to master the essential concepts, techniques, and best information security practices. Whether you're a seasoned IT professional or just starting out in the field, this guide will help you develop the skills and confidence to succeed on the exam and in your cybersecurity career.

Inside, you'll find:

- In-depth coverage of all the exam objectives, from threats and vulnerabilities to cryptography and access control, presented clearly and concisely.

- Practical examples, case studies, and hands-on exercises that reinforce your learning and help you apply your knowledge to real-world scenarios.

- Hundreds of practice questions and multiple full-length practice exams to test your understanding and prepare you for the format and difficulty of the actual exam.

- Expert tips and strategies for studying effectively, managing time, and overcoming common exam challenges and pitfalls.

- Access to online resources, including bonus practice exams, electronic flashcards, and a searchable glossary of key terms and concepts.

But this book isn't just about passing the exam. It's about gaining the foundational knowledge and practical skills essential for success in today's rapidly evolving cybersecurity landscape. You'll learn to assess and mitigate risks, implement and maintain robust security controls, and respond effectively to security incidents and breaches.

Whether you want to advance your career, meet job requirements, or simply enhance your cybersecurity knowledge, the "CompTIA Security+ SY0-701 Certification All-in-One Exam Guide" is the ultimate resource. It's the only guide you need to prepare for and pass the exam, and it's the perfect reference to keep on hand as you navigate the complex and ever-changing world of cybersecurity.

So why wait? Invest in your future and cybersecurity expertise by getting your copy of the "CompTIA Security+ SY0-701 Certification All-in-One Exam Guide" today. With this comprehensive and up-to-date resource at your fingertips, you'll have everything you need to succeed on the exam and in your cybersecurity career.

Don't miss out on this must-have guide for anyone serious about cybersecurity. Buy the "CompTIA Security+ SY0-701 Certification All-in-One Exam Guide" now and start your journey to becoming a certified cybersecurity professional!

Defense Information Systems Agency (DISA) Security Technical Implementation Guides (STIGs): Best Practices for Secure Government and Military Systems

"Defense Information Systems Agency (DISA) Security Technical Implementation Guides (STIGs): Best Practices for Secure Government and Military Systems" is the ultimate resource for IT professionals, government agents, and military personnel responsible for implementing and maintaining secure systems in compliance with DISA STIGs. This comprehensive guide provides in-depth coverage of STIG requirements, best practices, and real-world case studies, empowering readers to navigate the complex landscape of government and military cybersecurity effectively.

Written by a renowned expert with years of experience in cybersecurity and compliance, this book offers a clear and concise approach to understanding and applying STIG guidelines across various technologies and platforms. Readers will gain valuable insights into the STIG development process, the role of automation and tools, and strategies for overcoming common challenges and pitfalls.

The book features detailed explanations of STIG categories and structures, step-by-step guidance on implementing STIGs in diverse operational environments, and best practices for STIG compliance and auditing. It also explores the latest trends and developments in government and military cybersecurity, including the integration of STIGs with emerging frameworks like zero trust architecture and continuous monitoring.

Whether you're a seasoned cybersecurity professional looking to enhance your expertise or a newcomer to the field seeking to build your skills, this book provides the knowledge and tools you need to excel in your role and contribute to the mission of securing our nation's critical assets and infrastructure.

With its comprehensive coverage, practical insights, and real-world examples, "Defense Information Systems Agency (DISA) Security Technical Implementation Guides (STIGs): Best Practices for Secure Government and Military Systems" is an indispensable resource for anyone involved in government and military cybersecurity. Don't miss this opportunity to elevate your skills, advance your career, and make a lasting impact on the security of our nation's most sensitive systems and data.

Hacking the Hacker: My Top 10 Unconventional Cybersecurity Techniques

Are you tired of relying on traditional, reactive cybersecurity methods that always seem one step behind the hackers? Do you want to take your organization's cyber defense to the next level and proactively prevent, detect, and respond to even the most advanced and persistent threats? Then this book is for you!

In "Hacking the Hacker: My Top 10 Unconventional Cybersecurity Techniques," renowned cybersecurity expert and author Edgardo Fernandez Climent reveals his arsenal of cutting-edge, battle-tested techniques that go beyond the conventional wisdom and compliance checklists. Drawing on his decades of experience in the trenches of cybersecurity and his deep knowledge of the hacker mindset, the author presents a comprehensive and practical guide to implementing unconventional approaches such as:

- Behavioral biometrics for continuous authentication and fraud detection

- Deception technology for deceiving and trapping attackers with decoys and honeypots

- AI-driven threat hunting for proactively identifying and neutralizing hidden threats

- Quantum cryptography for unbreakable encryption and secure communication

- Security orchestration, automation, and response (SOAR) for streamlining and accelerating incident response

- And much more!

Whether you are a seasoned cybersecurity professional looking to expand your toolbox or a business leader seeking to understand and implement the latest and most effective cyber defense strategies, this book has something for you. This book explains each technique in clear, concise, and engaging language, with real-world examples, step-by-step instructions, and practical tips for success. It also provides a strategic framework for integrating these techniques into a cohesive and adaptable cybersecurity architecture that can evolve with the changing threat landscape.

With "Hacking the Hacker," you will learn how to:

- Think like a hacker and anticipate their moves before they make them

- Identify and prioritize your organization's most critical assets and vulnerabilities

- Implement unconventional techniques that can detect, deceive, and deter even the most advanced and persistent threats

- Integrate these techniques into a comprehensive and adaptive cybersecurity strategy

- Measure and communicate the effectiveness and value of your unconventional approach

- Foster a culture of proactive, innovative, and collaborative cyber-security in your organization

Please don't wait until it's too late. Invest in your cybersecurity knowledge and skills today, and start hacking the hackers before they hack you. Get your copy of "Hacking the Hacker: My Top 10 Unconventional Cybersecurity Techniques" now, and take your cyber defense to the next level!

Implementing NIST Cybersecurity Framework 2.0: A Comprehensive Guide for IT Professionals in SMEs

"**Implementing NIST Cybersecurity Framework 2.0**" serves as an indispensable guide tailored for Information Technology (IT) professionals navigating the complex landscape of Small and Medium-sized Enterprises (SMEs). In this comprehensive handbook, readers will find a detailed roadmap to fortify their organization's cyber defenses using the latest National Institute of Standards and Technology (NIST) Cybersecurity Framework iteration.

This book demystifies the intricacies of cybersecurity implementation, offering practical insights and step-by-step instructions to align SMEs with the robust security measures outlined in the NIST Cybersecurity Framework 2.0. Authored by seasoned experts in the field, the guide provides a holistic approach to addressing the evolving cyber threats SMEs face.

Whether you are an IT professional, cybersecurity practitioner, or SME decision-maker, "Implementing NIST Cybersecurity Framework 2.0" is your go-to resource for fortifying your organization's defenses in the digital age. Arm yourself with the knowledge and tools needed to safeguard against cyber threats proactively, making cybersecurity a cornerstone of your business resilience strategy.

ISO/IEC 27001:2022
STEP BY STEP
IMPLEMENTATION, AUDIT, AND
CONTINUOUS IMPROVEMENT
EDGARDO FERNANDEZ CLIMENT

ISO/IEC 27001:2022 Step by Step: Implementation, Audit, and Continuous Improvement

In a world where information security has become a priority for organizations of all sizes, the ISO/IEC 27001:2022 standard emerges as the gold standard for establishing, implementing, maintaining, and continually improving an Information Security Management System (ISMS). "ISO/IEC, 27001:2022 Step by Step" is your definitive guide to understanding and effectively implementing this essential standard.

This book is designed to guide you through the complex ISO/IEC 27001 certification process, breaking down each stage into transparent and manageable steps. From initial planning and risk assessment to implementing security controls and preparing for the certification audit, this book covers everything you need to know to secure your information and achieve certification.

This book offers a deep insight into the standard's requirements and their application in different organizational contexts through detailed explanations, practical examples, and case studies. Additionally, it provides valuable strategies, tips, and tricks to overcome common challenges in implementing and auditing the ISMS.

"ISO/IEC, 27001:2022 Step by Step" is aimed at IT and information security professionals, managers, and those responsible for implementing the standard in their organizations. With a clear focus on continuous improvement, this book is an indispensable tool for keeping your ISMS aligned with best practices and adapted to technological changes and new security threats.

Whether you want to certify your organization for the first time or update your existing ISMS to the latest standard, this book is your perfect companion. It provides expert guidance and the necessary resources to achieve your information security goals.

Mastering NIST SP 800-53: A Small Business IT Professional's Roadmap to Compliance

"Mastering NIST SP 800-53: A Small Business IT Professional's Roadmap to Compliance" is an indispensable guide tailored specifically for IT professionals operating within the dynamic landscape of small businesses. Authored with a keen understanding of the unique challenges faced by smaller enterprises, this book serves as a comprehensive roadmap to demystify and master the intricacies of the NIST Special Publication 800-53 framework. It goes beyond the theoretical by providing practical insights and actionable steps for implementing and maintaining NIST SP 800-53 controls, offering a holistic approach to information security. With real-world examples, best practices, and a focus on accessibility, this book empowers small business IT professionals to navigate the compliance landscape confidently, fortify their organizations against cybersecurity threats, and elevate their overall security posture. "Mastering NIST SP 800-53" is not just a manual for compliance; it is an essential companion for IT professionals seeking to safeguard the digital assets of their small businesses effectively.

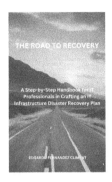

The Road to Recovery: A Step-by-Step Handbook for IT Professionals in Crafting an IT Infrastructure Disaster Recovery Plan

Disasters lurk around every corner, threatening to cripple your organization's IT infrastructure and disrupt critical operations. As an IT professional, you are the guardian of resilience, safeguarding data, resources, and business continuity in the face of the unforeseen. **The Road to Recovery** is your comprehensive roadmap to crafting a robust disaster recovery plan, empowering you to navigate adversity confidently.

This step-by-step guide delves into the core concepts of disaster recovery, equipping you with the knowledge to identify potential threats, from natural disasters like earthquakes and floods to cyberattacks and data breaches. Through a thorough IT infrastructure assessment, you'll learn to map critical systems, identify dependencies, and evaluate potential impact, gaining valuable insights to inform your decision-making.

The heart of the book lies in crafting a comprehensive disaster recovery plan. You'll gain a clear understanding of defining recovery objectives, establishing Recovery Time Objectives (RTOs) and Recovery Point Objectives (RPOs), and exploring a diverse range of recovery strategies tailored to your organization's specific needs. Whether implementing backup and restoration procedures, leveraging hot or cold sites, or utilizing cloud-based solutions, you'll have the knowledge to build a truly effective plan.

But creating a plan is only half the battle. **The Road to Recovery** emphasizes the crucial role of testing and maintenance. Learn practical testing procedures and simulation techniques to identify weaknesses and ensure your plan can withstand real-world challenges. Ongoing maintenance and monitoring are also covered, highlighting the importance of continuous adaptation to reflect evolving technology and threats.

This book is your indispensable companion for safeguarding your IT infrastructure. With its expert guidance and practical strategies, you'll be empowered to:

Proactively identify and anticipate threats to your IT infrastructure.

Conduct a thorough assessment of your critical systems and dependencies.

Craft a comprehensive disaster recovery plan aligned with your organization's specific needs.

Implement effective testing and maintenance procedures to ensure plan effectiveness.

Adapt your plan to evolving technology and threats, guaranteeing long-term resilience.

The Road to Recovery is more than just a handbook; it's an investment in your organization's future. By taking control of disaster preparedness, you ensure business continuity, minimize downtime, and emerge from challenges stronger than ever.

Is your IT infrastructure ready for the unexpected? Start your journey to recovery today.